Putting Women on the Agenda

Putting Women on the Agenda

Edited by Susan Bazilli

Ravan Press  Johannesburg

Published by Ravan Press (Pty) Ltd
PO Box 31134 Braamfontein 2017 South Africa

© Susan Bazilli, 1991

First published 1991

ISBN 0 86975 422 X

Cover by Ravan Press
Typesetting and design by Ravan Press
Printed and bound by Clyson Printers, Cape Town

Contents

Preface

*T*he contributions to this book originated as papers presented at a conference entitled *Putting Women on the Agenda*, organised by Lawyers for Human Rights, and held at the University of the Witwatersrand during Johannesburg in November 1990.

Some of the papers appear in the form in which they were presented at the conference; others have been revised by the authors to include some of the discussion that occurred at the conference itself. The length and style of the papers varies greatly. However, that should not detract from the importance of this collection. Rather, it should be seen in the context of the various debates and discussions taking place in South and Southern Africa about feminism, women and law, and the constitutional dispensation.

Many more people participated in presentations at the conference than are represented here, and their contributions should be acknowledged regardless of the fact that they did not prepare formal papers.

This book is not addressed specifically to lawyers, to academics, or to women alone. The current debate to formulate policies on gender issues involves everyone. But first and foremost, this contribution hopes to empower women to participate in all the crucial aspects of the transformation of South Africa.

It is hoped that these essays will be used as a basis for discussion and education in analysing the complexities of gender, race and class in the South African context. They should be seen as a contribution to the putting of women on the agenda for change.

Thanks is due to DANIDA (Denmark), the Canadian Embassy, the French Embassy, and Lawyers for Human Rights, who provided the financial support necessary to organise the conference; and to Interfund, which assisted in meeting the costs of publishing these essays.

Susan Bazilli
Johannesburg

Contributors

SUSAN BAZILLI holds degrees in sociology and a law degree from Osgoode Hall Law School in Toronto, Canada. She has worked as a community and feminist activist and has practised law in the areas of labour, sex discrimination and gender equality. After spending some time as a legal researcher and journalist in South Africa, she organised the *Putting Women on the Agenda* conference.

SANDRA BURMAN is a Wingate Research Fellow at Queen Elizabeth House, University of Oxford, and holds a research fellowship at the University of Cape Town, where she directs the Socio-Legal Unit. Her publications have included books on the imposition of law, on women and work, and on childhood in South Africa. Over the past decade her research has focused on the effects of urbanisation and apartheid legislation on legal and family structures.

JACKLYN COCK is an associate professor of sociology at the University of the Witwatersrand in Johannesburg. She has been involved in struggles around feminist issues, the environment, and militarism for many years. An activist in the Black Sash, the End Conscription Campaign and Earthlife Africa, she is the author of numerous publications, including *Maids and Madams*.

UNITY DOW practises law in Gaborone, Botswana. Recently, she successfully challenged the citizenship laws of Botswana, forcing legislators to give equal citizenship rights to women and children. She is presently setting up a human rights centre in Gaborone.

DOROTHY DRIVER is a senior lecturer in the Department of English Language and Literature at the University of Cape Town. Besides the contribution in this volume, and a previous essay on women and the ANC, she has published essays on South African women writers, and was recently awarded the Pringle Prize for Literary Articles for '"Woman" as Sign in the South African Colonial Enterprise', *Journal of Literary Studies*, 1, 1988, pp1–20. Her book on Pauline Smith is forthcoming from David Philip Publishers.

BIENCE GAWANAS is a Namibian advocate who spent many years in exile before independence. She worked at the Legal Assistance Centre before taking up a recent appointment as one of only two women on the new Public Service Commission. She is, however, first and foremost an activist who has worked for many years with Swapo and the Swapo Women's Council in exile.

FRENE GINWALA holds several law degrees and is a member of the British Bar. She also has a PhD in political economy. Presently she is the Director of Research for the Office of the President of the African National Congress and has written extensively on policy issues for the ANC.

NOLULAMO GWAGWA studied at the University of the Transkei, completed her MSc at the London School of Economics, and is currently working on a PhD on low income resource allocation for housing and urban planning. Her research involves gender and policy issues with regard to housing, local goverment, and urban planning.

DESIRÉE HANSSON holds a BSc Hons (Natal); M Soc Sc (Cape Town); and MA Clin Psych (Cape Town). She is a senior lecturer in the Institute of Criminology at the University of Cape Town and the chair of the Social Justice Resource Project. A registered clinical psychologist, a consultant in areas of women and law, and an active member of Rape Crisis (Cape Town), she is also a co-editor of *Towards Justice? Crime and State Control in South Africa*.

DIANNE HUBBARD received her law degree from Harvard Law School. Her publications include *Crisis in Crossroads: A Report on Human Rights in South Africa*, published by the Lawyers Committee for Human Rights in New York. She is presently a legal reseacher in Namibia and is involved in a number of projects relating to women and the law. She is a member of Women's Solidarity, an activist women's organisation in Windhoek.

BRIGITTE MABANDLA, who holds a law degree from the University of Zambia, is a member of the constitutional committee of the African National Congress and the convenor of a sub-committee on gender and children. She is presently a human rights research officer in the Community Law Centre at the University of the Western Cape, focusing on gender in constitution making and researching the legal status of children in South Africa.

MARY MABOREKE teaches in the Faculty of Law at the University of Zimbabwe in Harare. She completed her MPhil in Zimbabwe, in association with the University of Oslo, on a study of custody and maintenance and their effects on women. She teaches Women's Law, amongst other courses, and is a member of the Women and Law in Southern Africa Research Project.

CHRISTINA MURRAY is an associate professor in the Department of Public Law at the University of Cape Town. Her main interests are in constitutional law, human rights law, women and law and contract. She is an editor of the *South African Journal on Human Rights* and co-edited *No Place to Rest: Forced Removals and the Law in South Africa* with Catherine O'Regan.

THANDABANTU NHLAPO has a BA (Law) from the University of Botswana, Lesotho and Swaziland, an LLB from the University of Glasgow, and a DPhil from the University of Oxford for his research on 'Women's Rights in Traditional Family Law'. He is presently a senior lecturer at the University of Cape Town, teaching family and customary law. His primary area of interest is human rights in domestic law with an emphasis on women and children. He has published numerous articles, and was co-author, with Alice Armstrong, of *Law and the Other Sex: The Legal Position of Women in Swaziland*.

CATHERINE O'REGAN is a senior lecturer in the Department of Criminal and Procedural Law at the University of Cape Town, specialising in the areas of procedure, labour and gender. She holds a PhD from the London School of Economics, is the present editor of the *IMSSA Arbitration Digest* and was the co-editor, with Christina Murray, of *No Place to Rest: Forced Removals and the Law in South Africa*.

HELEN REES is a medical practitioner in Johannesburg, the women's health representative of the National Medical and Dental Association, and a lecturer in Family Medicine at the University of the Witwatersrand. She serves on the board of the Women's Health Project and is a regular contributor to *Speak* magazine.

ELIZABETH SHEEHY is an associate professor of Law at the University of Ottawa, Canada, where she teaches Criminal Law and Women and the Law. She is co-editor of the *Canadian Journal of Women and the Law* and is on the Board of Directors of Lawyers Against Apartheid (Ottawa). She has written extensively on women and the law, and her article 'Canadian Judges and the Law of Rape: Should the Charter Insulate Bias?' was awarded the Marion Porter prize for the most significant feminist research article in 1990.

CARLA SUTHERLAND is a researcher for the Committee of Enquiry into Sexual Harassment at the University of Cape Town. This committee, established in 1990, was the first of its kind in Southern Africa. As such she is recognised as one of the experts in this field in South Africa.

LINDA ZAMA is a practising human rights attorney in Durban, and a member of several organisations and commissions. She is secretary of the National Association of Democratic Lawyers, and works with grass-roots organisations on issues affecting human rights.

Introduction

Susan Bazilli

Keep in mind always the present you are constructing. It should be the
future that you want.[1]

*I*t is important that the history of the *Putting Women on the Agenda*
conference be chronicled. It is situated within the context of an ongoing
discussion in South Africa on gender, women's oppression, and women
and the constitution. Hence, reference will be made to some of the many
conferences and meetings that have taken place both inside and outside
South Africa over the past couple of years.

By drawing together various threads of feminist thought in such a
way, the cloth that is woven will be uneven and rough in texture, but it is
necessary in order to locate the very specific task of the struggle for the
emancipation of women within the particular, and peculiar, South
African context.

I will attempt to characterise some of the discussion that has taken
place within Southern Africa. Wherever possible, I will refer to Southern
African sources and reference material to acknowledge the depth of the
work that has taken place, and to make the discussion pertinent and
accessible to South Africans. However, this should not be seen as an
attempt to provide any definitive review of the literature. That would
comprise a volume in itself. Ideas, concepts, bodies of thought, and conceptual frameworks will be referenced which can then be pursued by

readers on their own. I will refer to specific papers in this text, but make
no attempt to summarise the work: the authors' words speak for themselves. Some concepts such as feminism, gender oppression, patriarchy
and so on, will be given 'working definitions'.

Women's issues *are* on the agenda: of trade unions; political organisations; aspects of civil society; at universities; within grassroots
structures – but wherever women are on the agenda, they are only there
because women have put themselves there. And this was accomplished
only through struggle. The work of the authors in this book is a contribution to that struggle.

History

The events and circumstances that led up to the Lawyers for Human
Rights (LHR) conference need to be set out in chronological form. They
illustrate that the process of 'putting women on the agenda' has particular antecedents within the South African context. We acknowledge our
collective past in order to define our vision of the future.

In 1988, the African National Conference (ANC) released the first
draft of its constitutional guidelines. These guidelines were circulated
within the country, an activity that was, at the time, illegal. Various
organisations and individuals began to comment on and write about the
guidelines. Early in 1989, the South African Law Commission released
its draft bill of rights. Again, academics and legal practitioners began to
comment on this document. In April 1989 there was a women's conference in Harare, hosted by the Institute for a Democratic Alternative
for South Africa (Idasa), where Zimbabwean women urged the women
of South Africa to organise *now* to ensure that they attain full and equal
rights, given the experience of women in the region. This is the same
message that Mary Maboreke exhorts in her paper in this collection. This
Harare meeting, part of the development of 'safaris' by various groups
and individuals to meet with the ANC in countries to the north of the
Limpopo, provided the first major access for this exchange to occur between South African women from inside the country and those in exile.

In August 1989 Idasa organised a conference on *Women and the
Constitution* in Cape Town. In December 1989 there was an ANC in-
house seminar held in Lusaka with the ANC legal/constitutional
committee and the ANC women's section. All aspects of ANC policy
with regard to women and gender were discussed, and an attempt made
to formulate national policy for the emancipation of women. One of the
primary issues dealt with was 'family policy' for a future South Africa.
Nolulamo Gwagwa's paper in this volume had its genesis at that meeting. In January 1990 approximately 350 women from South Africa and

women in exile met in Amsterdam at the Malibongwe conference. Papers were presented from all the regions of South Africa, with a particular focus on organising women rather than academic research.

In that same month, an article appeared in *Cosmopolitan* magazine reviewing these various drafts of the constitutional guidelines and the bill of rights. After many years of struggle by women on the ground, within organisations, and academic work, both within the country and by women in exile, the *Cosmo* article signalled that these issues had made the 'mainstream': hitting the newsstands in CNA and Checkers.[2]

Dorothy Driver's paper on language and the constitution, which was referred to in this article and discussed by the ANC constitutional committee, is published here in a revised and updated form.

And then there was February 1990. With the release of Mandela and the unbanning of political organisations, nothing in South Africa would ever be the same again.

The ANC's national executive committee issued a statement on 2 May 1990, regarding the emancipation of women[3] which enshrined the rights of women as a fundamental policy. This was the first comprehensive statement on women's emancipation released by any political party or organisation in South Africa, and to date it still is.

In October 1990, the South African Council of Churches hosted a *Women and Constitution* conference in Durban. They published various proposals and recommendations that were then circulated and discussed at the LHR conference. The importance of this initiative becomes clear when noting that over 70 per cent of South African women belong to some form of church organisation.

Subsequently, in November 1990, the Lawyers for Human Rights conference, *Putting Women on the Agenda*, was held. The week following that conference, the ANC's constitutional committee held a commission on gender in Cape Town, entitled *Gender Today and Tomorrow*.[4] In February 1991, there was a conference held at the University of Natal in Durban entitled *Women and Gender in Southern Africa*. In this introduction, many of the references will refer to papers presented at that conference.

Such an on-going process of meetings, involving some of the same individuals and work, but more importantly canvassing other opinions and ideas, allows for the dynamic evolution of discussion around women and gender and the constitution, a bill of rights, and the proposed Women's Charter. The importance of this on-going process cannot be stressed enough. This collection of papers, while clearly not representative of the process as a whole, at least provides access to the debates for those who did not attend these conferences.

This chronology is, of course, incomplete. There have been other conferences and meetings inside the country, notably the Congress of South African Trade Unions' (Cosatu) women's conference. There have also been conferences that have taken place in places as far afield as Venezuela, Amsterdam and elsewhere, where the issues pertinent to women in South Africa have been discussed. It is an essential part of the problem that much of this work has not been available to women in South Africa, and that which is available is usually only accessible to a small group of academics.[5] It is hoped that this volume will go a small way to redressing this problem.

Feminism

It seems that few words can more easily polarise people than 'feminism'.[6] I want to explain here what I mean by this concept; and later on, look at what I think it means in the context of the South African struggle for women's liberation.

In her opening paper, Jacklyn Cock says that we are facing an overcrowded 'agenda of struggle' and that priorities are ordered differently depending on one's ideological background. She goes on to stress that at the very least, women should agree on a broad principle to provide some kind of 'fulcrum' around which much of our debates can turn. We are a long way from achieving any kind of 'fulcrum', let alone 'consensus' on what 'feminism' is: and the debate itself is more instructive than the rhetoric. But as Cock continues: '[T]hat principle is social justice.' That is, perhaps, our best beginning.

We are now seeing the gestation of a human rights culture that hopefully will give birth to not just a new South Africa, but a culture that will be democratic, non-racist and non-sexist. Feminists see that feminism is an integral component of such a process. It is an emancipatory project, the essence of which is social justice. It aims to examine women's oppression, expose the dynamics of male domination and female subordination and, guided by that analysis, fight for women's liberation.[7] In so doing, it addresses the need to redress gender oppression and all of its effects: in essence, providing a liberation for all people from the oppressive gender roles in which they are enslaved. This is the essence of the 'humanist' nature of this struggle, referred to by Linda Zama. Feminism then can be seen as both an intellectual process and a political movement.

As an intellectual process, feminist analysis provides a perspective that takes the point of view, or standpoint, of women as an oppressed category, and assumes that the cornerstone of the social construction of reality is based on patriarchal notions of society, and given a particular face by various forms of colonialism, imperialism, capitalism, and all of the other 'isms'. Whether we are examining law, the economy, the family, or the state, a feminist analysis attempts to expose, to peel away the layers, of that male bias, sometimes called 'malestream thought'[8] or 'malevolent thought'.[9]

No single dimension of social life, whether biological, sexual, economic, psychological, political, or historical, is adequate to explain the origins and persistence of gender hierarchies. Theorists have sought to understand women's situations as fundamentally structured by the power relations of ideological and material forces. Feminist theory itself has gone through quite a metamorphosis from its early days of the western women's movement. There has been the attempt to provide a recovery of women who have been 'hidden from history',[10] and as such, to make visible the invisible. There has been the deconstruction of existing theories to reveal the 'androcentric' (male-centred) biases that they are based on. Then there was a reconstruction of theories that took into account the role that women play, for example, in the family, work, the economy and so on. Finally, there has been a critique of all of these methods, by feminist theorists, so that feminism and feminist analysis is not a static theory or 'ism', but is constantly being criticised and revised to take into account the dynamics of social change and theoretical refinement. The papers in this collection have sought to incorporate some of these various aspects of feminist theory or theories.

Feminism as a political movement has organised and mobilised women to struggle for change; it has sought to lobby for policies and changes to laws that reflect this understanding of the need for gender sensitivity and awareness in all social, political and economic life; and it has, more recently, attempted to, itself, recognise the fundamental relationship between race, class and gender. In so doing, it also recognises that no single theory can explain the oppression and subjectivities of race, class and gender.[11] This paradox brings us to the acute problem of feminism in a South African context.

A South African dilemma

There is a long standing cliché that we must distinguish between 'western' feminism and 'African' (non-western) feminism.[12] This was one of the main debates that took place in Nairobi during the 1985 women's conference which was held at the end of the United Nations Decade for Women. The end of the United Nations' decade, however, was really the beginning of raising these debates and conflicts.

Feminism often assumes a 'myth of sisterhood'[13] which can and most often does obscure the very important differences among women –

those of class, race, geographical location, political ideologies, ethnicity, age, sexual orientation, ability, and so on. Recognition and accountability for these differences is seen as vital to the effort to build general theories which genuinely account for women's oppression. Analyses of sex/ gender systems and sexism have all too often assumed that the experiences and perspectives of white, middle class, Western European and North American women can be generalised for all women. This criticism is just as true in America as it is in Africa.[14] The critique in South African terms has been that much of this perspective was 'imported' into earlier analyses by white academic feminists. Essential to the central task of feminism is the *validation* of the differences; our task is to empower all women so that they can speak for themselves.

The major fundamental characteristic of South African apartheid society is its deep divisions based on race and class. And while these divisions are deeply entrenched within a patriarchal structure, they manifest themselves differently for women located in the different spheres.[15] South African feminism needs to develop a historical-contextual approach with emphasis on the different kinds of gender oppression in the country.[16] In short, while all women are oppressed, they are not oppressed equally. There is inequality within inequality. However, while stating this, we also need to realise that the notions of 'double' and 'triple' oppression, or 'hierarchy' of oppressions, should be reconsidered. All women are oppressed, but 'not in the same way'.

How a South African feminism develops will also, as with everything, depend on political priorities. Manifestations of feminist thinking have probably been as fragmented as the history of all other political debates within the country. This problem will not be solved in the near future; nor can it or should it be 'solved'. But it has begun to be addressed by an integrated analysis. Generally, theorists speak about things or people as if everything can be put in a box and labelled as a category of social life. All too often, feminism speaks of the 'oppression of women', the need for the 'liberation of women', as if 'women' was a single category. Another 'category' that is often used too glibly is that of 'black women' or 'African women'. It smacks of 'us' and 'them'. It is trite for the reasons with which we are familiar, that most of the academic research that has been done in South Africa 'on' 'black women' has been carried out, documented, and theorised, by 'white women' academics. This issue of the objectification of black women was raised at the LHR and other conferences.[17] We must take cognisance of this fact. It must be 'put on the agenda'.

Some African feminists say: 'The feminist movement itself should be seen in context. It is a reformist rather than revolutionary movement in the West, initiated and sustained by middle-class women of [European] white origin.'[18] And there is no doubt that this is at least partly true.[19] Further:

> African womanhood has been an increasingly topical subject for writers in recent years. Unfortunately, however, the majority of them have not themselves belonged to the community of African women. This is in itself problematic, since the non-African who studies this rather complex issue is inevitably an observer rather than a participant. The limitation is further complicated by the fact that European authors tend to employ theoretical assumptions and a methodology which hampers or in some cases precludes a realistic assessment of the subject matter.[20]

But also too:

> Black women should not reject the term 'feminist' because of its association with white women... [R]ather we should re-claim the term and re-work it so that it speaks directly to our lives... [P]roblems arise not when white women choose to write about the experiences of non-white people, but when such material is presented as authoritative.[21]

And, 'If we get over the stage where our perception of the women's question is always blurred by the spectre of "western feminism" then we should get on with the business of addressing the crucial question as expected and demanded of us by history.'[22] This is, indeed, the 'historic charge and task' that Linda Zama urges upon us in her paper, exhorting us to work together.

Feminist struggle in South Africa must relate to the specific conditions in this country. Our actions and analysis must therefore include a recognition of the right of *all* women to speak in their own voices. 'African women must speak for themselves. They should also decide for themselves who they are, where they are going, what obstacles face them and how to remove these.'[23]

The challenge is more than acknowledging and incorporating into our theorising the complex connections between racial and gender oppression in the lives of black women. We need to build a feminist solidarity by confronting the divisions of race and class that divide women from one another and weaken our collective power. If the experiences of women are to be understood, addressed, and incorporated, then *all* women must participate in the building of theory. In a South African context, then, that means that those of us who are privileged need to facilitate, empower, and respect, this process for and with other women.

This book evolved out of a historical process, of which the conference was only one manifestation. If we do not address this fundamental issue in the development of our theories and analyses, then the policies that stem from such a process will not speak for the majority of women in South Africa.

Gender

There has been a leap between 'the women question' and 'gender analysis' which has only recently occurred in South African parlance. The word 'sex' denotes an individual as male or female, and derives from the individual's biological attributes. The word 'gender' extends these physical attributes to create an ideological construct which is based on the way that society understands those biological differences between men and women. What we recognise and experience as 'masculine' and 'feminine' is socially and culturally constructed as our 'gender', which involves a whole constellation of roles, expectations, social and sexual behaviours.

What we are looking at is the interrelationship between 'women's rights' and 'gender relations', as Frene Ginwala outlines in her paper. When we speak about 'gender relations' we raise relations of power. And gender is an integral part of all forms of power. In Ginwala's paper she examines the differential impact on men and women in terms of economic policies, and economic power. Both men and women need to be seen as *gendered beings*. The ways in which men and women operate in society is not natural and given, but is historically and culturally constructed and socially located.[24]

We must regard gender as an essential component of the national liberation struggle. 'We are engaged in a national democratic struggle against the apartheid regime, and the national question in South Africa needs to be reformulated to ensure that the struggle becomes a gender conscious struggle for a new transformed South Africa.'[25]

In putting women on the agenda, we are really addressing the need to put gender on the agenda: but in so doing, we recognise that we have a dilemma. We talk about gender oppression, and we mean human rights and social justice for all people, *and* we mean equality and recognition of the rights of women. We have to talk about women's rights, and not gender rights, because we do not want 'rights' to accrue to our socially constructed roles.[26] We do not use the term 'gender' simply to be polite and not offend men, we use it because it is the only way that we can try to explain why the social relations between men and women are so fraught with dissonance.

We must take 'gender' seriously, but we need to be cautious about its use. 'Gender' has been conceived as synonymous with 'women', retaining 'women' as the central focus of analysis of oppression under patriarchy.[27] This has had a two-pronged effect. The use of the term 'gender' without any kind of broad-based education has attempted to make men and women responsible for addressing issues that are still considered to be 'women's work'.[28] The reduction of the meaning of 'gender' as being synonymous with women has continued to focus gender analysis on areas of social life traditionally regarded as female domains such as the domestic sphere, the family, and so on.[29]

Patriarchy

'It is a sad fact that one of the few profoundly non-racial institutions [in South Africa] is patriarchy.'[30] I would say it is the *only* one!

This is another term that is used as if it means the same thing to all people. Obviously the experience of patriarchal power relations impacts differently on different women, depending on their social location – as does apartheid. Some of the fundamental ways in which men exercise social, political, sexual and economic control over women's lives across lines of culture, class and race can be outlined in broad terms as including:

> ... men's ability to deny women their sexuality or force it upon them; to command or exploit their labour or control their produce; to control or rob them of their children; to confine them physically and prevent their movement; to use them as objects in male transactions; to cramp their creativeness; or to withhold from them large areas of the society's knowledge or cultural attainments.[31]

Patriarchy, then, is the ideology of male supremacy that results from the social construction of gender which in turn justifies the social, economic and political distinctions between men and women. While feminist theorists have debated the various historical and material conditions that have created, or resulted from, these distinctions, the term 'patriarchy' remains the most useful description and is the one that is most often used.

Men and women are different, ie, they are not the same. Male supremacy – or patriarchy – has defined these differences as if what is male is better, and hence benefits are rewarded to the 'better half'. Male supremacy then created concepts like neutrality and objectivity and enshrined them in law. This had the effect of rendering invisible, or hiding, this 'gendering' of social constructs which are the foundation of social thought. The concept of 'equality' was introduced into the modern culture of rights, which were defined as individual. But the problem is that 'equality' is seen as 'equal', that is 'sameness' and is not able to translate difference and value. Patriarchy is upheld by means of a web of laws, public and private structures, including the family, religion, traditional practices, and ideological apparatus such as schools, the media, and so on.[32] We need to understand how patriarchal structures operate in order to construct policies and laws that do not further entrench gender oppression in the new society that we are forging.

The family and women

It is often said in feminist literature that the family is the central site of the oppression of women. This is so regardless of whether it is African or western families being discussed. And the family is by nature contradictory. For as it is a site of oppression, so too it is a site of resistance in a struggle against colonial domination and apartheid.

Our beginning point, in any discussion of 'the family', should be the actual lives people lead.[33] The 'family' is, at best, an enigmatic term. But we should not begin with some abstract and idealised model of the perfect family.[34] What do we mean by the 'family' when it is referred to in a constitution that argues for the 'protection of the family'? Our perspective seeks to locate the family within society and to understand its social construction as opposed to its operation: 'What is required is a total reconstruction of social relations.'[35]

This is addressed in several of the papers in this text. In our African context, we have to look closely at customary law regarding the practices which provide social cohesion and those which are harmful to people, especially women. As Frene Ginwala and Thandabantu Nhlapo note, we have to protect what is positive and reject what is negative. Nhlapo's paper on customary law provides such an analysis in very cogent terms. He cautions us, too, that the process of constitution-building in a new South Africa will be above all an exercise in negotiation and consensus-seeking. Therefore, it is extremely important to try to avoid cultural shocks to the majority of the population, when we talk about customary law.

Mary Maboreke provides us with some lessons from Zimbabwe about the difficulties that we will face. 'What about lobolo?' was a question often asked at many of the conferences referred to. It is a crucial issue, and one that Brigitte Mabandla attempts to answer when referring to ANC policies regarding customary practices which are, without doubt, fundamental to people's understanding of their culture.

There is no institution in South Africa that has been more violently affected by apartheid than the family. But all too often family policies have been discussed as if they are based on the nuclear family. In fact, a significant number of families are single-parent women-headed families. This fact must have a major impact on any policies that are created regarding the family, whether they be social welfare, maintenance laws or housing planning. Sandra Burman's socio-economic examination of the polices that have affected, and will affect, the family, provides an important analysis of the ways in which we are going to have to re-allocate limited resources.

The ideological underpinnings of our varied and complex notions of what constitutes the 'family' must be exposed. Nolulamo Gwagwa's paper compares the ANC's position on the family with that of the present South African state. Such an analysis is crucial if we are to understand what we want to put in place for the future. All social and economic policies will impact on the family. For example, all social security, maintenance laws, and family law, are based on a specific conception of the 'family'. And conceptualisations of the family are an intrinsic part of the various forms of nationalism in South Africa. Responsibility for the family is placed fundamentally on women: whether it is in the policy of 'separate development' or in the ANC's historical claim that motherhood is the ultimate symbol of women's political heroism.[36] Any political philosophy that continues to locate women primarily within the private realm of the family is fundamentally disempowering for them.

This continual relegation to the family and to the roles that women assume as, above all, the revered mother, is an issue that has been addressed in South Africa. But it needs a much stronger analysis. If we are seen to be attacking motherhood, we are viewed as the most heinous of villains, or perhaps at best, western bourgeois feminists. The slogan 'A Woman's Place is in the Struggle', aside from yet again telling women where their place should be, usually is followed by a second slogan, 'Mothers of the Nation'. Women can be in the struggle, but as wives and mothers. As Mamphela Ramphele has said:

> Look at how women define themselves and their issues. They always speak up in their capacities as mothers or as wives, acting for the sake of their husbands and children. They never articulate their issues, as citizens, who happen to be women, and are therefore entitled to equality. By limiting their self-definition to their roles as child-raisers and home-makers they are clinging to some of the very stereotypes that perpetuate their oppression.[37]

Often this was the only way women could make political space for themselves,[38] but those days are over now. In illustrating the parallels between the ANC and the state's deification of the family, and women's place therein, Nolulamo Gwagwa cautions us about the effect this will have on our future policies and laws regarding the family.

The state and women

It is pertinent to look at the state from a feminist vantage point. But in South Africa we are talking about a state where the majority of the people have not had *any* democratic rights. This must be understood when we examine any 'feminist critiques of the state' that have stemmed from western writings.

Frene Ginwala discusses the obligation on the state to end sexism, in a similar way that a new constitution may place an obligation on the state to end racism. 'The responsibility for ensuring equality, racial as well as sexual, should be placed upon the State, and entrenched in the constitution.'[39] This is of fundamental importance, for to do otherwise places the onus on the oppressed to 'claim' their 'rights', a procedure fraught with inequities. This is a very difficult onus for any state to bear.

A new constitution which includes gender would have to take into account both the dimensions of the universal issues affecting women and men, and the specific forms that apartheid has given to gender domination.[40]

Feminist theorists have pointed out that the state, in its relation to society as a whole, and in its specific relation to institutionalised masculine dominance, urgently requires our sustained analysis. While the origin of this analysis is grounded in critiques of western democracies by white western feminists, it has begun to be applied to the South African context.[41] Although apparently gender neutral in its formulation, state policy has profound and far-reaching implications for women. 'Policy is designed to concretise specific conceptions of a desired social and economic reality, but it is articulated and implemented in an arena of already existing social relations.'[42]

Our concern with the state is linked to the twofold nature of feminism's political project: first, to understand the nature of the social, political and economic relations through which women's subordination is constructed and maintained; and second, to dismantle these structures in the process of creating a society which is free from relations of dominance and subordination that stem from gender, class or race differences.[43] The lessons that we can benefit from stem from struggles that the women's movement has waged in other countries around the world. We have two important examples of this: from Canada, by Elizabeth Sheehy, and from Zimbabwe, by Mary Maboreke.

The question that we have to pose is how to incorporate these lessons into the very transformation process that we are engaged in here. We must query the extent to which our new state will be autonomous from, or will itself reinforce, male dominance. We know that any political strategy that regards the state as a lever for progressive social change necessarily emerges from a position that is essentially 'reformist'. And in South Africa we are not talking about reform, we are talking about transformation and reconstruction.

A large part of the state's support of gender oppression or sexual inequality exists at the level of ideology. But ideology has a material base and the ideology of male supremacy has had a tangible impact on shaping the everyday practices and circumstances of women's lives – and the form of this impact is clearly dependent on their race or class. If we are to expect state power to be used as one of the strategies to achieve the goals of women's emancipation, we are expecting the power of the state to be responsive and responsible to the demands of women.

What are 'women's rights'?

When we talk about the liberation of women, or address the oppression or subordination of women, we often characterise the struggle as one of fighting for 'women's rights'. But the concept of 'rights' is also an ideological one. As Frene Ginwala, Catherine O'Regan and Christina Murray have pointed out in their papers, we are not simply talking about addressing 'discrimination' against women; we are not simply talking about 'equality' as an abstract notion.

In fact, we want to distinguish between what has been called 'women's rights feminism', which addresses the notion of equality, and 'women's emancipation feminism', which takes us beyond mere equality to a vision of the transformation of society as a whole rather than focusing only on the improvement of the relative status of women.[44] It is a particular perspective on the whole of our society that we are seeking to transform. And that is precisely why these authors have sought to address the notions of gender oppression and equality.

We have often used the terms 'rights' and 'human rights' to characterise what we have been fighting for. From the 1948 Universal Declaration of Human Rights, the attainment of fundamental human rights has come to symbolise the essence of our struggle, most eloquently framed in the Freedom Charter. But what do we mean by women's rights? When 'rights' intersect with 'law' the real issue is 'power'. Who has the power to demand and who has the power to cede these rights? How do we attain our rights in the face of structural and systemic inequality? And in South Africa, the legacy of the legislated and instituted inequality of apartheid is legion. The history of 'rights' has developed from the liberal notion of equality under the law in an individual capacity, and not from the structural inequalities of race, class and gender. But the extension of 'rights' is associated with the foundations of democracy and freedom: the protection of the weak against the strong, the individual against the state. 'To couch a claim in terms of rights is a major step towards a recognition of a social wrong.'[45] Such a 'right' gives legitimacy to a claim. Where we must be vigilant is to recognise that *if* the gender power relations remain the same, legal individual rights do not resolve problems but rather transpose the problem into one that is defined as having a legal solution.[46]

In seeking legal redress, or having recourse to legal remedies in the traditional legal system, the individual must prove that her rights have been violated. Women then take the hazardous risk of having the law work against them by resorting to law that is structured on patriarchal precedents, as Elizabeth Sheehy so clearly illustrates. This is not to say that we should ignore earlier struggles for law reform (in other countries) but we should be mindful of the fact that history has shown us that women's oppression is not simply a matter of equal rights or discrimination under the law.

The same caution holds true for issues of race and class, and can often be illustrated in ways that appear more concrete than talking about the more nebulous notion of gender. For example, if the law, as it is presently constituted, retains its inherent bias in favour of white middle class men then the recourse to justice through the judicial process for black people, for marginalised poor people, for rural illiterate people, for working class people, will be just as impossible as it is now.

In Britain, the Sex Discrimination Act 1975 and the Race Relations Act 1976 have been largely unsuccessful in changing discrimination against women or people of colour. In Canada, women have lost much more under the Equality Section of the Charter of Rights and Freedoms than they have gained, as it is white middle class men who have used the section to protect *their* rights. In America today the analysis of feminists, of progressive legal practitioners, and of the black community in general suggests that the notion of enshrining 'civil rights' in law has ignored the fact that the majority of the 'poor' (as a category) are condemned to the black underclass, and that the access to law for the majority of women remains a 'right' on paper only.[47] The failure of the Equal Rights Amendment (ERA) also attests to this.

For example, the law may concede a 'right' to decent health care, or the 'right' to safe abortions, or the 'right' to legal representation, or the 'right' to a clean environment, or the 'right' to a living wage: but if the coffers of the state and capital refuse to fund the administration of these policies as 'rights', then the right becomes no more than the 'plight' it once was.

Finally, there is one point that cannot be emphasised enough! The experiences of women throughout the world have shown us that there is often no relationship between the attainment of national liberation, through struggle, and the attainment of women's rights. Unless women's rights are taken seriously during a society's transition, they will not miraculously appear afterwards.[48] As Mamphele Ramphele says, '[Women] fought side by side with their men for liberation, and afterwards they were sent back to the cooking pots and told to get on with the business of child-rearing. Their exploitation has not ended.'[49]

The law and women

What is law? Law typically incorporates a community's customs and values, whether domestic, economic, religious or moral; and law acts primarily as a means of social control which entrenches these values in the interest of the society's dominant class. Because the law reflects the interests of the dominant, or ruling, class in both practice and theory, it therefore reflects the interests of patriarchal control over women's lives. In fact, all notions of what 'law' is can be reduced to one: power.[50]

In the present South African climate, we are faced with the task of determining the future of law and its relationship to women. To do so, we must always be cognisant of narrowing the gap between law and justice. We know all too well that there has been little, if any, relationship between law and justice in South African history. In terms of gender oppression, as in other areas, this is not just a semantic distinction.

The word of law, whether statutory or judicial, is a 'sub-category of the underlying social motives and beliefs from which it was born'.[51] Law as we usually understand it refers to written laws, codes and systems of control, retribution and remedies. But justice is the inclusion – in law – of the more ethical, abstract dimension that contemplates the purpose behind the rules and the effective implementation in a justiciable – and justifiable – way. The first priority for a feminist analysis of law is to look to both the letter and the spirit of the law. The Rule of Law provides, in theory, that no one is above the law or exempt from it, and all citizens are equal before and under the law. The law must be applied equally and impartially to all citizens. We know that the Rule of Law is fiction in South Africa – for the majority of men *and* women. Legal ideology conceives of law as exempt from politics. We do not.

Practical implications

Research into the problems women face has many components which must be undertaken before we can change, redress and transform the legal situation of women. We first need to find out what the law is – the official law, the law on the statute books – and whether and how it discriminates against women. Many laws appear to be neutral, but adversely affect women because of the economic and social conditions of their oppression. Some of the most far-reaching implications affect women in the workplace. Catherine O'Regan and Christina Murray have examined the history of protective employment legislation and its effect on women. In so doing, they examine the debates around equality: for women to be equal to men does not mean being the same as men. This sameness/difference argument has a long history in feminist legal theory[52] and is the basis for the necessity for redress through affirmative action policies.

Some laws may be ambiguous, and leave their remedies up to judges or administrators who are male. Some laws may be extremely inappropriate to the local conditions, such as those that undermine the positive aspects of tradition or, for example, communal property ownership in rural areas.[53]

Some laws are obviously *prima facie* – on the face of it – discriminatory against women. For instance, we can clearly see the discrimination against women applied by the reduction of women to minors through the application of Roman-Dutch law, and especially by the colonisation of customary law by Roman-Dutch law. The history of matrimonial and family law in South Africa attests to this.

Other laws may adversely affect women because of what is left out, rather than prescribed, by them. The application and the administering of the law(s) also impact adversely on women. Some laws may appear to be fair and to treat women and men equally, but are not enforced or adhered to in practice by either the judiciary or the legislators. The laws themselves, or the remedies decreed by the laws, may not be administered effectively, or even at all. This is glaringly obvious when we look at maintenance laws. Not only do they constantly deny meagre financial resources to women and children, but women are better off widowed than abandoned. Mary Maboreke illustrates this problem in Zimbabwe.[54] But if women do not have access to the information or the economic resources to use the law, even in cases where the laws may exist and remedies may be given, the law is ineffective.

Perhaps most importantly, we have to determine the real needs of women, and whether and how the law can be used to meet those needs. Whatever the law or statute or regulation is in any given jurisdiction, such legislative instruments will affect people. And at least half, if not more, of the people, are women. So the laws must be sensitive to the specific needs of women, in other words, they must be gender sensitive, so that they do not discriminate against either women or men in their application.[55] We do so, cognisant of the contradiction Frene Ginwala points out, that while we seek to change the law, and to use the law to seek redress, law itself is what has been used to oppress us.

In tackling these problems, we must re-emphasise that the starting point must be the perspective of women ourselves. We need to focus on narrow laws that affect women specifically, such as the administration of welfare benefits or the private law of maintenance. This is, in essence, what has been termed 'women's law'.[56] We need to focus on laws that appear gender neutral but have a disproportionate impact on women. We need to focus on the language that goes into the constitution and the bill of rights, in practice and in process.

We have much to learn from the experiences of women throughout the world. Most importantly, we can learn from the women in the Southern African region: here we present the work of Mary Maboreke, Unity Dow, Bience Gawanas, Dianne Hubbard, and the Women and Law in Southern Africa Research Project.[57]

Acute gender questions

In the early days of feminism, the slogan 'the Personal is Political' was coined. This saying derived from the dichotomy between the public and private spheres. Productive activity was seen to take place in public, in the market, and by men. Women bear the labour of reproduction – reproducing the labour force and taking care of the workers at home, in the private sphere. Women's place, then, is in the home, whether it is in the bantustans, the townships, or the suburbs. This is a very simplistic reduction, but it serves to illustrate that by relegating women to the private realm, women's problems become private. It is a basic tenet that whatever is privatised is harmful to women – whether it is the privatisation of health care or violence in the home.

Economic activity is seen to be a productive, public and male activity. Frene Ginwala peels away the layers of this assumption when she talks about paid and unpaid labour. This is a crucial distinction that must be understood when we look at making economic policies accountable for women's labour. According to United Nations statistics,[58] women *worldwide* make up slightly more than one-half of the population, perform two-thirds of the world's work, receive one-tenth of the world's income, and own one-hundredth (one per cent!) of the world's property.

Perhaps nowhere has the argument for the struggle for substantive equality been made more persuasively than with respect to the issue of reproductive freedom, which is an 'essential precondition to full and equal participation in society'.[59] While Jacklyn Cock cautions us that such issues have to be seen in different cultural contexts, there can be no argument that control over one's body is the *most* basic human right. In Helen Rees' paper, she defines reproductive rights as the right of women to decide when and how to have their children. That simple statement underlies one of the most contentious battles that women have fought throughout the world – legally, socially and politically. The right to safe contraception, the right to safe delivery and pre and postnatal care, and the right to terminate a pregnancy are preconditions to women's basic human rights. An estimated 300 000 illegal abortions per year in South Africa is not only horrific, it is an indication of what can only really be called women's domestic enslavement.

It should be a constitutional right that a woman herself is able to make the decision about if and when she becomes pregnant or if and when she chooses to terminate a pregnancy.[60] But there must be the political will, the economic resources, and equal access to facilities and technologies before such a right is translated into reality.

Violence against women through rape, domestic violence, sexual harassment and sexual assault is seen to be a 'private' matter. There are two papers on rape in this collection, by Desirée Hansson and Dianne Hubbard. The estimates are that one rape takes place every minute in South Africa. Count the minutes that it has taken you to read this far: now imagine those battered, bruised and violated women. Dianne Hubbard's paper on rape in Namibia culls from much of the international and regional literature on rape. It serves as a very useful example of the kind of research that needs to be documented in order to lobby and advocate change in a newly independent country. Desirée Hansson's paper exemplifies the ways in which academics and activists in South Africa can work together to draft concrete proposals for legislative change.

Sexual harassment is an all-too-common violation experienced by women. It occurs to domestic workers in the home; to workers in the factories, offices and corporate headquarters; to workers and students in universities; and it happens all too frequently in our own political organisations: in fact, it happens so frequently that even defining it and speaking about it publicly is a recent development. Carla Sutherland's insightful analysis of the first and only reported judgement on sexual harassment indicates the long way we have to go in overcoming, not only the problem, but the attitudes towards women that it represents.

The state perpetrates and perpetuates violence against women in a multiplicity of ways: through action, omission, practice, endorsement, neglect. One aspect is the 'second assault', described in the papers on rape as what happens to rape survivors when they have to deal with the legal system – the police, the lawyers, the court, the judges. The 'private' now intersects with 'public' violence.

In South Africa, we have further heinous examples of state violence against women: forced removals; denial of land, shelter, clean water, enough food to eat; lack of literacy and education; the violence and brutality carried out by the security forces and their agents.

Another area where we need to ask acute gender questions is that of women and work, women and the economy. Issues of maternity benefits, protective legislation, equal pay, recognition of unpaid labour, agricultural and domestic sectors, health and safety regulations, working conditions, the informal sector, the participation of women in trade unions and definitions of economic activity: all these and more need to be critically examined and discussed. Since it is assumed that the key to women's liberation is through organising, we can take cognisance of the lessons that can be learned from the women in the trade union movement in South Africa.

Women's participation in forging the future

In our struggle to achieve liberation for all South African people, we have to pay special attention to all the changes that we will demand: in making new laws, creating law reform and transformation, drafting and instituting the new constitution and the bill of rights, and so on. In order to do so, we need to analyse the fundamental underpinnings of many of the concepts that appear to be taken for granted in the basic rhetoric of a democratic society.

A constitution is a written document that sets out the legal framework of the government.[61] It is the most important law of a country – the supreme law. A constitution describes how the government will be elected and how the courts will work, what rights the citizens have, and what powers the government can and cannot have. And this law sets out the rules as to how all other laws will be made. A constitution sets out the way the government is to be elected and defines the institutions through which the governing will be done; the legislature which makes the laws, the executive which does the actual governing in terms of the law, and the judiciary which ensures that the laws are obeyed by the citizens and the government itself.

But as Frene Ginwala has discussed, it is no good saying we want this or that in a constitution if we elect an all-male constituent assembly or we have only a few women in positions of power. It is only through the participation of greater numbers of women, throughout the entire process, that we will come anywhere near *really* putting women on the agenda.

The fundamental rights and freedoms of the people are enshrined in a constitution through a bill of rights.[62] Our bill of rights will no doubt include several levels – or 'generations'[63] – of rights: the right to speech, privacy, association, opinion; economic and cultural rights such as the right to education, health and social security; and collective rights such as the right to a clean environment. A bill of rights also establishes specific mechanisms for ensuring that those rights and freedoms are respected. But these mechanisms are only as good as the means of enforcement, which traditionally have been the courts. An independent, non-racial, *non-sexist*[64] and representative judiciary would go some way to ensure that the principles in a bill of rights are respected. However, as Elizabeth Sheehy indicates in the Canadian experience, women will lose far more than they will gain when it is the judiciary that is empowered to make decisions. The Canadian experience is very instructive here when we look at the power of the judiciary versus parliament in interpreting sections of the charter of rights and the constitution.

Other instruments that could be put in place to ensure that people have recourse to enforcing their rights exist at a multiplicity of levels: criminal law, administrative laws, human rights commissions, an office of a commissioner of justice or ombudsperson, community courts, industrial courts, family courts, pay equity commissions, constitutional courts, sexual harassment commissions of inquiry, labour relations boards, workers' compensation tribunals, social assistance or welfare review tribunals, maintenance courts, and so on. These would provide a forum for complaints, a mechanism for enforcing the rights of an individual, and application of remedies for redressing wrongful or discriminatory treatment.

Affirmative action mechanisms will provide one essential mechanism for achieving some of the redress that is demanded, both in terms of race and gender. Political power was the sub-text of the Lawyers for Human Rights conference. Formal equality is worth little if it is not supplemented by affirmative action that will help to destroy the structures and behaviour patterns created by centuries of gender oppression, of discrimination against women.[65] This is a crucial indication of what we want to do: 'put flesh on the constitutional skeleton', as Bience Gawanas puts it in the Namibian context.

At the LHR conference, there were several calls to hold a separate workshop or conference on affirmative action. But the point, precisely, is that affirmative action needs to be examined in each and every issue. It cannot be compartmentalised or ghettoised. This was clearly recognised by the resolution that was passed during the last session: 'This conference proposes that all delegations engaged in negotiations on the future constitution of South Africa should be composed of equal numbers of men and women.'[66]

Conclusion

All proposals for change need to be combined with a radical and aggressive re-education process; to give women confidence, to empower women to demand their rights and to re-educate the men – from the legislators to the judges to our companions, co-workers and comrades. We have to be constantly vigilant to ensure that our past will not set limits on what is possible for our future.

Our primary goal will be to develop policies and mechanisms to eradicate systemic discrimination and gender oppression *before* we build the new South Africa. We need to ensure that we build strong, independent, autonomous organisations to represent the needs and demands of women. This must be integral to the democratic process: the negotiations for the terms of the transfer of power, the election procedure itself, and participation in all levels of government and state organs.[67]

'The ultimate test of feminist politics is the extent to which it can provide women with the skills to challenge a male vision of the world, and provide an alternative to that vision.'[68] Part of the challenge that we face in South Africa is that this vision will not be the same for all women: we have to find commonalities in both our language and our vision, so that we can work together to transform the nature of South African society.

Finally, there are two essential aspects to working in a feminist context that must be stated here, and I cannot stress them enough. These are, quite simply, affirmative action and networking. Affirmative action should be the basis of how we work as feminists in South Africa. This means that we have to re-define what we consider academia to be. Those of us who are privileged enough to have the skills to do research, to write, to speak at conferences, have to share those skills, and provide opportunities and the sharing of resources, with others. Privatisation of resources appears to go hand in hand with academia. We need to overcome this by networking, which allows us not only to learn from women throughout the world, and the Southern African region, but also, and more importantly, from each other. Part of redefining what we need to try to overcome through affirmative action translates into very practical realities like access, language, financial resources, priorities of research, skill sharing, and so on. There never will be such a creature as 'unified feminism',[69] nor is that the goal. But what feminism should mean, in theory and in practice, is that we share our resources and our skills, and we learn from each other.

While this should hold true for all aspects of academic endeavours in the future South Africa, here quite clearly I am focusing on feminism as a methodology.

Bience Gawanas made a very valuable point at the conference when she referred to Namibia's policy of 'national reconciliation'. She said that 'we are going to have to beat each other up first before we can have reconciliation.' My plea is that we address our conflicts, we

acknowledge them, and we deal with them openly, honestly and publicly.
Liberation, as well as feminism, will mean very different things to different people. In order for us to really understand that, we must make it a
priority for all the voices of women not just to be heard, but
acknowledged. This is not just our challenge, it is our obligation. It cannot be stated often enough: national liberation struggles do not result
automatically in the 'emancipation' of women. We, all of us, must work
hand in hand to ensure that the present we are constructing will be the
future that we want.[70]

Notes

1. Alice Walker, *The Temple of My Familiar*, London: The Women's Press,
    1989. As a point of interest, Walker coined the term 'womanist' as a way of
    avoiding identification with 'feminism'.
2. D Paice, 'The Great Men-Daba', *Cosmopolitan*, January 1990. CNA is the
    Central News Agency; Checkers is a supermarket chain in South Africa.
3. See Appendix 1.
4. Reported in B Mabandla, Dr M Tshabalala, E Sisulu and C Murray,
    'Women's Rights: A Discussion Document', University of the Western
    Cape: Centre for Development Studies, December 1990. This is a full report
    of the discussion and suggestions for revision and amendment of the ANC
    proposals for the constitution and bill of rights.
5. For a thorough review of 'women's studies' in South Africa, see I Dubel,
    'South African Women's Studies: An Overview and Future Research
    Priorities', paper presented at *Development Alternatives in Southern Africa*,
    Uppsala, May 1987. This paper was revised as 'South African Women's
    Studies Beyond the Legacy of Apartheid', presented at *Women and Gender
    in Southern Africa* conference, 1991, forthcoming in *Agenda*. For a critique
    of what is defined as 'academia' from a feminist perspective in South
    Africa, see S Bazilli, 'Feminist Conferencing', *Agenda*, 9, 1991, p44. See
    generally entire issue of *Agenda*, 9.
6. I am not going to refer to the various debates over the various ideological
    positions of feminism, but for a very useful over view, see M Friedman,
    J Metelerkamp and R Posel, 'What is Feminism?', *Agenda*, 1, 1981, p3.
7. M Luxton and HJ Maroney (eds), *Feminism and Political Economy:
    Women's Work, Women's Struggles*, Toronto: Methuen, 1987.
8. M O'Brien, *The Politics of Reproduction*, London: Routledge & Kegan
    Paul, 1981; D Smith, *The Everyday World as Problematic: A Feminist
    Sociology*, Boston: Northeastern University Press, 1987.
9. C MacKinnon, *Feminism Unmodified*, Harvard: Harvard University Press,
    1987.
10. S Rowbotham, *Hidden from History*, London: Pluto Press, 1973 – the first
    feminist text on this subject, where the phrase comes from. For South
    African references, see H Bernstein, *For Their Triumphs and for Their*

Tears, London: IDAF, 1985; C Walker, *Women and Resistance in South Africa*, London: Onyx Press, 1982; C Walker (ed), *Women and Gender in Southern Africa to 1945*, Cape Town: David Phillip, 1990; papers from *Women and Gender in Southern Africa* conference, Gender Research Group, University of Natal, 1991.

11. C Smart, *Feminism and the Power of Law*, London: Routledge & Kegan Paul, 1989; and 'Law's Power, the Sexed Body, and Feminist Discourse', *Journal of Law and Society*, 17(2), 1990, p194.

12. D Driver, 'Draft Essay on the Position of Women in the New ANC Constitutional Guidelines, 1990'. Author's unpublished draft.

13. See E Spelman, *Inessential Woman: Problems of Exclusion in Feminist Thought*, London: The Women's Press, 1990, for a challenge of the assumption of homogeneity that underlies much of feminist thinking. See also C Ramazanoglu, *Feminism and the Contradictions of Oppression*, London: Routledge Chapman & Hall, 1989. I am indebted to Desirée Hansson for this reference. See also CT Mohanty (ed), *Third World Women and Feminist Politics*, Bloomington: Indiana University Press, 1991.

14. E Thornhill, 'Focus on Black Women!', *Canadian Journal of Women and Law*, 1(1), 1985; M Kline, 'Race, Racism and Feminist Legal Theory', *Harvard Women's Law Journal*, 12, Spring 1989; B Ehrenreich, *Fear of Falling: The Inner Life of the Middle Class*, New York: Harper Row, 1990; T Amott and J Matthaei, *Race, Gender and Work: A Multicultural Economic History of Women in the United States*, Boston: South End Press, 1990; G Joseph and J Lewis, *Common Differences: Conflicts in Black and White Feminist Perspectives*, New York: Doubleday, 1981.

15. A van Niekerk, 'Towards a South African Feminism', paper no 9, *Women and Gender in Southern Africa* conference, 1991. See also S Nene, 'Black Feminism: The Dilemma and the Dialectic', paper no 49, *Women and Gender in Southern Africa* conference.

16. Van Niekerk, 'Towards a South African Feminism'.

17. For a review of the debates that arose, specifically at the *Women and Gender in Southern Africa* conference in Durban, see Bazilli, 'Feminist Conferencing'.

18. C Qunta (ed), *Women in Southern Africa*, London: Allison & Busby Ltd, 1987. See Preface. See also C Obbo, *African Women: Their Struggle for Economic Independence*, London: Zed Press, 1980.

19. See Ehrenreich, *Feminism and Class Consolidation*.

20. Qunta, *Women in Southern Africa*.

21. B Hooks, 'Talking B(l)ack', *Fuse*, 13(4), 1990, p22. See also B Hooks, *Ain't I a Woman: Black Women and Feminism*, Boston: South End Press, 1981; and B Hooks, *Talking Back: Thinking Feminist, Thinking Black*, Toronto: Between the Lines Press, 1989.

22. B Kgositsile, 'The Woman Question: Are the Chains Breaking?', *African Communist*, First Quarter, 1990, cited in P Horn, 'Towards the Emancipation of Women in a Post-apartheid South Africa' paper no 34, *Women and Gender in Southern Africa* conference, 1991, p27.

23. Qunta, *Women in Southern Africa*.

24. S Hassim, 'Where Have All the Women Gone? Gender and Politics in South African Debates', paper no 36, *Women and Gender in Southern Africa* conference, 1991.
25. Horn, 'Towards the Emancipation of Women'.
26. This point was made by Elizabeth Sheehy at the ANC constitutional committee meeting 'Gender Today and Tomorrow' and can be found in the recommendations in Mabandla, 'Women's Rights'.
27. L Manicom, 'Ruling Relations: Rethinking State and Gender in South African History', paper no 5, *Women and Gender in Southern Africa* conference, 1991.
28. T Shefer, 'The Gender Agenda: Women's Struggles in the Trade Union Movement', paper no 19, *Women and Gender in Southern Africa* conference, 1991.
29. Manicom, 'Ruling Relations'.
30. A Sachs, 'Judges and Gender: The Constitutional Rights of Women in a Post-Apartheid South Africa', *Agenda*, 7, 1990, p1.
31. K Gough, 'The Origin of the Family', in R Reiter (ed), *Towards an Anthropology of Women*, New York: Monthly Review Press, 1975.
32. Horn, 'Towards the Emancipation of Women'.
33. A Sachs, 'The Constitutional Position of the Family in a Democratic South Africa', *Agenda*, 8, 1990, p40.
34. Sachs, 'The Constitutional Position of the Family'.
35. A Charman, 'A Response to Albie Sachs: What is the Family?, *Agenda*, 8, 1990, pp55–60.
36. J Wells, 'The Rise and Fall of Motherism as a Force in Black Women's Resistance Movements', paper no 39, *Women and Gender in Southern Africa* conference, 1991; Hassim, 'Where Have All the Women Gone?'.
37. H Zille, 'Life in Transition: An interview with Mamphela Ramphele', *Leadership*, 6(5), 1987, pp65–7.
38. Wells, 'The Rise and Fall of Motherism' and J Wells, 'The History of Black Women's Struggle Against Pass Laws in South Africa', unpublished PhD Dissertation, Columbia University, 1982.
39. F Ginwala, in this volume. See also F Ginwala, 'Formulating National Policy Regarding the Emancipation of Women and the Promotion of Women's Development in our Country', paper presented at the Lusaka ANC Workshop on Gender, December 1989.
40. Sachs, 'Judges and Gender', p1.
41. M Barrett, *Women's Oppression Today*, London: Verso, 1983; Z Eisenstein, *Feminism and Sexual Equality*, New York: Monthly Review Press, 1984; S Findlay and M Randall (eds), 'Feminist Perspectives on the Canadian State', *Resources for Feminist Research*, 17(3), Toronto: Ontario Institute for Studies in Education, September 1988; M McIntosh, 'The State and the Oppression of Women', in A Kuhn and A Wolpe (eds), *Feminism and Materialism*, London: Routledge & Kegan Paul, 1978; C MacKinnon, 'Feminism, Marxism, Method and the State: An Agenda for Theory', *Signs*, 7(3), 1982. For South Africa, see Manicom, 'Ruling Relations'; Gender Policy Group, 'State, Gender and Restructuring in South Africa in the 1980s', *Women and Gender in Southern Africa* conference.

42. Gender Policy Group, 'State, Gender and Restructuring'.
43. M Randall, 'Feminism and the State: Questions for Theory and Practice', in Findlay and Randall (eds), 'Feminist Perspectives on the Canadian State'.
44. A Miles, 'Feminism, Equality and Liberation', *Canadian Journal of Women and the Law*, 1(1), 1985.
45. Smart, *Feminism*; Sachs, 'Judges and Gender'.
46. Smart, *Feminism*.
47. P Williams, 'Spirit-Murdering the Messenger: The Discourse of Fingerpointing as the Law's Response to Racism', *University of Miami Law Review*, 42, 1987; also P Williams, 'The Obliging Shell: An Informal Essay on Formal Equality', *Michigan Law Review*, 87, 1989.
48. For various references on this question see: Horn, 'Towards the Emancipation of Women'; A Armstrong (ed), *Women and Law in Southern Africa*, Harare: Zimbabwe Publishing House, 1987; L Mukurasi, *Post Abolished: One Woman's Struggle for Employment Rights in Tanzania*, London: Women's Press, 1990; 'Women and Law', *The Tribune*, New York: International Women's Tribune Centre, United Nations, July 1990; S Urdang, *And Still They Dance: Women, War and the Struggle for Change in Mozambique*, New York: Monthly Review Press, 1989. (Unfortunately the women from Mozambique who were invited to attend the conference were unable to get their visas in time.)
49. Ramphele, quoted in Zille, 'Life in Transition'.
50. Smart, *Feminism*.
51. Williams, 'Spirit-Murdering the Messenger'.
52. Basically, the two main opposing views are that women's differences, for example regarding maternity and reproductive roles and employment opportunities, should allow women to be treated equally, but differently, versus the view that such demands by women to recognise the differences and provide differential treatment will serve to further disadvantage them.
53. Armstrong (ed), *Women and Law in Southern Africa*. See her Introduction for a detailed elaboration of these points in 'Identifying the Problems'. The Women and Law in Southern Africa (WLSA) Research Project is a long term research project into laws that affect women in six countries in Southern Africa. Each country has a national co-ordinator, and the whole project is co-ordinated in Harare by the regional co-ordinator. For articles that have looked at some of the legal issues affecting women in South Africa, see: B Mabandla, 'Women and Law in South Africa', paper presented at the Malibongwe conference; P Andrews, 'The Legal Underpinnings of Gender Oppression in Apartheid South Africa, unpublished paper; J Segar and C White, 'Constructing Gender: Discrimination and the Law in South Africa', *Agenda*, 4, 1989; S Meintjes, 'Ideologies of Female Subjectivity and the Gendered Nature of Legal Practice in South Africa', paper presented at the *Women and Gender in Southern Africa* conference, 1991. See also F Ginwala, M Mackintosh, and D Massey, ' Gender and Economic Policy in a Democratic South Africa' paper presented at *Gender Today and Tomorrow* workshop, forthcoming publication by the Open University, London, 1991.

54. Elizabeth Gwaunza of the Women and Law in Southern Africa Research Project delivered a paper at the conference on the research into maintenance laws in Zimbabwe. Unfortunately there was not enough space to reproduce her paper in this volume.

55. Armstrong, *Women and Law in Southern Africa*.

56. T Stang-Dahl, 'Taking Women as a Starting Point: Building Women's Law', *International Journal of Sociology of Law*, 14, 1986.

57. See Armstrong (ed), *Women and Law in Southern Africa*, for an explanation of this approach in the Women and Law in Southern Africa Research Project. Also see Mary Maboreke in this volume.

58. United Nations statistics cited in B Roberts, 'Trends in the Production and Enforcement of Female "Dependence"', *Canadian Journal of Women and Law*, 4(1), 1990, pp217–34.

59. S Gavigan, 'Women and Abortion in Canada: What's Law Got to Do With It?' in Luxton and Maroney (eds), *Feminism and Political Economy*. See also Helen Rees in this volume. For a comprehensive history of abortion in South Africa, see H Bradford, 'Herbs, Knives and Plastic: 150 Years of Abortions in South Africa, c. 1840- 1990', paper presented at the *Women and Gender in Southern Africa* conference, 1991.

60. See Mabandla, 'Womens' Rights'.

61. This definition and discussion of a constitution is taken from 'What is a Constitution?', ANC constitutional committee, 1990.

62. *A Bill of Rights for a New South Africa: A Working Documnet by the ANC Constitutional Committee*, University of the Western Cape: Centre for Development Studies, 1990.

63. These are referred to, in sequence, as first, second and third 'generation' rights.

64. My emphasis.

65. Sachs, 'Judges and Gender'.

66. For a full report of the discussions at the LHR conference, see the report in *Rights: A Lawyers for Human Rights Publication*, 1, February 1991, Lawyers for Human Rights, National Directorate. The same was true of the *Gender Today and Tomorrow* workshop held by the ANC constitutional committee, see 'Women's Rights: A Discussion Document'. At the ANC conference there was a very specific call for the ANC constitutional committee to practice affirmative action by appointing more women to the committee. At present there is only one woman, Brigitte Mabandla, on a committee of 20 people.

67. S Westcott, 'Legitimating Constitutions: Albie Sachs Conveys the ANC Vision', *Sash*, September 1990, p16.

68. Hassim, 'Where Have All the Women Gone?'.

69. See Desirée Hansson, 'A Patchwork Quilt of Power Relations: A Challenge to South African Feminism', paper delivered at the International Feminist conference on *Women Law and Social Control*, Montreal, Canada, 1991.

70. I want to acknowledge the support, constructive criticism, ideas, discussions and sustenance that I received while writing this introduction from Elizabeth Sheehy, Brigitte Mabandla, Jacklyn Cock, Desirée Hansson, Gcina Mhlope, Colleen Brady, Ann Oosthuizen and Anne Mullins.

Putting Women on the Agenda

Jacklyn Cock

*N*either 'women' nor 'the agenda' are self-evident categories. I think it is important that we talk about 'women' not in isolation but within a system of gender relationships; relationships which privilege men and subordinate women. These relations are differently inscribed in different cultural traditions. Similarly the priorities on the overcrowded agenda of struggle in South Africa are differently ordered by people of differing ideological commitments. I think all of us in debating the place of women in the future can agree on one broad principle to provide a kind of fulcrum around which much of our debates can turn.

That principle is social justice. In simple terms this means that all South Africans should enjoy equality of opportunity. But this should be measured not in terms of access but by outcome. It means that the social composition of our decision-making bodies must reflect the social composition of our population. In other words the race and gender characteristics of our leaders must reflect those of the population at large. This understanding of social justice also implies that the race and gender characteristics of our most prestigious professions, and the graduates of our universities should also reflect those of the population at large. If not, there has been injustice.

I think we can all agree on the importance of this goal though we probably disagree quite sharply on how to define and achieve it. Clearly the inequalities of the past mean that it is going to be very difficult to achieve. Equality of opportunity can only have meaning if those who begin with unequal chances are given unequal support. The constitutional guidelines of the African National Congress (ANC) specifically require affirmative action to eliminate discrimination between the sexes. However, how to implement such action is an extremely controversial topic.

In tackling the question of putting women onto the agenda we are faced with a number of difficulties. At the *Weekly Mail* Book Week in November 1990 Nadine Gordimer began her talk by saying, 'Progressive forces in our country are pledged to one of the most extraordinary events in world social history: the complete reversal of everything that, for centuries, has ordered the lives of all our people.'[1] It is a extraordinary event and we are all privileged to be part of it. However, Nadine Gordimer went on to talk exclusively about violence and racism.

I think that points us to the first problem we confront in putting women on the agenda – the fact that the agenda of struggle has been dominated by apartheid. The outcome is a kind of reductionism; a tendency to reduce all our problems to apartheid. The implication is that with the dismantling of apartheid, women's oppression will disappear. In April 1990 there was a joint workshop of the ANC/Cosatu Economic Trends Group in Harare which produced some recommendations on economic policy. This is what the Harare document has to say about women: 'One of the legacies of apartheid and its economic system is discrimination against women.'[2]

Now maybe we should be grateful that the Harare document talks about women at all, but the way in which it does so illustrates precisely this kind of reductionism. As we know, discrimination against women has got far deeper roots. Therefore the ANC has acknowledged that this issue has to be addressed separately. A May 1990 statement of the national executive committee of the ANC on the 'Emancipation of Women in South Africa' notes:

> The experience of other societies has shown that emancipation of women
> is not a by-product of a struggle for democracy, national liberation or
> socialism. It has to be addressed in its own right within our organisation,
> the mass democratic movement and in society as a whole.[3]

The second problem we face in putting women on the agenda is directly due to the poverty and social dislocation caused by apartheid. It is a fact that for many women in South Africa the goal is physical survival. As Ruth Mompati said in a recent interview, debates about how to free women from the kitchen sink have little meaning for women who lack a kitchen, or access to clean water and nutritious food for their households.[4] We have to be sensitive to these different realities, meanings and experiences.

Even apparently straightforward women's issues, such as violence against women or reproductive rights, have to be understood in their different cultural contexts. We know that there is a lot of violence against women in South Africa. The figure for rape is about 1 000 a day.[5] One practising psychologist at an academic conference estimated that 60 per cent of South African husbands beat their wives.[6] He maintained that most cases were not reported because many families thought a certain amount of violence was 'normal'.[7] At a recently reported meeting, a KwaZulu chief said that if a Zulu man told his wife to fetch water and she did not, he must ask one more time, and if she failed once again to fulfill her duty then the man must hit her.[8]

The issue of reproductive rights might appear to be clear cut in a society where there are an estimated 300 000 illegal abortions a year. But the problem goes beyond traditional male resistance. Discussing the prevalence of AIDS and the use of condoms, a random survey among women reported that many women maintained that condoms deprived them of the joy of sex. One woman said, 'I want sperms not rubber'. Other comments were, 'It should be flesh to flesh'. 'Sperms have proteins and I need those proteins.'[9]

What this means is that in putting women on the agenda we in South Africa will *have* to go out and talk to people to find out what their needs and demands are. This is an advantage in one way – it means we can avoid much of the elitism and class-bias which has weakened the women's movement in the advanced industrialised societies of the north.

We are an industrial society of a special type. Many of the demands of the feminism coming from urban-industrial societies are inappropriate here. There are no blueprints of appropriate agendas that we can transpose automatically from other contexts to our own. Whereas women in the west have identified the family as a site of women's oppression, women in South Africa point to the destruction of family life as one of the most grievous crimes of apartheid. The diversity of family forms in South Africa is just one example of how we have to take account of very different meanings and experiences.

I think the third problem we face in putting women on the agenda is that many of us – including myself – are blinkered. The years of apartheid repression and isolation have damaged us in far more ways than we know. We have been cut off from much contact and information. We have also developed a tendency to romanticise other revolutionary struggles such as those in Cuba and Nicaragua with which we identify. We are inspired by the accounts from Cuba of how a dozen men and women armed with guns and a simplistic revolutionary theory could land in an old boat and two years later were ruling their country. But those struggles have made mistakes. The Family Code in Cuba which attempted to make it compulsory for men to do their share of domestic labour is an example of such a mistake. We also have a tendency to look to very different societies for solutions. For example, there has been much written about the Swedish model of child care which has extensive and flexible rights for parents. But Sweden is not only a more developed society than ours, it also has a degree of homogeneity that we lack. South Africa is an extremely diverse society. Unlike most modern industrial societies it has not been homogenised by social forces such as public education, mass culture or universal military service. Gender relationships are differently defined in different cultural traditions.

But – and this brings us to the fourth difficulty I think we face in putting women on the agenda – we have no historical tradition of gender equality in South African society. The European communities from which the white settlers came, as well as the indigenous societies of Southern Africa were male dominated and patriarchal. In pre-colonial Africa the majority of women were subordinated to male authority. This is still a reality for many women.

Our problems are daunting. In South Africa employment rates have been increasing among women of all races since 1960. Today women constitute about 40 per cent of the economically active population. Yet South Africa has no national policy of leave for maternity, paternity or parenting at all, no national policy encouraging flexible working arrangements and part-time and shared jobs and no national policy to provide child care for those who need it.

There are some difficult questions here. In demanding maternity rights and benefits for women are we potentially weakening women's position in the labour market by making them more expensive to employers? In demanding maternity rights and benefits for women are we not reinforcing the sexual division of labour which allocates child care to women? Should we not rather focus our demands on the rights and responsibilities of parenthood?

Another difficult question concerning the relation between equal rights for women and equal responsibilities, relates to military service. Historically conscription has been linked to citizenship. Does equal responsibilities mean that women should also be conscripted and required to do military service? There is quite an extensive debate developing about the integration of the SADF and MK into a new South African army. But I have heard no mention of the role of women in this new army. 'Putting women onto the agenda' means that the gender dynamic has to be present in *all* our debates on how to transform our society.

We should mobilise our energies as women to transform our society. By overcoming the passivity rooted in our sense of ourselves as powerless victims; by drawing on the caring and nurturing qualities that many ordinary women display every day of their lives; by refusing to imitate male styles of competition, and adopting male models of 'success' and 'achievement', we can contribute towards achieving social justice in South Africa.

This involves change at both the structural and the personal levels. Rudolph Bahro wrote, 'Change can only proceed from the changed.'[10] The new South Africa calls for very different people – people with a capacity for sharing resources and participating in decision making; people with confidence, energy, tolerance and courage.

The change required in South Africa cannot be brought about by atomised, isolated individuals. We need to work together to deepen our understanding and develop our collective strength. We can draw on the forms of organisation that the women's movement has developed which are democratic and non-elitist. This presents an alternative to the traditional forms of political organising – of large meetings and platform speakers which intimidate and silence people and fail to generate any active mass involvement. We need different political practices which overcome rather than reproduce existing hierarchies – forms which are truly democratic, egalitarian and supportive, which build the confidence and participation of all involved.

Our struggle for a vision of social justice, which includes gender as well as race and class, will not be an easy one. But we have certain clear advantages over feminists in other societies; we must take these advantages into consideration. Firstly we can avoid the deep divisions which have splintered feminism in other societies. Analytically a feminist perspective recognises gender as a significant social relation, which structures our social experience and shapes the social world so that women have distinctive and specific experiences, compared to men. It is very obvious to us here that gender is not the only or even the most significant social relation which shapes experience. Therefore it is impossible for us to overlook the importance of class and race. In the process we avoid the kind of oversimplification of positing a common female oppression that is shared by all women; an understanding that has bedevilled feminist organising in other societies.

Furthermore we are not operating in a political wilderness. We have the commitment of a political organisation with mass support. Despite its flaws, the ANC's most famous document, the Freedom Charter, clearly states the importance of equality for women. The 1988 constitutional guidelines take the spirit of the Freedom Charter further and commit the ANC to address actively the inequalities between men and women *both* in the home and in society at large. The feedback received by the ANC to this document is informing policy issues being debated within the organisation at present. This is tremendously encouraging. It means we are not some tiny marginalised group working for an eccentric goal. We have the support of a mass-based movement which not only shares our goals but which provides us with the space to formulate demands.

Of course there are problems within the ANC at present, and we have to be open and honest about acknowledging those problems. But I think there's a danger that in all the years of anti-apartheid activity we've developed the habit of thinking critically rather than constructively. This is a particular danger for academics like myself because we are trained and rewarded for being critical rather than appreciative.

The constitution and the legal framework of the new South Africa should guarantee social justice, but the new constitution must also be a nation-building document. Our nation contains many different cultures and traditions and clearly the constitution must protect this diversity. Until now the differences between South Africans have been the grounds of discrimination and denial. The challenge facing us now is to create a new society which celebrates this diversity; a society in which power is more equally shared, relationships are more stable and trusting, and human beings, both men and women, are more complete and able to experience the full range of human alternatives.

Notes

1. *Weekly Mail* Book Week, Market Warehouse, Panel Discussion on 'Violence in South Africa', November 1990.
2. The Harare Document was produced at a workshop held in Harare in March/April 1990 by representatives from the ANC, UDF, Cosatu and the Economic Trends Group. See *Transformation*, 12, 1990, p5.
3. This statement is found in Appendix 1.
4. *Daily Mail*, 3.7.1990.
5. This is a National Institute for the Prevention of Crime and the Rehabilitation of Offenders (NICRO) estimate quoted in the *Weekly Mail* 17.2.1989.
6. *Sunday Star*, 29.9.1985.
7. *Sunday Star*, 29.9.1985.
8. *Weekly Mail*, 1.6.1990
9. *Sowetan*, 30.5.1990.
10. R Bahro, *Socialism and Survival*, London: Heretic Books, 1982.

Putting Women into the Constitution

*Christina Murray and Catherine O'Regan**

*I*n 1990, when the ANC was unbanned, Nelson Mandela released, and when the prospect of a peaceful settlement in South Africa brightened, some women's groups became concerned that their interests would not be considered as politicians constructed a new political and legal order for the country. A colleague of ours was invited to address one of these groups on constitutions, constitution making and on the role women could play in the process. She pointed out that the responsibility for protecting the interests of women is largely left to women. A member of her audience agreed and said that she had already done something in this connection, she had written to the state president making the point that there were issues relating particularly to women that needed addressing and asking for reassurance that women were not going to be left out of the process of constitution making. She received no reply for quite some time and so, when she next saw the state president, she asked what had become of her letter. He explained that he had handed it on to his wife.

This anecdote sums up the position of women in South African life. Women's issues are private, domestic issues. They (like a wife) belong in

* The discussion between pages 33 and 36 is a summary of the introductory comments to 'Whose Freedom? Which Charter?' made at the November conference.

the home. They are not the concern of the men who are intent on nation-building, on creating the 'new' South Africa.

Such a view of the world, which is thought by many to be natural and obvious, must be changed and there are many ways in which one can attempt to do this. One important way is to establish non-sexist values in a constitution. It is likely that a new constitution in South Africa will incorporate a bill of rights and will set up structures to enable legislation, executive action and perhaps even private action to be judged in terms of the bill. This would mean that legislation, for instance, could be challenged and overturned for being unconstitutional, for being contrary to the basic values enshrined in the bill of rights. One of the values that we may expect a bill to protect is freedom from discrimination on the basis of sex or gender and the equal treatment of men and women.

Women in South Africa have protested about their subordinate legal and social status and demanded the equal treatment of men and women for many years. This demand is reflected, for instance, in the Women's Charter of 1954, in a Federation of South African Women (Fedsaw) document submitted to the Congress of the People in 1955 and in the Freedom Charter itself. But, alongside the claim for equal treatment, women usually also demand recognition of their role as wives and mothers, a role which, it is suggested, requires special protection.

Using a legal notion of equality to challenge the oppression of women is not easy and the matter is complicated by the necessary claim for the recognition of the special circumstances in which women find themselves which sometimes conflicts with equality claims.

The first problem with the notion of equality is that, unlike that of justice or fairness, it requires a comparison to be made. It asks, 'Equal to whom?' And, of course, the answer seems always to be, equal to men. This has enabled lawyers to argue that equality is relevant only when people are alike. In other words, a woman is entitled to claim equality with a man only if she can show that she is like the man in a particular situation, that she has the same qualifications, does the same work or bears identical responsibilities. The reality of women's experience is that we very often cannot (or do not wish to) be like men. We are given different education, work in different places, and bear different responsibilities. These differences constitute, in part at least, the oppression of women. This means that formal equality cannot offer much to women in their oppression. While women are prevented from getting into the same jobs as men, for instance, an equal pay provision will not assist them.

The second problem with using the concept of equality to deal with the subordination of women is that there are ways in which women differ from men biologically. Relatively few biological differences matter and their significance is intermittent and variable. But, in the case of childbearing, for instance, you cannot compare women to men and the notion of equality as judges and lawyers usually understand it, provides no answers.

These problems with the concept of equality might be dealt with in different ways. First, one might build into an equality clause an express provision stating that where women are biologically different from men, they shall not be prejudiced as a result of that biological difference. This would deal with the problems of maternity and pregnancy, as special treatment relating to childbearing could not be challenged on the basis that it deprives men of equal treatment. Of course, any special protection like this carries with it the danger that, by possibly requiring employers to provide benefits to women when they bear children, it will make women more expensive to employ and will price us out of the labour market.

A provision that accommodates biological differences between women and men would still fail to deal with the cultural and social patterns of difference that women experience. A classic example of this occurred in South Africa in the mid-1980s when legislation protecting women from working at night was abolished. Until then, women were not permitted to work at night unless a special exemption was given to their employer. But, as part of a move to introduce racial and sexual equality into the workplace, South African labour law was changed to allow women to work at night. The vulnerability of travelling when transport is risky, the dangers of walking home in the dark and the fact that nightwork frequently involves leaving children alone, for instance, are circumstances that do not really affect the men who work at night.

We could deal with these social and cultural differences between women and men by putting another provision into the constitution, saying all women and men shall be equal, except in relation to biological differences, and except in relation to social and cultural differences. But the great danger with this is that it would build gender stereotypes into the constitution. By making existing (and oppressive) social structures constitutionally proper we would entrench them.

There is a completely different route one could take and that is to try to reconstruct our notion of equality. Instead of limiting the notion of equality to one which requires only people who are similarly situated to be treated alike, it might seek to equalise outcomes. This might mean that the fact that women may differ from men for biological or social and cultural reasons would not justify treatment which disadvantages one group. It might mean, for example, that if women take time off for child-bearing, they need to be compensated for their loss of seniority. In other words, we could try to develop a notion of equality that looks at the substantive experience of women, not at the formal notion of likeness.

Whatever formula is used in a constitution, its effectiveness will be determined by the way it is implemented. Changing the law will not change our lives. The experience of women in Canada bears testimony to this. Between 1985 and 1988, the first three years of the equality provision in the Canadian constitution, 44 cases relating to sexual equality were brought before Canadian courts. Of these, 35 were brought by men and only nine by women. This must show us that a constitution will be of no use at all unless we organise around it and use it as a weapon for furthering women's interests. We cannot expect lawyers and judges to develop a notion of equality that will echo women's experience rather than reflect present cultural patterns unless we are insistent in our claims to be heard.

Whose Freedom? Whose Charter?

The fact of women's oppression is sometimes disputed, but it can clearly be shown that women are less wealthy, less well-educated[1] and less likely to occupy positions of power than men.[2] Although more likely to be unemployed,[3] they do more work because they are responsible for household labour. And even when employed, women earn substantially less than men do. The reason for women's oppression is more difficult to isolate. We do not believe that it stems purely from the biological differences between women and men, but that it is also shaped by material forces.[4] As a result, women from different class and racial backgrounds in South Africa experience a different oppression. Black working-class women are triply oppressed, by apartheid, by capitalism and by patriarchy.[5]

The African National Congress's Freedom Charter of 1955 acknowledges this oppression and claims: 'The rights of the people shall be the same regardless of race, colour or sex'; 'Every man and woman shall have the right to vote for and stand as a candidate for all bodies which make law'; 'Men and women of all races shall receive equal pay for equal work'. At the same time the need for some kind of 'special treatment' for women is asserted and their domestic role is emphasised: 'There shall be... maternity leave on full pay for all working mothers'; 'Free medical care and hospitalisation shall be provided for all with special care for mothers and young children'.

These passages reveal two apparently contradictory approaches to ending the subordination of women: one based on equality, asserting that sex should not be a basis for treating women and men differently, and one that responds to women's difference from men and claims some sort of special or protective treatment for them.

Using the claims for equality and protection in the Freedom Charter as a basis, this paper examines the way in which law may operate to alleviate the oppression of women. It begins with an examination of two documents on women's issues which preceded the Freedom Charter, indicating the dual nature of women's claims in them. Once again, these are claims for equality and claims for protection. We then sketch the relationship between women's oppression and law, focusing on the workplace and the home. We show that the concerns informing the drafting of the two earlier documents remain important and indicate the ways in which law reinforces women's subordination to men. In the last part we pursue the theoretical problems relating to equality and protective legislation that we raised earlier, and explore ways in which the oppression of women may be remedied.

Political organisation of women in South Africa has always been (and still is) overshadowed by what are considered to be the central, most important issues – race and economics.[6] Noticeably absent from the Freedom Charter is a commitment to rectify existing discrimination on the basis of sex. While 'all shall be equal before the law!', it is only those 'laws which discriminate on the grounds of race, colour or belief' which will be repealed. For instance, 'the preaching and practice of national, race or colour discrimination and contempt shall be a punishable crime', and 'the colour bar in cultural life, in sport and in education shall be abolished', but sex discrimination is not earmarked for direct action. Perhaps even more telling is the rallying cry in the preamble that 'and therefore we the people of South Africa, black and white, together equals, countrymen and brothers adopt this Freedom Charter'.[7]

The ranking of discrimination against women as a secondary problem in the charter is not altogether surprising. Raymond Suttner has described the Freedom Charter as 'the document for liberation in South Africa, the programme that is accepted by most South Africans as providing the basis for freedom from oppression and exploitation'.[8] He continues, '[i]t is the response of a people denied their right of self-determination, a people struggling for self-determination'. In this statement is a hint of the dual political function of the charter. It is intended as a proposal for a future, just South Africa but it is also a rallying point and manifesto for people engaged in the struggle against apartheid now.[9] The importance of the second function partially explains the limited attention paid to sexual oppression in the document. Addressing the oppression of women is an extremely complex matter. Many will deny that such oppression exists, others will disagree about the type of action to be taken and, perhaps most problematically, the charge of sexual oppression is directed not only at white rulers but also at men committed to liberating South Africa from apartheid rule. To a movement concerned with unity, the issue could easily be perceived as divisive rather than strengthening. The history of women's organisation in South Africa reflects these tensions.

The women's clauses in historical context

The 1910s and 1920s saw some feminist organisation: a small, white suffragist movement and action by a small group of Native and coloured women in the Orange Free State between 1913 and 1920 in the Anti-Pass Campaign.[10] In 1913 a Bantu Women's League was established within the ANC but the ANC itself did not grant women full membership status until 1943. It was at this time that the ANC Women's League, to which all women members of the ANC automatically belonged, was established.[11] Even then, however, the general attitude to women was essentially conservative. As Walker comments:

> by directing women into a separate body, the ANC was also perpetuating the existing sexual divisions within its organisation. This tended to reinforce stereotypes about 'women's role' and 'women's work', and subtly undermined the formal equality of the sexes that had been proclaimed'.[12]

At the same time, women themselves were relatively inactive politically. Matters had changed by the 1950s. The significant role of women in the 1952 Defiance Campaign is now well-documented. Shortly after the end of the Defiance Campaign Fedsaw was launched and, at the founding meeting, a 'Women's Charter' was adopted. This document and a second one, 'What Women Demand', drafted by Fedsaw women for submission to the conveners of the Congress of the People, provide a background to the treatment of women in the Freedom Charter and a starting point for understanding the concerns of women at the time that it was adopted.[13] Both reflect the tension between claims for equality and claims for special treatment later found in the Freedom Charter.

The Women's Charter seeks the liberation of all people, the common society of men and women. It clearly asserts that freedom from poverty, and race and class discrimination alone, cannot achieve this.[14] Until equality between men and women is realised, a struggle for liberation is not over: 'We shall teach the men that they cannot hope to liberate themselves from the evils of discrimination and prejudice as long as they fail to extend to women complete and unqualified equality in law and in practice.' The position in the Women's Charter is that a struggle for economic and racial liberation addresses only part of the issue. Without tackling the oppression of women, an organisation committed to freedom is inadequate; the one issue does not take priority over the other as racial and sexual discrimination are interlocked manifestations of oppression. This position was as controversial then as it is now. The women who drafted the Women's Charter were committed to struggling with men for freedom, but acknowledged that '[a]s women there rests upon us also the burden of removing from our society all the social differences developed in past times between men and women, which have the effect of keeping our sex in a position of inferiority and subordination'.

The Women's Charter deals with a range of ways in which women have been oppressed in South Africa, but two, connected themes run through the entire document. The one concerns the 'laws, regulations, conventions and customs that discriminate against us as women'; the other relates to the relationship of dependence of children on their mothers. In confronting the issue of legal and customary oppression, the charter refers to the way in which women's access to property and economic security and independence is denied by marriage laws and laws relating to status:

> Not only are African, Coloured and Indian women denied political rights, but they are also in many parts of the Union denied the same status as men in such matters as the right to enter contracts, to own and dispose of property, and to exercise guardianship over their children.

In some past, ideal period in which 'men and women were partners in a compact and closely integrated family unit' these traditions 'no doubt served purposes of great value'.

In modern society they do not correspond to 'the actual social and economic position of women'. Here the second theme of the charter is visible. In the modern South African economy, women fend for themselves and their children. While 'women share with our menfolk the cares and anxieties imposed by poverty and its evils', it is

> as wives and mothers [that] it falls upon us to make small wages stretch a long way. It is we who feel the cries of our children when they are hungry and sick. It is our lot to keep and care for the homes that are too small, broken and dirty to be kept clean. We know the burden of looking after children and land when our husbands are away in the mines, on the farms, and in the towns earning our daily bread...

And through these two calls, a call for equality and a call for recognition of a woman's additional responsibility in the family (the double shift), the Women's Charter seems to assert that rights for women cannot be separated from the unequal burdens and responsibilities of their lives.

The parallel concern about equality and the special circumstances in which women find themselves is reflected again in the eight specific

aims set out for Fedsaw at its founding meeting. Alongside a commitment to fight for political rights, Fedsaw aimed to strive for 'equal rights
with men in relation to property, marriage and children, and for the
removal of all laws and customs that deny women such equal rights' as
well as

> the development of every child through free compulsory education for
> all; for the protection of mother and child through maternity homes,
> welfare clinics, créches and nursery schools, in countryside and towns,
> through proper homes for all, and through the provision of water, light,
> transport, sanitation, and other amenities of modern civilization.

'What Women Demand' was drawn up in May 1955, a year after the
Women's Charter was drafted. It was discussed and approved at a Fedsaw meeting in Johannesburg attended by over 200 women.[15] Once
again, the demands set out reflect the harsh conditions in which the
majority of women were (and still are) living:

- We demand four months maternity leave on full pay for working
  mothers; properly staffed and equipped maternity homes, ante-natal
  clinics, and child welfare centres in all towns and villages, and in the
  reserves and rural areas...

- We demand compulsory free and universal education from the primary
  school to the University; adequate school feeding and free milk for all
  children in day nurseries, nursery schools, and primary and secondary
  schools...

- We demand... indoor sanitation, water supply and proper lighting in
  our homes.

- We demand... more dairies, and full supplies of pasteurised whole
  milk... subsidisation of all protective foods... controlled prices for all
  essential commodities...

- We demand... peace and freedom for our children.

Towards the end of the document, after these and other similar demands
for all people are listed, is a brief but far-reaching section of demands for
'all women of South Africa':

- The right to vote.
- The right to be elected to all State, Provincial or Municipal bodies.
- Full opportunities for employment in all spheres of work.
- Equal pay for equal work.
- Equal rights with men in property, in marriage, and in the guardianship
  of our children.

A month later, on 26 June 1955, the Freedom Charter was adopted by the Congress of the People at Kliptown.[16] The charter contained the provisions relating to women are set out on page 38. Each of these documents claims equality for women and, both expressly and implicitly, each proposes protective legislation.

Law and the oppression of women today

The claims in the Women's Charter and 'What Women Demand', reflect the experience of the women who participated in their drafting. For instance, the demand for equal access to and remuneration for work in the public sphere, and the demand for recognition of the double shift and its impact on women's ability to perform in the workplace are couched in terms which underscore the hardship of the role of women. But the insistence on recognition of women's role in the home and as mothers runs the risk of entrenching these roles rather than liberating women. At the same time, for the women who drafted these documents to have ignored the conditions in which they found themselves would have been to neglect the real conditions of their oppression.

The workplace

Despite some startling developments in labour law since the 1950s,[17] similar contradictions are reflected in women's experience in the 1990s.[18] A brief indication of the shortcomings of the present legislation will show that the demands women made in the 1950s have still not been met.

Such legislative protection as has been given to women, has excluded domestic workers and farm workers. Domestic work particularly, is almost entirely undertaken by women, and domestic workers enjoy no security of employment, no minimum conditions, and no right to maternity benefits, pensions, or workmen's (sic) compensation.[19] In addition, organising domestic workers into effective trade unions is hard because the isolated and individualised nature of their employment means that they cannot combine to exercise collective power against their different employers. Instead pressure will have to be brought to bear on the state in an attempt to improve minimum conditions.

Even those women who seek jobs in industries which are covered by the general labour legislation are still not guaranteed equal access to employment. Labour legislation protects employees only once they have entered employment, and employers are entitled to discriminate on grounds of sex (or for other reasons) in choosing their employees.[20]

Once in a job which falls within the scope of the Labour Relations Act,[21] women may be protected from discrimination on the grounds of sex. The Act states that it is an unfair labour practice for an employer 'unfairly to discriminate' on the grounds of sex.[22] However, despite the potential of this provision as a weapon women may use against sexual discrimination, very few cases have been brought to court. Indeed, perhaps the leading case on the provision to date concerned the dismissal of a senior managerial male employee for sexual harassment. The employee sought to argue that his dismissal was unfair, but the employer successfully relied upon the unfair sexual discrimination provision to justify it.[23]

The paucity of unfair labour practice litigation concerned with sexual discrimination illustrates a major difficulty with the unfair labour practice definition and procedures. Litigation in the industrial court is both costly and likely to antagonise employers. The weak position of most women employees means that it is improbable that any individual woman will successfully interdict sexual harassment or any other form of sexual discrimination under unfair labour practice provisions unless she has financial and organisational support. Although trade unions are the obvious organisations to provide working-class women with this assistance, they have not yet done so.[24] Their failure to do so is once again evidence that the women's struggle has not been a priority – the central concerns have been issues of class and race. The inability of women to use the unfair labour practice definition to improve their position indicates the inadequacies of legal attempts to overcome discrimination, an issue we will raise later in this article.

Another major piece of legislation which seeks to ensure the equality of women in the workplace, but with more controversial implications, is the Basic Conditions of Employment Act, 3 of 1983. This legislation repealed some of the protective provisions contained in earlier legislation such as the Factories, Machinery and Building Work Act, 22 of 1941, most notably the provisions prohibiting women from working at night. The repeal of this legislation was met with mixed feelings by women workers and feminists. On the one hand, it seemed to be a step towards the liberation of women; on the other, the liberation it implied included longer working hours, the vulnerabilities of travelling to and from work when public transport is poor, if available at all, and the aggravated problems of seeking child care at night.[25] Protective legislation, while perhaps not giving women formal equality, often recognises and compensates for their subordination in the household. The lesson of the nightwork provisions is that repealing legislation which is perceived to prejudice women should not be done without first consulting the affected women and their organisations.

Although the inclusion of sexual discrimination in the unfair labour practice definition goes some way to meet the demands for equality expressed in the Freedom Charter, women's demands for maternity leave remain unmet. The Unemployment Insurance Act of 1966 provides for a limited maternity pay scheme in terms of which a woman who has been in employment for three years may receive maternity benefits at a rate of 45 per cent of her previous salary for six months.[26] This provides limited protection but it does not assure women of a right to return to work within a stipulated period after the birth of their child; the benefits are not sufficient; and like the Labour Relations Act, the Unemployment Insurance Act does not cover women working in domestic service, on farms or in the civil service.

The demands for state assistance in relation to child care have been ignored. There are no legislative provisions concerning child care, nor are there any tax incentives given to women to use child care. Those women who are the primary caregivers in relation to their children face real difficulties in entering a labour market where no provision for child care is made. The problem is most severe for working-class women who mostly must rely on family members or elderly members of the community to assist them; either gratuitously or for minimal compensation.[27] The problem of the double shift must be dealt with if women are to be given a fair deal in the labour market. Even if the concept of an unfair labour practice as it is defined now were to succeed in obtaining equality for women in the workplace, and were the legislature to provide women with equal opportunity and full maternity benefits, women's ability to succeed in the labour market would still be determined by the fact that most women bear the primary responsibility for child care and household labour. The double shift means that women are simply not able to compete as equals with men in the labour market. So providing women with equality in the workplace will not render them equal until there is a change in the sexual division of labour in the household.

The home

One can assert as a general proposition that although women bear the major responsibility in the home, running it and caring for children, the power to control finances, make choices and enforce decisions is generally the man's. However, it is not simply the presence of a man in the family that is oppressive, just as every man does not dominate women. It is through the patriarchal structure of South African society that men are dominant. This structure determines women's lone domestic responsibility and the characterisation of domestic work as women's work. It affirms that men are engaged in the work that matters, work outside the home, and that, in the home, it is men who control while 'their' women labour.

The subordination of women to men within the family is reinforced by legal structures. For instance, the man is legally designated 'head of the household', a status which symbolises his authority over his family and which gives him the power to make certain decisions which his spouse cannot legally veto.[28] Then, violence in the home is inadequately dealt with by the law, adding to the man's administrative status in the family a sense of physical authority. So, a husband cannot be convicted for the rape of his wife. Rape, our legislature declared only in 1989, cannot occur between married couples.[29] And battery or systematic violence against women in the home is treated lightly by the law. The substantive law, criminal procedure and the attitudes of prosecuting authorities work together to allow men to escape accountability for violence in the home and thus indirectly reinforce the notion that such abuse is legitimate. In addition, for many women there is no possibility of equal access to economic wealth. The practical position that men have greater access to the economy is reinforced by rules which limit the right of many women to own or dispose of property. Thus women married by customary law may own only very limited forms of property (in particular, possession of the most valuable property, land and cattle, is usually not allowed) and, formally at least, their right to economic activity is dependent on the approval of their husbands.[30] Until recently many women married by civil law, the dominant legal system in South Africa, were placed in a position very similar to that of a child, dependent on their guardian's, that is husband's, approval if they wished to enter the economy in any way.[31] For middle-class women there are numerous other niggling legal reminders of their husbands' superior status – usually it is only the husband as main breadwinner who is entitled to valuable housing subsidies; women are frequently compelled to join the medical aid scheme of which their husband is a member; forms for income tax are the responsibility of the husband, not the wife.

The structural nature of the oppression of women in relation to the family is starkly revealed by the position of women in single-parent families. In every section of South African society there is a high number of single-parent families: mothers who are not married caring for their children; women married by customary law whose husbands have taken other wives and, particularly where the structure of customary society is weak, who are unable or unwilling to support earlier families; the wives of migrant labourers who have little contact with their husbands in the cities; divorced women looking after children. Here no man dominates in the home but such women may well suffer greater economic and social disabilities than their counterparts in two-parent families. Formally the law requires men to support their children, whether or not they are living with them and whether or not the children are classified as legitimate.

The practice is very different. In an important study on single-parent families in South Africa, Sandra Burman has shown that the private maintenance system does not support children adequately:

> Awards are too low, the default rate extremely high, and unless a woman displays the utmost determination in instituting the case and subsequently pursuing arrears, she may well receive no maintenance at the end of the period.[32]

The state maintenance system fails to remedy this. As Burman's study shows, it is available to a small number of people only and provides very meagre grants.

There are other reasons, too, for the failure of the maintenance system. Maintenance courts and offices are understaffed, dated systems of office management and filing encumber the process, telephone enquiries are not dealt with – women must go in person to see if maintenance for their children has been paid and it is often difficult to trace the men who must pay.[33]

These problems are symptomatic of a society that is not primarily concerned with the needs of women. As the society is confident that, whatever their social and economic circumstances, women will do their best for their children (and if they do not, welfare organisations will declare their unsuitability as parents), it relies on the legal theory that fathers must maintain their children. When they do not little urgency is attached to the problem.

The structural nature of the oppression of women and the fact that it cuts across lines of race and class makes it difficult to address. In addition, the role of women as wives and mothers, subordinate to their husbands in particular and male society in general, is often considered 'natural' and right. It is a role that is reaffirmed in cultural and religious institutions and to challenge it is to attempt to destroy a 'natural' order. Nevertheless, a programme for the liberation of South Africa which does not take the issue of gender discrimination seriously is incomplete. For there is no evidence to support the claim that, if apartheid and capitalism are dismantled, sexual oppression will end too. Indeed, the experience in liberated colonial states suggests the reverse.[34]

Implementing rights for women

Implementing the claims made in the Freedom Charter will not necessarily end the subordination of women. To think it would, would be to accept the 'myth of rights'[35] and to posit an automatic relationship between legislation and social change. Changing the law does not change society. But that does not mean that for women there are no gains to be made in enacting the claims in the Freedom Charter.

First, legal rights can in certain circumstances be used to change social relations. But it is necessary to jettison the view that legal rights are goals achieved, they are weapons which may be used to alter power relations in society.

> Rights are no more than a political resource which can be deployed... to spark hopes and indignation. Rights can contribute to political activation and organization, thus planting and nurturing the seeds of mobilization... Mobilization thus emerges from this perspective as the strategy, litigation as a contributory tactic, and rights as a source of leverage.[36]

Once rights are seen as weapons of political mobilisation it is possible to see how enacting the demands of the Freedom Charter could be a step towards ending the subordination of women. For rights enshrined in a bill of rights could be used as social demands around which women could be mobilised and organised, particularly in the workplace. Just as labour legislation has provided worker organisations with tools to re-structure the balance of power in the workplace, even if only to a moderate extent, legislation for women could be used in a similar way.[37]

However, the methods usually used by legal systems to address the subordinate position of women are problematic. The traditional concept of equality which is enshrined in the Freedom Charter and the 1990 ANC draft bill of rights (along with most other modern constitutions) is poorly equipped to tackle the problem. Legal systems generally adopt an Aristotelian approach to equality and seek to treat like people alike.[38] Implementing equality at this level means ensuring that women with qualifications equivalent to men are given similar opportunities to their male counterparts. This approach cannot work when women are not like men, for instance in pregnancy and childbirth, where an Aristotelian-based equality simply emphasises differences. As Littleton has noted, 'legal equality analysis "runs out" when it encounters real differences'.[39] But even when judges accept that men and women are formally alike, traditional equality analysis may obscure real differences which arise from the structural nature of women's oppression.

As we have indicated above, women's oppression means that they are structurally excluded from social and economic power primarily through the maintenance of a sexual division of labour. This division stereotypes 'appropriate roles' for women and their 'natural' place.[40] So, women do 'women's work' in the factories – which not surprisingly at-tracts low wages; and when they get home, they do the domestic work – 'chores'. The Aristotelian notion of equality allows substantial inequalities and is unable to overcome differences rooted in the sexual division of labour.

A further problem with using equality to address the oppression of women is that the concept itself has a male bias. For equality tends to judge women by men's standards. It does nothing to address the hierarchy in terms of which activities stereotyped 'male' are valued more highly than 'female' ones. The argument that equality is male-biased is based on the perception that dominant social institutions are themselves male-biased, a perception that is supported by an analysis of the legal system which reveals

> ... the male domination of the legal forum in terms of its personnel; the male domination of the legal system in terms of the legislature and powerful interest groups; and the construction of disputes in individual terms and their resolution through a closed system of reasoning.[41]

It is thus the male-bias of equality that prevents the police from understanding that the under-policing of family violence is an issue of gender discrimination – that the view that 'as a family matter' battery is less important is based on men's, not women's, perceptions.[42] Consequently many feminists argue that women do not want to occupy space that may be made for them in such institutions and Andrea Dworkin declares:

> Some of us have committed ourselves in all areas, including those called 'love' and 'sex' to the goal of 'equality'... Others of us, and I stand on this side of the argument, do not see equality as a proper, or sufficient, or moral, or honorable final goal. We believe that to be equal where there is not universal justice, or where there is not universal freedom is, quite simply, to be the same as the 'oppressor'.[43]

'Protective legislation' or 'special treatment' is another way of addressing the position of women in society. Such legislation, sometimes referred to as being concerned with 'asymmetrical equality',[44] recognises women's differences, for example by providing maternity benefits or by prohibiting women from doing nightwork or excessive overtime. Legislatures have had mixed motives in using this approach. Often it has been adopted in response to demands by women but to some extent it has been used to structure the workplace in a way that provides better opportunities for men.[45] In recognising cultural differences related to gender, protective legislation may entrench women's oppression by confirming the position they occupy in society.[46] In addition, it may be argued that as long as women are treated differently in some areas their status will be subordinate to that of men. The experience of 'separate but equal' in the area of race will apply to sexual and gender discrimination as well.

MacKinnon puts it more forcefully: 'For women to affirm difference, when difference means dominance, as it does with gender, means to affirm the qualities and characteristics of powerlessness.'[47]

The theoretical difficulties with using equality and special treatment to remedy discrimination have been amply demonstrated in practice both in the context of discrimination on the basis of race or colour and in that of sex or gender discrimination.[48] Nevertheless it seems rash to jettison the legal tools of equality and special treatment entirely. A claim for equality carries enormous rhetorical and political force;[49] that all people should be treated equally regardless of race, colour or sex is basic to twentieth-century notions of justice. And equality is not meaningless. It is important that men should not be preferred merely on account of their sex. Accordingly some feminists have argued that the concept of equality should be reconstructed to avoid constant comparison with the male norm. Various proposals have been made for a more useful concept of equality. For instance, Littleton has argued for a reconstructed concept which accepts and values differences, '[making] difference costless'.[50] Lacey proposes that we address the idea of equality not in terms of equality of opportunity as liberal models usually do but in terms of 'welfare, power, resources and goods'.[51] Other writers suggest supplementing the concept of equality with concepts of responsibility[52] or caring.[53] The task of how to move towards a new construction of equality must be considered; the negotiation of a new constitution and a new bill of rights makes the matter pressingly urgent.

Similarly, some form of protective legislation or special treatment may be the only method of accommodating legitimate claims that women should be guaranteed rights while recognising that physical characteristics and social institutions may place special burdens on them. It is useful to recognise that there is a difference between protective legislation which is based on biological differences between men and women, notably maternity legislation (which must always be necessary)[54] and protective legislation based on a socially determined sexual division of labour, for example, child care provision and nightwork prohibitions. Special treatment arising out of the sexual division of labour is controversial and should be addressed anew in each set of circumstances after careful consultation with the women concerned and their organisations.

The draft bill of rights issued by the constitutional committee of the ANC in 1990 invokes other devices for addressing the problem of structural oppression: affirmative action and positive action.[55] Article 13 of the bill of rights provides that nothing in the constitution shall prevent the enactment of legislation, or the adoption by any public or private body of special measures of a positive kind designed to procure the advancement and the opening up of opportunities, including access to education, skills, employment and land, and the general advancement in social, economic and cultural spheres of men and women who in the past have been disadvantaged by discrimination.

This article ensures that attempts to remedy oppression by favouring particular disadvantaged groups are not blocked by the equality provision in the bill. Affirmative action would avoid some of the problems of a special treatment approach by emphasising its role as remedying social injustices; affirmative action programmes would address women because, historically and culturally, they have been subject to discrimination on the basis of their sex and not because they are inherently different to men in ways that are legally relevant.

In addition, article 14 and article 7(3) of the draft bill of rights provide for a programme of positive action which commits the state to implementing affirmative action programmes. Article 14 envisages a state that will actively work towards realising rights, and although its main focus is on the creation of a non-racial democracy, it also encompasses action which 'recti[fies] the inequalities to which women have been subjected'.[56] This commitment to an active programme of social reconstruction is crucial.

In requiring a commitment to the question of the oppression of women in all areas of state action, the ANC proposals go beyond what is often described as affirmative action. They recognise that it is not sufficient to ensure that qualified men do not always get jobs ahead of equally qualified women. If positive action and affirmative action are to succeed, programmes will have to be developed which address the oppressive nature of family structures,[57] which ensure that women's experiences of the criminal justice system are heard and which educate women and men for a society in which male supremacy is as distasteful as white supremacy. Welfare programmes must tackle the economic debility of single-parent families as an issue as urgent as the educational inadequacy of Bantu Education. The status of women in the workplace must be dealt with with as much commitment as the establishment of an accountable police force. Violence against women can no longer be minimised or ignored.[58]

It is important that such programmes avoid the problems of formal equality. An attempt needs to be made to draw on the experience of women.[59] Once one accepts that legal structures are patriarchal and generally unresponsive to women's experience, this is hard. How is the legal system persuaded that violence against women in the home is as serious as football hooliganism? Sachs suggests that adopting a women's charter may provide an answer. Such a charter would

> aim to be declaratory, affirmative, educational and operational, that is, it would declare the rights that women and men have, it would establish a programme of action to be undertaken to realize the rights in practice, it would serve as a point of reference for the whole of society, and it would establish appropriate mechanisms for enforcement.[60]

It would be formulated 'essentially but not exclusively by women'. In Sachs' scheme such a charter would be additional to a bill of rights, expanding on it and providing 'a point of reference for its interpretation'. It would have legal force but be easier to amend than the bill of rights itself. This is an attractive idea as it acknowledges the need to compensate for the exclusion of women and to provide formal structures in an attempt to do this. It raises a myriad of constitutional and political questions which Sachs does not address[61] but, even if such a charter were not formally incorporated into the constitution it could be a powerful document. Its drafting process would require women to try to understand and articulate our experience of the world. A charter could become a powerful political document, providing a standard against which to judge legislation and public action politically, if not legally.

Implementing the demands made in the Freedom Charter, together with the introduction of a progressive affirmative action and positive action programme suggested in the 1990 ANC draft bill of rights could assist in ending the subordination of women. But we must not be naive about the impact of constitutionally enacted rights. Such rights will only make a difference if they are used as political resources by women's organisations in their struggle for a more equitable society.[62] If the declaration in the preamble to the Freedom Charter[63] that all must enjoy equal rights is to be not merely the promise of a brotherhood but that of a common society of men and women, then there must not only be a clear constitutional commitment to women's rights in a democratic South Africa, but continued efforts by women themselves to establish that society.[64]

Notes

1. According to an HSRC survey, while 61 per cent of South African men over 20 years of age had received formal education beyond Standard 3, only 41 per cent of women had. See C Ellis, *Literacy Statistics in South*

Africa 1980 (excluding Transkei, Bophuthatswana and Venda), Pretoria: HSRC, 1987.
2. See, for instance, JD van der Vyver, 'Women in Politics and Public Administration', *South African Journal on Human Rights*, 1, 1985, p63.
3. For a full discussion of women's unequal status in the labour market, see Pundy Pillay, 'Women in Employment in South Africa: Some Important Trends and Issues', *Social Dynamics*, 11, 1985, p20.
4. See, for a full discussion of this point, S Coontz and P Henderson (eds), *Women's Work, Men's Property: The Origins of Gender and Class*, London: Verso, 1986.
5. See B Bozzoli, 'Marxism, Feminism and South African Studies', *Journal of Southern African Studies*, 9(2), 1983, p139.
6. See for instance, N Gordimer, 'The Prison-house of Colonialism', in Cherry Clayton (ed), *Olive Schreiner*, Johannesburg: McGraw Hill, 1983, p97.
7. Dorothy Driver would certainly conclude that women are excluded from the Freedom Charter. See her paper in this collection, which is a revised version of the paper 'Women and Language in the ANC Constitutional Guidelines for SA', *Die Suid-Afrikaan*, 23, November 1989, p15. The ANC constitutional guidelines of 1988 retained the ranking of the Freedom Charter, placing a constitutional duty on the state and all social institutions to eradicate race discrimination and the 'economic and social equalities' it has produced while no such urgency was placed on the issue of discrimination against women. However, the ANC draft bill of rights published in 1990 rectified this. Articles 13 and 14 recommend a programme of positive action to combat racism and sexism.
8. R Suttner, 'The Freedom Charter – the People's Charter in the Nineteen-Eighties', the 26th TB Davis Memorial Lecture, University of Cape Town, 1984, p13. Suttner adds that the charter should form a basis for political discussion.
9. C Walker, *Women and Resistance in South Africa*, London: Onyx Press, 1982. See Cherryl Walker's comment at p181, that the organisers of the People's Congress saw it as having a dual function: to act as a demonstration of mass support and to provide organisers with a focus around which to mobilise. For a political review of Walker's book, see D Budlender, S Meintjies and J Schreiner, 'Women and Resistance in South Africa: Review Article', *Journal of Southern African Studies*, 10(1), 1983, p131.
10. Walker, *Women and Resistance*, p27ff.
11. See Walker, *Women and Resistance*, pp88–9, and for a discussion of the history of the women in the ANC, see J Kimble and E Unterhalter, '"We opened the road for you, you must go forward". ANC Women's Struggles 1912–1982', *Feminist Review*, 12, 1982, p11.
12. Walker, *Women and Resistance*, p90.
13. Both the Women's Charter and What Women Demand, as well as a list of women known to have attended the inaugural conference of Fedsaw, are included in an appendix to Walker, *Women and Resistance*, p279ff.
14. See also Walker, *Women and Resistance*, p156ff.
15. Walker, *Women and Resistance*, p182ff.

16. For a description of the role women played at the congress, see Walker, *Women and Resistance*, p181ff.

17. Labour law has developed in two major ways: minimum standards and conditions of employment have been set, see for example the Basic Conditions of Employment Act, 3 of 1983; and legislative support for collective bargaining by black workers and their unions has been provided (see the Labour Relations Act, 28 of 1956 as amended).

18. See S Gordon, *A Talent for Tomorrow: Life Stories of South African Servants*, Johannesburg: Ravan, 1985. J Barrett, et al, *Vukani Makhosikazi: South African Women Speak*, London: Catholic Institute for International Relations, 1985. L Lawson, *Working Women: A Portrait of South Africa's Black Women Workers*, Johannesburg: Sached and Ravan, 1985.

19. For a discussion of the law relating to domestic workers in South Africa, see S Flint, 'The Protection of Domestic Workers in South Africa: A Comparative Study', *Industrial Law Journal*, 9, 1988, p1 and 187. See also Jacklyn Cock's pathbreaking sociological study, *Maids and Madams: A Study in the Politics of Exploitation*, Johannesburg: Ravan, 1984.

20. This is as a result of the definition of employee contained in section 1 of the Labour Relations Act, 28 of 1956, read together with the definition of unfair labour practice contained in the same section.

21. Section 2(1) of the Labour Relations Act excludes from its scope not only farmworkers and domestic workers but also employees of the state (many of whom are women) and university lecturers. It is also important to realise that workers in bantustans are not covered by South African labour legislation. However, farmworkers and domestic workers may be included within the scope of labour legislation in the near future.

22. Subpara (i) of the definition in section 1 of the Labour Relations Act.

23. *J v M* (1989), *Industrial Law Journal*, 10, p755. For a discussion of the law on sexual harassment, see JG Mowatt, 'Sexual Harassment – Old Remedies for a New Wrong', *South African Law Journal*, 104, 1987, p439. See also Carla Sutherland in this volume.

24. Some of the problems facing women in organisations are well described by Cheryl Carolus, 'Things don't happen automatically', in R Suttner and J Cronin, *30 Years of the Freedom Charter*, Johannesburg: Ravan, 1986, p152–7. See also G Jaffee, 'Women in Trade Unions and the Community', *South African Review*, 4, 1987, p75. The problem women experience in trade unions is not peculiar to South Africa. For a discussion of the women in the British trade unions, see N Charles, 'Women and Trade Unions in the Workplace', *Feminist Review*, 15, 1983, p3.

25. For a full discussion of this development see C Murray, 'Women and Nightwork', *Industrial Law Journal*, 5, 1984, p47.

26. For a full discussion of maternity benefits see N Caine, 'Maternity Rights for Black Working Mothers', *Responsa Meridiana*, 5, 1989, p444.

27. See J Cock, et al, 'Childcare and the Working Mother: A Sociological Investigation of a Sample of Urban African Women', Second Carnegie Inquiry into Poverty in South Africa, Paper 115, University of Cape Town, 1983.

28. See June Sinclair, *An Introduction to the Matrimonial Property Act 1984*, Cape Town: Juta, 1984, p15.

29. Section 1, Criminal Law and Criminal Procedure Amendment Act, 39 of 1989.

30. The position varies across the country and, in Natal, is governed by the KwaZulu Act on the Code of Zulu Law, 6 of 1981. For an introductory discussion see J Julyan, 'Women, Race and the Law', in Alan Rycroft (ed), *Race and the Law in South Africa*, Cape Town: Juta, 1987, p139.

31. This was under the marital power regime. The Matrimonial Property Act, 88 of 1984 provided that the marital power would not exist in marriages concluded after it came into force and the Marriage and Matrimonial Property Amendment Act, 3 of 1988 did the same for civil marriages concluded by black people after 2 December 1988. Neither Act affected the matrimonial regime of existing marriages and, of course, neither has any affect on the status of women in customary unions.

32. S Burman, 'When Family Support Fails: The Problems of Maintenance Payments in Apartheid South Africa', *South African Journal on Human Rights*, 4, 1988, pp194 and 334.

33. Burman's conclusions are corroborated by our experience in a number of maintenance offices. However, the recently published Maintenance Amendment Bill seeks to address some of the problems.

34. See, for example on Nigeria, H Seymour, 'Obstacles to Women's Participation in the Development Process', *Journal of African Marxists*, 8, 1986, p75; on Kenya, R Feldman, 'Women's Groups and Women's Subordination: An Analysis of Policies Towards Rural Women in Kenya', *Review of African Political Economy*, 27/28, 1983, p67; and on Mozambique, S Urdang, 'The Last Transition? Women and Development in Mozambique', *Review of African Political Economy*, 27/28, 1983, p8.

35. Stuart Scheingold's phrase which he defines as 'an approach that grossly exaggerates the role that lawyers and litigation can play in a strategy for change... The myth of rights is... premised on a direct linking of litigation, rights and remedies with social change.' See S Scheingold, *The Politics of Rights: Lawyers, Public Policy and Political Change*, New Haven: Yale University Press, 1974.

36. Scheingold, *The Politics of Rights*, pp204–5.

37. It is not easy for women to become politically active. The very nature of their oppression makes organisation difficult. After they have finished working outside the home they have to work in the home. Taking on a third role, that of political activist, is often virtually impossible. See Carolus, 'Things don't happen automatically'.

38. See Ann C Scales, 'The Emergence of Feminist Jurisprudence: An Essay', *Yale Law Journal*, 95, 1986, p1373 at 1374.

39. Christine A Littleton, 'Reconstructing Sexual Equality', *California Law Review*, 75, 1987, p1279 at 1306.

40. See for instance Catherine MacKinnon, *Feminism Unmodified: Discourses on Life and Law*, Cambridge: Harvard University Press, 1987, p32ff.

41. Nicola Lacey, 'Legislation Against Sex Discrimination: Questions from a Feminist Perspective', *Journal of Law and Society*, 14, 1987, p418. See

also, in the context of violence, MA Freeman, 'Violence Against Women: Does the Legal System Provide Solutions or Itself Constitute the Problem', *British Journal of Law and Society*, 7, 1980, p215.

42. LM Finley, 'The Nature of Domination and the Nature of Women: Reflections on Feminism Unmodified', *Northeastern University Law Review*, 82, 1988, p352 at 357.

43. A Dworkin, 'Renouncing Sexual Equality' in *Our Blood: Prophecies and Discourse on Sexual Politics*, London: Women's Press, 1976, p11.

44. See Littleton, 'Reconstructing Sexual Equality', p1292. For a discussion of the American literature, see Scales, 'The Emergence of Feminist Jurisprudence'.

45. For example, limitations on women's working hours were seen as a standard for the limitation of men's working hours through collective bargaining. See S Deakin, 'Equality Under a Market Order: The Employment Act 1989, *Industrial Law Journal*, (UK), 19, 1990, p1, and Murray, 'Women and Nightwork'.

46. See the discussion in relation to nightwork above.

47. MacKinnon argues that by affirming so-called women's values we affirm what we have been permitted – 'what male supremacy has attributed to us for its own use'. See MacKinnon, *Feminism Unmodified*, p39.

48. In the context of racial discrimination see, for example, L Lustgarten , 'Racial Inequality and the Limits of Law', *Modern Law Review*, 49, 1986, p68, and, on English sex discrimination legislation, see generally Evelyn Ellis, *Sex Discrimination Law*, Hants: Gower, 1988 and David Pannick, *Sex Discrimination Law*, Oxford: Clarendon Press, 1985. For a review of the usefulness of the new Canadian Charter of Rights in establishing rights for women see G Brodsky and S Day, *Canadian Charter Equality Rights for Women: One Step Forward or Two Steps Back*, Ottawa: Canadian Advisory Council on the Status of Women, 1989.

49. For a useful analysis of the importance of political terms, see M Edelmean, *The Symbolic Uses of Politics*, Urbana: University of Illinois Press, 1964.

50. Littleton, 'Reconstructing Sexual Equality', p1301.

51. Lacey, 'Legislation Against Sex Discrimination', p419.

52. See Lucinda M Finley, 'Transcending Equality Theory: A Way out of the Maternity and Workplace Debate', *Columbia Law Review*, 66, 1986, p1116.

53. Catherine T Bartlett, 'MacKinnon's Feminism: Power on Whose Terms', *California Law Review*, 75, 1987, p1555.

54. Here we are referring to maternity leave for childbirth and the period immediately thereafter. Parental leave to care for a newborn baby should not be restricted to mothers.

55. See articles 13 and 14 of 'A Bill of Rights for a New South Africa', ANC Constitutional Committee, CDS Cape, 1990. Neither the Freedom Charter, nor the 1988 ANC constitutional guidelines had contemplated affirmative action to remedy gender discrimination.

56. The notion of positive action introduced in article 14 is consonant with article 10's proposal to realise social, educational, economic and welfare rights. The European Council has a recommendation concerning the implementation of positive action for women. For a full discussion see

C McCrudden, *Women, Employment and European Equality Law*, London: Eclipse, 1987.

57. We would not argue that all aspects of the family are oppressive. In fact, in important ways women have autonomy in the family. This aspect of the campaign by conservative women against feminism, particularly in the United States is often not taken seriously enough by feminists. See also D Schalkwyk, 'Elsa Joubert: Women and Domestic Struggle in Poppie Nongena', in C Clayton (ed), *Women and Writing in South Africa*, Marshalltown: Heinemann, 1989, p253.

58. For discussions of attitudes to violence against women see, for example, C Hall, 'Rape: The Politics of Definition', *South African Law Journal*, 105, 1988, p67; S Estrich, 'Rape', *Yale Law Journal*, 95, 1986, p1087; H Rafter and EA Starke (eds), *Judge, Lawyer, Victim, Thief: Women, Gender Roles and Criminal Justice*, Chicago: Northeastern University Press, 1982.

59. To a certain extent women see themselves through male eyes and evaluate their problems in male terms. This is in the nature of oppression and mutes women's voices. But women are not totally trammeled by male standards and organised women learn from one another. Take rape-in-marriage, for example. A woman may believe that there is no such thing – that her husband is entitled to intercourse without her consent. Once she learns of the notion of rape-in-marriage past experiences take on a totally new complexion and unwanted intercourse may become rape.

60. A Sachs, *Protecting Human Rights in a New South Africa*, Cape Town: Oxford University Press, 1990, p62. For a discussion of the Women's Charter, see B Mabandla et al, *Women's Rights: A Discussion Document*, Cape Town: Centre for Development Studies, 1990, pp46–7.

61. One obvious difficulty lies in the mode of its adoption. Would an instrument drawn up 'essentially... by women' be incorporated in democratic constitutional structures? Our understanding of the nature of the oppression of women suggests not. Sachs envisages similar charters for other groups and has suggested that a Worker's Charter might address the particular problems of workers (see A Sachs, 'A Bill of Rights for South Africa: Areas of Agreement and Disagreement', *Columbia Human Rights Law Review*, 2, 1989). Such a charter would surely be negotiated with employers. Would the Women's Charter be negotiated with men? If so it would lose much of its usefulness. If not it would probably be unlikely to be given a constitutional role at all.

62. Perhaps Scheingold's analysis of the transformative character of rights as 'agents of political mobilization' (Scheingold, *The Politics of Rights*, p148) breaks down when we consider the household. As we have seen, the key to ending the subordination of women lies in restructuring the balance of power in the household. It may be that the peculiarly atomised position of women in the household means that it will be far more difficult for women to mobilise to alter power relationships in the jealously guarded privacy of the home than in the relative publicity of the workplace. Even so, effective organisation in the public sphere which may change women's position of social and economic subordination, will almost certainly impact on the balance of power within the household.

63. The section in the preamble is: 'We, the people of South Africa declare ...
    That our country will never be prosperous and free until all our people live
    in brotherhood, enjoying equal rights and opportunities.'
64. As Frene Ginwala commented in an interview, 'liberation can only be
    achieved by women themselves, by getting involved'. See 'ANC Women:
    Their Strength in the Struggle, *Work In Progress*, 45, 1986, p10.

Theories of Equality
Some thoughts for South Africa

Linda Zama

We are at a critical stage of our history where there is talk of white fears and business fears about the future economic policies of a post-apartheid South Africa. Already there are murmurs of disillusionment about the absence of women in decision and policy-making forums of progressive organisations. We are told in high-sounding slogans that 'all shall be equal before the law'. The question is whether equality will be automatic simply because we have a liberal constitution and good laws drafted by our best legal brains. The women's situation should be analysed in terms of the development of society. Development is a process, and there is no question of leaping over stages of development if we seek to understand the oppression and subordination of women. The oppression of women is not natural; it is something that came about as society passed through stages of development. It is a sad legacy of history which needs to be corrected.

It is often said black women face triple oppression: they are discriminated against in society, at work and at home where they are traditionally regarded as inferior because they are women. White women do not suffer the third yoke of being black. This discussion does not seek to overlook the race issue; however the gender issue will be treated as broadly as possible. It is time we concentrated on the substance, and not

the forms of discrimination. Women of all colours have a common problem, that of being victims of discriminatory traditional practices.

Contradictions

In October 1990 the South African Council of Churches held a conference on *Women and the Constitution*. One woman said:

> As a white bourgeois feminist I thought that the conference was
> characterised by, on the one hand, the constant reference for the need for
> a broad front of women across the divides of race, culture, ideology and
> class, to fight for women's emancipation, and on the other hand, the
> emphasis on 'unity with our men in the national liberation struggle'.

South Africa is a contradictory society and we need to address those
contradictions. As an African woman I do not have a problem with
carrying a baby on my back, or water on my head, or working at home,
or going to work in my law practice, or sitting down to write conference
papers. There are contradictions, but they will gell into amazing strength
for South African women. Alice Walker says in her book *The Temple of
My Familiar*: 'Struggle is endless, it has layers and layers; it is smelly
too.'

Post-apartheid South Africa

The struggle of women and men in South Africa is not just for majority
rule, a liberal democratic constitution and a justifiable bill of rights. It is
a struggle for the liberation of women and men to restructure our society
into a humanistic one. It is not incidental to our struggle for national
liberation. It is part of our broad struggle and we cannot separate one
from the other. When women are called upon to play their part in shaping a post-apartheid South Africa, they are being challenged to
participate in building an alternative society that is to be created and
moulded by them, but also by men and by children. Our vision is of an
anti-racist, democratic, non-sexist South Africa free from exploitation.
These are the ideals we should strive for. The question is how do we
strive towards the ideal? What follows is an attempt to deal with the
mechanics in a pragmatic way.

Participation

South African women, and particularly black women, have courageously
'held the fort' or 'kept the home fires burning' whether as poverty-
stricken wives of migrants, as mothers or as combatants on the battle

front. In Southern Africa millions of women played and are still playing an active and supportive part in the process of decolonisation. However, a general survey of the position of women in independent states in Southern Africa gives a depressing picture.

The situation in South Africa will not be an exception unless we address participation of women in decision making, and women learn to assert themselves. Participation presupposes activity. Women cannot participate if they fold their arms and keep quiet for fear of alienation if they take a firm stand. The struggle for participation is a fierce one in a patriarchal society like ours where recognition is not on merit but on colour, class and gender. Even the most democratic organisations have difficulty struggling beyond class and gender.

Space for participation will not be created easily by men. At the same time men cannot speak about participation in a non-participatory society like ours. There is enough space for all of us on this planet; women and men, black and white must share it. It is conceded that struggle for participation of women will be painful. Relationships will crumble but women must assert themselves and ensure the constitution and all legislation affirms their participation. Instead of simplistic slogans like 'freedom for all' and 'equality for all', our slogan must be *'struggle* against the oppressors and exploiters', and 'let the opportunity to oppress and exploit be abolished'.

The most fundamental question is whether women are channelling their energy in the right direction. For post-apartheid laws to be significant in the struggle for the emancipation of women they must move in the same direction as other social, political and economic institutions. If not, the law merely becomes 'the law' in the big books without any significance to the real life and daily toils of women. This is often the case in countries which enact laws decreeing equality of treatment and equality before the law for both sexes. Women remain economically and materially dependent on men because of men's control of, and better access to, productive sources. If the wealth of South Africa is to be shared, we must demand an economic policy that will make space for a percentage of women to prove themselves.

When the newly elected members of the ANC Southern Natal region executive committee were interviewed, journalists directed questions to the two women on the committee. They asked, 'haven't you been elected because you are women?' and the reply was, 'the calibre of the women who sit on this committee dismisses the myth that we are merely dressing up windows here. Give us six months and we are going to prove that to you'.

Women must assert themselves in demanding participation in the affairs of struggle for national liberation. They must agitate for participatory space in small community meetings, in civic structures, and in political organisations. Participation must start at a lower level; some women are still too scared because they have not been able to evolve their own self-confidence. Big things in local government and national government will be shaped by their effective participation. As long as the legislature remains dominated by men the enactment of just, fair and equitable laws to govern marital property rights of spouses will not mean a better deal for married women. If our country is dominated by exploitative institutional structures, it is argued that women themselves must attempt to mobilise the legal system to the advantage of their children and themselves.

A legal system for all

For a long time we have argued that the legal system in our country is shaped to protect privileges of the white male minority. This is a fact. In order to be systematic in our search for a just and equitable society let us look at women's legal problems in terms of the law 'on the books', the application of the law and the real needs of women. The following are a few suggestions highlighting what needs to be done.

The law 'on the books'

Those who research this aspect of law must determine what the law is and how it discriminates against women. The common law is not always clear, just as statutes may be ambiguous or unrelated to local conditions. What springs to mind here are unfair home ownership regulations for spouses married out of community of property. The concept of marriage out of community of property is itself questionable. It suggests that relationships are based on material connections. This law is a symptom of our perverse society. Another example is Section 21(5) of the KwaZulu Education Act, No 7 of 1978, which provides that 'any unmarried female permanent teacher who falls pregnant shall resign her post on 30 days notice and if she fails to do so shall be summarily discharged from the service of the Department as soon as her condition becomes known or apparent'. Some laws appear to be neutral whereas in practice they adversely affect women. For example, if a mother is very young, this is taken into consideration when determining custody during divorce action. The assumption here is that the woman cannot provide financially for her child. Even if she is employed she is relegated to the lowest paying job?

Administering the law

Maintenance laws, for instance, are a frustration for women. It is either that officials hesitate to apply them because they sympathise with their male-kind or they are bribed to ignore the transgressions of the defaulter. Some laws are ineffective because people do not know that they exist to protect their rights. Women in particular have a problem of occupying low positions in society. They are less likely to have access to information or institutions which can help them. A law which grants women the rights to own property becomes ineffective in a society where there are no jobs for women, and therefore no money to purchase property. Women will have to participate in administering the law.

Determining the real needs of women

Researchers must avoid researching for themselves. Research must be relative to existing conditions. In many cases, perhaps because of the Christian values that predominate in our society, legal reformers seeking to improve the status of women begin by concentrating on marriage laws, tax laws, divorce laws, marital property rights, etc. In Southern Africa there is irrefutable evidence that a vast number of women are not married and therefore marriage laws are largely irrelevant to them. Can we not look at laws regulating co-habitation without marriage or rights of so-called illegitimate children? What about poverty and underdevelopment? Can we not agitate for laws which work towards alleviating poverty for all, and encouraging economic development?

It is hoped that the message here will serve as a catalyst for fundamental change in not just the substance and form of our laws, but in the very ways that we examine, research and formulate policies for changes that will have a real and necessary impact on changing and challenging the situation of the oppression of women in South Africa.

Women and the Elephant
The need to redress gender oppression

Frene Ginwala

When considering any aspect of our subject – putting women on the agenda – we have to begin with a clear and common understanding of how we perceive the relationship of women and society. It is therefore important to identify and define the problem with which we are trying to deal. What we are talking about is not discrimination against women. The phenomenon that we have to address in this country is gender oppression.

Discrimination is more a symptom than a cause. It is the product of the whole way in which society works. To attack it, then, we have not only to legislate and act against it itself but also to work for shifts in the deeper causes which underlie it. As the ANC national executive committee's statement on the emancipation of women says: 'To achieve genuine equality, our policies must be based on a real understanding of gender oppression and the way in which it manifests itself in our society.'

The word sex is a biological definition, while gender is a socially constructed understanding of what it is to be a man and what it is to be a woman, with defined characteristics which are encompassed in the notion of femininity and masculinity in our society. We derive these understandings from the way society is organised and from the way in which we experience it. We are all aware from our own experience that this social construction is loaded with psychological and physical traits which are artificial and attributed to all men and all women.

From this it follows that 'men's role' and 'women's role' in the family, the economy and society generally are not biologically determined (apart from pregnancy and childbirth), but are culturally allocated, and the relationship between the two is not one of equality but of oppression.

What we must address therefore are the power relations in society. Given that gender oppression is socially constructed, we must examine and aim to change the social relations which construct it. Our aim must be to reform gender relations so that they exist on a more equitable foundation and provide the basis for the full and free development of both men and women.

Let us consider for a moment some of these characteristics that are attributed to women and how they affect us in our daily lives: Supposedly men are rational, and women are intuitive. Women are small and frail, men are tall and strong. In western societies, this has given rise to the notion that men are stronger and suited to physical and manual work, they are logical and hence better at science and able to understand machines, and because they are allegedly immune from emotional judgements and operate on pure reason they make good managers and executives. In contrast, women are weak, supposedly better at arts and with a particular talent for the 'caring professions' and social sciences; they are given to emotional outbursts and intuitive judgements and hence incapable of taking on any major responsibility in business and industry.

These notions of what are female and male characteristics are not only inaccurate but totally artificial – they are cultural constructs and vary between places and with time. For example, although today in South Africa women are considered most 'suitable' for domestic work, up to the beginning of the twentieth century in Natal and the Transvaal men, and not women, were the domestic workers, and still are in many parts of Asia. In times of war women replace men in most categories of civilian employment. They do heavy work on the land and in industry, drive and repair trucks and cranes, operate heavy machinery, etc. In South Africa, African women had traditionally been the cultivators of land. This did not fit in with the Victorian notions of the missionaries on the role of women in society, and hence when schools were established African women were trained to be the domestic workers and were excluded from the agricultural training provided for African men.

Divisions between jobs done by men and jobs done by women become self-perpetuating because in turn they shape the jobs and tools and the work environment. Decisions about the size and weight of loads, the force required to move levers, the design of tools, even the length of spade and pick handles are based upon assumptions about which sex is doing the work. In office furniture, desks for managers are sized according to male physiques, secretarial ones for women's!

All of us are victims, and tend to accept social, political and economic relations based on artificial assumptions about men and women as real. As a result we are guilty of accepting the world and our society as given. It is there, and we have to fit women into it. We try and shape women, to accommodate a given society and its underlying assumptions, rather than challenging the assumptions and reshaping society. We all tend to do this.

As academics, and as activists in the liberation movement, we have participated in numerous conferences and written papers around the themes of women and education, women and health, women and society, women and the law, women and the constitution and so on. The logic of this is almost to write a paper entitled 'women and the elephant', because the assumptions in this approach are that women are homogeneous and we are considering and relating women to something like the elephant, that is outside of women, and whose shape and character is unaffected by that something called women.

By following this approach women are identifying themselves as 'outsiders' seeking entry into a society that is normal and acceptable to women. When we deal with racism in our society we have come to reject such notions. For many years there was the perception that there existed a 'civilisation' to which blacks had not contributed, and blacks had to be raised to certain levels before they could qualify for the vote and otherwise participate fully in civilised society. These ideas have been rejected in most parts of the world, and even to an extent among the ruling circles in our country. Why then in gender relations do we now put up and acknowledge a standard which we women have to fit into?

One of the fundamental changes facing South Africa is its emergence as a democratic country, as an African nation with an African culture on an African continent; not as a European nation with a European culture artificially located on the African continent. Similarly, we have to build our democracy as a gender-neutral society, one whose institutions, patterns of behaviour, values and norms are people-shaped rather than man-shaped. Both processes are part of the liberation struggle.

Further, if we continue to look at women as homogeneous we will not be able to assess and take into account questions of class and race in our society. It is the interface of race, class and gender which has shaped our society and is the fundamental issue that we have to confront. If we continue to see our problems as simply a matter of discrimination, then we will not be able to deal with the fundamental basis on which the status and condition of women in South Africa has been determined.

The focus of a great deal of research in this country has been on the oppression of black women. By ignoring the position of white women, the impression is created that black women are the only oppressed women in South Africa. The spotlight has also been on the liberation movement's policies and the failure of women activists to raise feminist issues. This research and criticism has very often come from white academics. While much of what has been said may have been factually correct, the context was wrong and the understanding of the liberation struggle faulty.

The failure to look at the position of white women in society was initially shared by the liberation movements. For example, those who framed the Women's Charter of the 1950s referred to the absence of property rights for African women, but ignored the reality that white women had only limited property rights at that time, and for some purposes white women were also treated as minors.

The result of the critical spotlight being focused on black women by mainly white women had the effect of setting back the cause of feminism. It made black women and the liberation movement defensive, and allowed those who were anxious to maintain the status quo to exploit the situation. Hopefully, we have moved away from this, and can now look at gender issues as they affect all South Africans, and not exclusively in racial and ethnic terms. We need also to address white women in our country and ask: what have you done with the relative power that you have had? Where are white women in the political, social and economic life of our country? Did comfort and privilege blind you to the national oppression around you and to your own subordinate status?

There is an additional aspect now being added to the situation of maids and madams in our society. There are growing numbers of black 'madams'; and what is more, both madam and maid are in the same ANC branches. This is a major challenge for the liberation movement, and will provide a demanding test for the principles and values we have advocated in struggle.

The ANC's understanding of gender oppression was set out in the NEC's statement of 2 May 1990:

> Gender oppression is everywhere rooted in a material base and is expressed in socio-cultural traditions and attitudes all of which are supported and perpetuated by an ideology which subordinates women. In South Africa, it is institutionalised in the laws as well as the customs and practices of all our people. Within our racially and ethnically divided society, all women have a lower status than men of the same group in both law and practice. And as with racism the disadvantages imposed on them range across the political, economic, social, domestic, cultural and civil spheres.

Thus there is a material base with social, cultural and ideological underpinnings. These are all interdependent and each of them has to be addressed. Is it possible to address these equally, or must it be at the expense of one or another? More importantly, the interdependence emphasises that we cannot put gender into a box and say these are gender issues which we must look at in isolation from the general problems of society.

Those engaged in women's studies in particular must consider whether it is possible to have a viable gender policy. Are we in danger of putting women in a ghetto of our own making? Should we speak of women's rights or of gender relations?

Women must consider whether the way in which we formulate the issue harms us, and the danger of ghettoising women. Are the issues being discussed of concern only to women, or to all democrats? While we welcome the fact that Lawyers for Human Rights organised a conference around these matters and recognised the issues as ones of human rights, we must also take note of the fact that very few male lawyers participated in the conference. This reflects a failure on the part of both women and men to recognise the nature of gender oppression, and their own responsibility to redress it.

The issue cannot be compartmentalised. Gender policy cannot be treated as something separate. The question of gender relations must permeate all policy. This means that we must begin to challenge the structures and institutions that we tend to accept as given. Such an approach leads to some surprising conclusions as we found when instead of looking at women from the perspective of economists, one looked at the economy from the perspective of women.[1]

Generally, women disappear when economists look at economic issues. In South Africa's statistics, there is serious under-enumeration of Africans, and even more so of African women. But the real problem is universal, and economic policy and the whole terrain of economic debate tends to be deeply biased against women. We found that:

- Economic concepts *exclude* women and the perspective of men is wrongly perceived as the universal objective perspective.
- The economic activities of women are systematically *devalued* and omitted in the economic statistics and argument.
- Economic analysis largely *omits* the economic relation between the genders, for example, at work and within the household, hence:
- Aspects of the operation of the economy are systematically *misunderstood*, hence:

- Economic policy is based on some false premises and can systematically work to the further relative and absolute *detriment* of women.[2]

Clearly there is a need for a rethink of some of the basic categories of economic analysis and policy making; and a redefinition of many of the supposedly gender-blind concepts of economics. One example will suffice to illustrate: All women are familiar with the notion that domestic labour consists of 'chores' and is not 'work'. But why must we recognise such definitions as acceptable? Should the terms used by economists not be redefined so that 'labour' includes both paid and unpaid work, and 'work' and the 'working day' included unpaid work so recognising and valuing women's total working day.

In the light of the ANC policy on the emancipation of women, its economic policy has to begin to address such issues. Internationally also, there are UN resolutions which call for recognition of the unpaid work done by women as a contribution to creating wealth.

Women must begin to look at other areas of society in a similar way, challenging the fundamental definitions and institutions that are usually taken as given.

This must include both the laws and the legal system. There is a danger that our objectives will be limited by demanding simply that blacks and women should be put on the *existing* bench and the law should be made 'accessible'. Let us instead put the laws and the legal system under a microscope and examine the fundamentals as they should apply in a gender-neutral society.

Our experience of the law has not been that it is necessarily a liberating force, on the contrary laws are what oppressors have used to control people, and in particular to subordinate women. Let us then scrutinise legal systems, legal structures and institutions, legal ideas with women's eyes, and formulate what it is that we need. Simply having a woman judge will not solve our difficulties. Women must approach law as a system of regulating society in a creative way, starting from the pooling of our collective experiences.

However, this is not to suggest that until this is done women should not look at the laws within the existing legal system. In particular, women have to articulate their demands in relation to the constitution of a new South Africa. It is important that even while we are challenging structures, institutions and systems, we make sure that what is being proposed does not work to as great a disadvantage to women as it might do without our intervention.

When women in the ANC looked at our proposed constitutional guidelines, a number of changes were proposed which need to be included in the constitution of a democratic non-racial, non-sexist South Africa. We believe it is necessary to place an obligation on the state to end sexism, in a similar manner to the obligation to end racism. Otherwise, the equal rights accorded to women can be no more than rhetoric. We cannot expect women with little education, and scant resources to find out that the constitution guarantees them certain rights, and then to set about the complicated legal procedures to claim those rights, especially as those rights might have to be asserted against male members of the family. Such types of constitutional rights are devoid of meaning.

Another recommendation made was that any law, custom or practice that discriminates against women should be held to be unconstitutional. Again, in the proposed guidelines there was the idea of democratising the traditional office of chiefs. However, the traditional powers of chiefs included judicial functions, and in most societies women were not even admitted to the courts. Hence it was argued that the democratising of traditional institutions must include the democratising of judicial and other powers. Similarly, proposals were made regarding the family: the need to recognise various types of family systems, and to remove the structural subordination of women in any new family law.

Now my final point is on the subject of this conference: 'putting women on the agenda'. Who should be doing this? Quite simply it has to be women. We will not do so by having a conference about it. It is going to have to be done by struggle. The one thing the ANC has learnt is that no one will give us our freedom, we have had to fight for it. Women are going to have to struggle for their emancipation. Despite the ANC's excellent policies, we do not have excellent practices. Gender relations are imbalanced and it is a power relationship. At the moment we have to talk about political power. Women have got to put themselves on the agenda. The only way we are going to ensure that the laws which we want in future are there is if women are part of the law-making machinery. It is no good saying we want this or that in the constitution if we elect an all-male constituent assembly or we only have a few women.

So part of what we have to do is to talk about how we are going to organise, how we are going to make sure that we put women on the agenda. We have to elect women into positions of power and then by that process of participation we will achieve the kind of gender-neutral society which I think we need to move towards.

Postscript

After the longest and most intense debate of the 48th ANC National Conference (July 1991), a proposal by the ANC Women's League that a

30 per cent quota for women should be instituted at all levels of the ANC including its national executive committee was not accepted.

This was not a surprising development and was a consequence of tactical errors by the Women's League and political failure by the ANC. The debate revealed a lack of understanding of affirmative action policies and the mechanisms through which they can be implemented. The result highlighted the dilemma faced by a women's organisation located and operating within a national liberation movement.

The ANC in exile has adopted very progressive positions on the emancipation of women, positions that are far in advance of other national liberation movements, and of many western governments and political parties. However, the adoption of such policies owed more to the persuasive advocacy of some women members than to the level of understanding of either the membership or the entire leadership. As a consequence, both in exile and in the reconstituted legal ANC in South Africa, little regard was paid in practice to the question of women's emancipation, and on a number of occasions the ANC leadership failed to act in conformity with its policy pronouncements. This was evident, when very few women were on the interim leadership structures appointed by the NEC to establish the ANC inside South Africa. Again despite the very strong political demand that there be the widest possible political participation in the constitution-making process, the ANC's own constitutional committee has consisted of 19 men and one woman.

The debate at conference revealed the failure of the organisation to take its own policy on gender issues seriously and to educate the membership on these policies. Women members, and the ANC Women's League also failed to engage the membership in debate prior to conference or to promote and project the policies they wanted conference to adopt. In the months following the decision of the Women's League Conference to put forward the quota, its own activities focused almost exclusively on campaigns around issues such as the release of political prisoners, and the violence that was unleashed against the people with the connivance of the police and security forces. In practice the League functioned simply as an arm of the ANC, mobilising women into the organisation and the current national struggles. There was little in its approach or activities that was specific to women.

Not only did the League fail to engage in educational programmes around emancipation and the quota, but by allowing the broader national issue to overwhelm it, the League lent substance to those critics who have long argued that a woman's organisation attached to the ANC would inevitably subordinate women's interests.

It is not too harsh to suggest that the League failed its first test, and its membership will have to engage in critical self examination as to its future role. However, it is not yet possible to definitively answer whether the ANC Women's League can prioritise women's issues.

Affirmative action

The proposal for a women's quota in the ANC's decision-making bodies is in conformity with the organisation's commitment to affirmative action policies in a democratic South Africa.

One needs to recognise that historic injustices create a legacy of disadvantage that will not be overcome automatically. Legislation that outlaws discrimination and provides for an extension of equal opportunities to all citizens will do little to redress historic imbalances if one operates on the assumption that those previously disadvantaged will already have the necessary skills, education, training and experience, and that all that is necessary is to introduce an element of 'free and fair' competition. In such circumstances there will be neither freedom, nor competition, and no fairness.

Further, one cannot permit a situation where those who are already privileged should have the exclusive responsibility of determining how education, skills and training are to be provided, while the disadvantaged are required to wait patiently until their standards are 'raised'.

Affirmative action is a form of positive discrimination in favour of these previously disadvantaged, and can be used as a transitional and therefore temporary measure to redress the imbalance. Affirmative action policies have been used in a number of countries in relation to groups disadvantaged on grounds of race, gender, language, ethnicity, etc. Such policies have been most commonly applied in the fields of employment and the provision of educational facilities and skills training. In most cases this has involved the imposition of quotas in favour of those whom the policy is intended to benefit.

The ANC has committed itself to a policy of affirmative action for women in a post-apartheid South Africa. In the sphere of employment this must go beyond simply giving preference to women among equally qualified candidates. To be really effective, affirmative action must extend to advancement and promotion and recruitment including an obligation to search for suitable women candidates. Many gifted and skilled women have been excluded through being 'rendered invisible' by existing hiring practices in all countries including South Africa. In addition there will need to be affirmative action in the provision of education, training and support, and the conscious elimination of stereotyping in the education and careers advisory systems.

Women are also rendered invisible when it comes to considering candidates to fill responsible jobs or positions in political organisations –

whether this is done by appointment or through elections. The absence of women in such positions in every country in the world establishes beyond doubt that in democratic elections choices are not based solely on merit. To argue that merit is the criterion being applied would be to subscribe to the view that women are genetically inferior to men, as there are so few women who have 'merited' selection so far.

The application of affirmative action in this area is much more contentious, and there has been considerable discussion on the relative merits of special 'women's seats' and quotas as well as on the actual mechanisms of selection.

The absence of women at decision-making levels is detrimental to the organisation concerned – as the experiences of more than half the population are excluded and do not inform the decision-making process. This is particularly important in political parties and liberation movements where the mobilisation of the entire population is so vital. Many political parties have set apart a number of seats in their decision-making bodies for women.[3] The mechanisms used vary. In some cases a certain number of seats are designated as women's seats. In others, a proportion of the overall membership of a committee must be women. In the first case, usually but not always, those selected are intended to represent women's interests, and are chosen by women. In the second, various mechanisms are used for the selection, but both men and women are involved.

In this way, women are able to function in decision-making committees. There is an educative value in women being seen to be among those who make important decisions, and women's experiences and perspectives to some extent begin to inform those decisions. On the other hand, there are negative aspects. There is a danger that these seats form a ghetto, limiting women's participation rather than expanding it. Rarely, if ever, is the quota allotted to women proportionate to their numbers in the population or membership, and the agreed initial number becomes an upper limit. In addition, whatever the intention, women are often seen simply as women's 'representatives' rather than as members of the committee or executives who happen to be women. They are then excluded from mainstream issues. At the same time, any questions relating to matters chauvinistically perceived as women's issues, such as catering, health and welfare, children and family, are automatically allocated to the women on the committee thus further entrenching divisions, keeping women isolated and the questions of emancipation outside of general concern and attention.

Last but not least, simple quotas often lead to resentment of capable women because some male or white feels he has been discriminated against and on the basis of 'pure merit' would have been appointed or elected. This resentment is often manifested in aggressive behaviour and hostility to women colleagues and confrontational response when affirmative action is being advocated.

Such attitudes are aggravated by particular mechanisms used as affirmative action, which pit individual men against women. The most commonly used system in elections is for there to be a common list of candidates, and regardless of the votes received a fixed percentage of women are deemed to have been elected. Unsuccessful males thus experience 'discrimination' in a very visible and direct way: they will have received more votes than a successful women candidate, or will claim to have done so. Individual women are targeted and the system provokes male hostility, while on occasions women feel guilty for being responsible for the exclusion of a capable male. In addition, such a mechanism does not overcome the ghettoising of women, and effectively operates in the same way as women's seats or women's representation does, with all the negative aspects already listed.

These considerations have exercised the minds of feminist activists and has deterred them from supporting quotas.

However, some of the negative factors are mitigated by applying affirmative action at the point of choosing rather than when votes are counted, that is by voters rather than electoral officers. Thus electors would be required to vote for a certain minimum percentage of women, and all valid ballot papers would have to reflect this. Those with the highest number of votes would be elected regardless of whether they were men or women.

Such a system has a number of advantages. It serves to educate the voter by promoting consideration of women candidates and overcoming the usual 'invisibility' of women. Women elected in this way are also more likely to be seen as having been elected on merit and as general or national leaders rather than as persons representing only women's interests. In addition, this mechanism can help to eliminate, or at least reduce, male hostility, as no woman would have been deemed elected if she has received fewer votes than an unsuccessful male.

In most countries where such mechanisms have been used, more women that the required minimum percentage on the ballot paper have been elected. However, such a result is not automatic. But the way is open for women to strategise, and by limiting the number of women candidates, to facilitate the election of larger numbers of women.

The Women's League Conference did not consider mechanisms when putting forward its proposals for a 30 per cent quota in all structures of the ANC. However, a number of those who promoted the adoption of the quota had been persuaded by the knowledge of the advantages of this type of mechanism.

The main argument used against such a system has been that it limits the voters' freedom of choice. This, however, applies to all forms of affirmative action. Yet as women's experience has shown, without such policies hierarchical and power relations are self-perpetuating.

In a democratic South Africa, blacks and women will bring with them the cumulative burden of their historic disadvantages.

Whites and men have for centuries enjoyed privileged education, health employment and power, and as a result in many areas of human activity retain a virtual monopoly of experience.

The argument that the 'standards' of blacks have to be raised before the introduction of democracy is now recognised as merely an excuse for maintaining the status quo and retaining minority rule. Similarly, in relation to the economy and in society generally, such an approach is a way of maintaining white and male privileges. For how can blacks and women acquire the skills and the experience to break the monopoly of effective power without affirmative action?

The organisation of the ANC conference did not allow for in-depth debate. The size of the commissions and the plenary sessions usually only permitted a single intervention of two or three minutes. There was therefore no opportunity to debate the case for or against affirmative action in general or in relation to women. However, the commitment to affirmative action remains, and will be put forward as part of the organisation's constitutional proposals.

No doubt in the negotiating process the issue will be contested in the name of democracy by white males desirous of maintaining their monopoly of power and privilege. Women will have to build alliances across racial and political barriers if they are to ensure that their interests are not lost in the process.

The ANC has to find means of translating its commitment to progressive policies into action, and of educating and enhancing the understanding of the membership to support such implementation.

When black men demand affirmative action for themselves, what arguments can be used to deny it to women? And if affirmative action is to form part of the ANC's proposals for the constitution of a democratic South Africa, can we fail to incorporate it into the constitution of the ANC?

Notes

1. Frene Ginwala, Maureen Mackintosh and Doreen Massey, *Gender and Economic Policy in a Democratic South Africa*, United Kingdom: Open

University Development Policy and Practice Working Paper No 21, April 1991.
2. Ginwala et al, *Gender and Economic Policy.*
3. Most but not all the political parties that have introduced a quota are members of the Socialist International. Among these, the Canadian New Democrats have a 50 per cent quota, the Norwegian Labour Party and the Danish and German SPD have 40 per cent and the British Labour Party 40 per cent by 1995. Following the introduction of a quota in Germany and Spain, the parties found that 80 per cent of new party members were women. In Norway and Denmark, the quota applies both ways: 'In all elections and nominations, there must be at least 40 per cent of both sexes.' In South Africa, the Conservative Party has a 30 per cent quota for women.

Promoting Gender Equality in South Africa

Brigitte Mabandla

Women have been integral to struggles waged and won against colonialism, racism, and fascism. They have been a major force in national liberation struggles. Yet the emancipation of women themselves has proved to be one of the longest struggles ever waged.

Numerous factors can be cited as inhibiting the struggle for the emancipation of women. But the most important factor impeding women's emancipation through liberation struggles is the tendency to subsume women's issues in the quest for national liberation. Usually the argument is advanced that women should not press hard for issues of concern to them because the 'time is not appropriate'. It is often argued that once national liberation is achieved, women's problems will necessarily be resolved and they will be emancipated – almost by default. History tells a different story. The experience of many women in liberation struggles around the world is that national liberation does not automatically bring about women's emancipation.[1]

As we debate the character of the new South Africa, we need to focus clearly on women's issues. We must anticipate differences between the various political organisations and their understanding of women's issues. These differences are a reflection of the general discord in the interpretation of human rights in South Africa.[2] As South Africa is poised for change, tension is reflected in the debates surrounding the drafting of the new constitution. In particular, tension exists over the meaning of democracy, equality and non-discrimination. Obviously, the major tension lies between the democratic forces and the present South African regime and its allies.

The democratic forces of this country are struggling to introduce a 'culture of rights'. The principle of non-discrimination is an established human rights principle recognised in modern democracies. Related to this is the concept of equality between the sexes at law and in practice. The adoption of the UN Convention on the Elimination of all Forms of Discrimination against Women introduced gender equality as a contemporary human rights principle.[3]

It is common knowledge that the equality of men and women is not on the agenda of most political organisations currently contesting power. It is therefore expected that just as most of these parties have difficulty understanding long-established human rights principles, they will have difficulty recognising women's rights and the concept of equality between the sexes. It may well be that when the democratic forces place women's issues on the agenda of the constitutional debate, these forces will respond by contesting proposals put forward.

While the ANC attempts to address women's emancipation, we must concede that the matter is still at a level of rhetoric, both in the ANC and the mass democratic movement (MDM).[4] We need to break this logjam! We must link the issue of women's emancipation to the struggle for a democratic dispensation.

This paper examines how, in this phase of struggle, we can ensure that women's rights are protected and gender equality is promoted in a democratic dispensation. It lists the most recent demands made by women, both in the ANC and in the broader democratic movement. It also raises questions pertinent to women's emancipation.

The protection of women's rights

The demand for the protection of women's rights and the promotion of gender equality in a democratic, non-racial and non-sexist South Africa was made unequivocally at an ANC in-house seminar in Lusaka in 1989 organised by the ANC women's section, the legal committee, and the constitutional committee.

The Lusaka seminar formed part of many similar gatherings organised both inside and outside South Africa to discuss the ANC's constitutional guidelines. While various formations of the democratic movement inside South Africa discussed the guidelines, the Lusaka seminar focused specifically on gender equality in a democratic dispensation. It covered a wide range of issues, such as the legal disabilities of women in general and African women in particular, the prevalence of gender oppression among all classes and races, and the necessity to address the material, cultural and ideological underpinnings of gender oppression.

In January 1990, about 350 delegates from the MDM and the ANC women's section attended the Malibongwe conference in Amsterdam. This meeting also addressed gender equality in a democratic, non-racial and non-sexist South Africa. The demands made at that forum are consistent with those made at the Lusaka seminar. Thus reference in this paper will be made to the recommendations of the Lusaka in-house seminar as it covered a broader spectrum of issues than the Malibongwe conference.

What are the demands of women in South Africa?

Some of the basic demands made by women at the Lusaka seminar were:

- The future state should be a united democratic non-racial and non-sexist state.
- Characterisation of our future society should be explicitly non-sexist.
- The constitutional guidelines should be comprehensively examined to ensure that patriarchy is not entrenched with regard to family, land ownership and the judicial system.
- Constitutional recognition should be accorded to a Women's Rights Charter which should be formulated through popular participation.
- The state should ensure the implementation of a programme of affirmative action.
- The constitution should protect women against non-democratic cultural and religious practices, domestic violence, sexual harassment and rape.
- The law should enable women to have full control over their bodies and they should therefore have a right to choose to have a child or terminate a pregnancy.
- Domestic labour should be socialised.
- Labour law should guarantee a living wage for women to be determined through consultations with trade unions and other interested parties.
- There should be protective legislation established in consultation with trade unions and women's organisations.
- A democratic government should ratify the UN Convention on the Elimination of all Forms of Discrimination against Women.[5]

Entrenching gender equality

The constitution

It is possible for the constitution to be structured to address the demands of women and yet not to impede gender equality. Its language should not be neutral, and there must be clear reference to men and women where such distinctions are necessary.[6] It must be stated unambiguously that South Africa is to be reconstituted as a democratic non-racial, non-sexist unitary state. Democratic principles should permeate the constitution which should conform to international standards. Thus discrimination on the basis of gender, race, colour, ethnic origin, language or creed should be outlawed.

Bill of rights

A bill of rights for a democratic dispensation should be one which entrenches the fundamental rights of the people of South Africa. We have the opportunity of formulating a bill of rights which conforms to the modern notions of democracy. This would include rights to information, privacy, freedom of expression, freedom from discrimination; general social, economic and educational rights; and other fundamental rights such as the right to a clean environment.[7]

A South African bill of rights should unequivocally entrench equality between the sexes. It must forbid discrimination on the basis of gender and protect single parenthood. It must provide for legislation to be enacted against sexual harassment and the physical abuse of women. It should discourage gender stereotyping in the media and in education. The rights of people to choose a partner for marriage should be protected. The partners in a marriage should be accorded equal status during the course of the marriage and at its dissolution. The rights of women workers should also be protected, particularly domestic and rural workers. The bill of rights must also provide for a programme of affirmative action which would provide mechanisms for redressing the discrimination against women, as well as other oppressed classes in South Africa.

Government

Government should be structured to facilitate gender equality at national, regional and local levels. The structure of government as manifested in the nature of the executive, the legislature and the judiciary has a direct bearing on power relations in the country. This structure is best determined by the balance of forces on the ground. The structure of government and its apparatus will necessarily determine choices made regarding mechanisms to achieve the emancipation of women. The pertinent questions include the following:

- Do we need an executive or a presidential system? The choice we make must enhance democracy in the new state.
- In the current constitutional debate there have been arguments in favour of a bicameral parliament and a constitutional court – would this bring greater constitutional democracy in the new South Africa?
- With regard to parliament, where will power be vested – in chamber X or in chamber Y? If power is vested in one chamber what then will be the function of the other chamber? How will the two chambers be constituted? How do we ensure that both chambers complement each other in their functions and are both of equal importance? Is this possible?[8]
- The most important question for women is how do we build mechanisms into the structure of government that will guarantee parliament is a strong instrument of democracy ensuring that women are not discriminated against?

The judiciary

The judiciary can be a powerful instrument for change but it may also retard change. The present judiciary is discredited in the eyes of the majority and the democratic forces in South Africa. There is a call for an independent judiciary and a constitutional court in the new South Africa.

- How do we ensure this?
- How will the new judiciary be constituted?
- Who will appoint the judges – what will the criteria be?
- Do we need special courts?
- Do we need a constitutional court?
- Do we also need quasi-judicial bodies?
- With regards to a constitutional court – how should it be composed?
- What should its functions be and how does it relate to the executive and to parliament?

To ensure women's emancipation is addressed, the judiciary needs to be structured to safeguard the representation of women at all levels. This means women must be included in the judicial process. Discrimination in South Africa has meant there is untapped potential amongst groups of people and there is fine legal expertise which has not been fully utilised. Amongst these groups are women.

The Charter for Women's Rights

The women's charter should embody women's rights as identified by women themselves. There are, however, questions that need to be addressed regarding the status of the document. The document may possibly be read together with the bill of rights in the interpretation of legislation, or it may also be used as guidelines in the enactment of subsidiary legislation. The debate on the status of the women's charter is ongoing; both in terms of its content and its inter-relationship with the bill of rights and the constitution as to its legislative and interpretive status. All parties who have discussed such a charter agree that it is a fundamentally important tool for the organising and mobilising of women in all sectors of South African society.

The UN Convention on the Elimination of all Forms of Discrimination against Women

The new democratic state of South Africa should ratify UN conventions, and in particular the human rights instruments. When the Convention on the Elimination of all Forms of Discrimination against Women is ratified we will have to establish the link between the bill of rights and the Charter of South African Women's Rights. This may well depend on the contents of the rights embodied in the charter and those in the convention.

If the charter was to be more radical than the convention, then the convention would be of little use in practical terms. It may well be that there are difficulties in establishing consensus on a number of issues canvassed for the charter, for example, religious and customary practices which may impede women's emancipation. In this case the principles of the convention may be invoked when necessary by the domestic courts. The other advantage of ratifying the UN convention is it may serve qualitatively to improve the struggle for women's emancipation in South Africa because the UN re-evaluates implementation of the convention from time to time.[9] This constantly keeps the issue of women's emancipation on the agenda of member states who have ratified the convention.

Conclusion

The democratic forces in our country regard constitution-making as a process in which all people should be actively involved. Constitution-making is a struggle in which people assert and determine their rights. The process has been ongoing for many decades. The Freedom Charter, on which the ANC bases its constitutional framework, is a policy document that came about as a result of struggles on the ground.

The current debate on a new constitution is enhanced by people's struggles to dismantle apartheid and determine the nature of democracy in our country.

Women, who in South Africa make up 53 per cent of the population, must be part of these struggles in order to understand the issues, and qualify to take part in decision-making processes. Women in the struggle must take the lead in highlighting gender issues in their organisations as well as in society at large. The proposed women's charter is a milestone in addressing the question of women's emancipation in South Africa. This process needs the full support of all democratic forces in our country.

Notes

1. In Mozambique, Zimbabwe and Namibia more attention to women's emancipation occurred after national liberation.
2. John Hund, 'Scepticism about Human Rights in South Africa', *South African Journal on Human Rights*, 5, 1989, p26. JD van der Vyver, 'Comments on the Constitutional Guidelines of the ANC', *South African Journal on Human Rights*, 5, 1983, pp141–4.
3. Adopted by the United Nations General Assembly in December 1979.
4. ANC president Oliver Tambo, in his opening address to the ANC women's conference in Luanda in 1981, urged his movement to address women's emancipation: 'If we are to engage our full potential in pursuit of revolutionary goals, as revolutionaries, we should stop pretending that women in our movement have the same opportunities as men.' See also ANC policy statement on women released in May 1990.
5. 'Gender Family and Children in Constitution Making', unpublished draft report of ANC in-house seminar, December 1989.
6. Dorothy Driver, 'Women and Language in the ANC's Constitutional Guidelines', *Die Suid-Afrikaan*, 23, October–November 1989, pp15–18. The critique is a persuasive study and it should influence construction of language in constitutional drafting.
7. *A Bill of Rights for a New South Africa: A Working Document by the ANC Constitutional Committee*, University of the Western Cape: Centre for Development Studies, 1990.
8. Advocate Dullah Omar, 'National Party Proposals', paper delivered to South African Municipal Workers Union at the National General Council meeting, Cape Town, November 1990, pp8–10.
9. Margaret Wadstein, 'Commemorative Seminar on the Convention on the Elimination of all Forms of Discrimination against Women', *UN Report Reference CS/CEDAW/1990/WP4*, 2–12 September 1990, pp2–12.

The ANC Constitutional Guidelines in Process

A feminist reading

Dorothy Driver

'*F*ew would deny', Albie Sachs said recently, 'that gender is on the agenda' of the 'new South Africa'.[1] So important a part does gender seem to be playing in the contemporary political arena that the ANC constitutional committee, having first drafted its constitutional guidelines for a democratic South Africa to include a clause on equal rights for women, later agreed to revise these guidelines and this clause in the light of a set of proposals from the ANC women's section. Speaking in July 1990, well after the first guidelines[2] had been released, Frene Ginwala said that the ANC had finally acknowledged that women's liberation was not going to be simply a by-product of the liberation struggle. She also suggested that the *new* ANC constitutional guidelines would repair current attitudes on women as well as the material base of gender oppression.[3] That this was an optimistic position to take at the time is evident if one looks closely at the first revision, published in November 1990.[4] However, important changes *were* made to the original constitutional guidelines, and it is to these changes that the first part of this paper is devoted, in acknowledgement of the fact that the ANC is the only political organisation in South Africa with a detailed policy on gender, and that it is only due to the ANC's recognition of women as a political force (first through the agency of the women's section and then of the Women's League) that gender *is* 'on the agenda' at all.

Since the constitutional guidelines are still in process, one should not treat the first revision as if it were final.[5] Nevertheless, however ephemeral this first revision turns out to be, it is worth addressing the changes as they occur. The purpose is partly to indicate the *gradual* nature of the amendments, for they seem to signify masculinist resistance, which must be taken into account by feminists, and partly to record a particular moment where feminist appreciation turns into dissent. This close reading might, moreover, serve as a model of at least one kind of feminist analysis, against and through which other kinds might develop, in the interests of promoting South African feminist theory. The sticking points in the shift from the original to the new constitutional guidelines presumably presage some of the difficulties this charter will have in gaining wide-based support in the black community, to say nothing here of the extreme resistance likely to be encountered in the white community as well, which has yet to engage at an official, governmental level with the subordination of women upon which its own versions of patriarchy have been based.

The ANC's first revision was drafted during a four-day meeting between the constitutional committee and the women's section. The preamble to the guidelines had originally noted that the constitution should 'promote the habits of non-racial and non-sexist thinking [and] the practice of anti-racist behaviour'. Given the distinction set up between 'thinking' and 'behaviour', only anti-racist and not anti-sexist behaviour was to be promoted. While no change was made to this apparently small but troubling distinction, the revised preamble now says that 'special attention has to be paid to combatting sexism, which is even more ancient [than] and as pervasive as racism'. Although the focus of the preamble remains on reparations to the damage done by apartheid, the reference to the need to fight sexism, and above all the acknowledgement that sexism is 'even more ancient' than racism, provide welcome contradiction of the insistence elsewhere that the practice of subordinating women was brought to Africa by the colonisers.[6]

In the new guidelines themselves, following this generally progressive trend, there are some major changes. The most striking is the set of emphatic references to 'men and women' instead of, simply, 'the people'. In the original guidelines, 'the people' had a dubious reference, for although the term theoretically includes women, the addition of a special clause on women (in the original) had helped cast doubt on the referent of 'the people': to give women a special clause suggested that they might not have been catered for elsewhere, in clauses regarding economic life, for example, and, indeed, the original constitutional guidelines *do* define women as no more and no less than mothers, whose proper sphere is domesticity.

A second major change, linked to the first, is the revision of the original clause on women (clause w), now amended to refer to women and men. The original clause read: 'Women shall have equal rights in all spheres of public and private life and the state shall take affirmative action to eliminate the inequalities and discrimination between the sexes.' The new guidelines amend this to refer to the requirement that the state and social institutions 'take affirmative action to eliminate inequalities, discrimination, and abusive behaviour based on gender'. The inclusion here of 'abusive behaviour based on gender' corrects the implicit exclusion of sexist behaviour in the preamble, which is an important step. The reference to affirmative action in social institutions, which would presumably include hospitals, schools, religious organisations and so on, is also notable. Clause w, however, defers full discussion of equal rights between men and women to a charter of gender rights, which 'shall be incorporated into the constitution'. More of this later.

Under economy, clause s says that the state should promote the acquisition of 'managerial, technical and scientific skills among all sections of the population, especially the blacks', and now adds the words, 'and shall take special steps to remove the barriers to women participating fully in economic life'. And the land clause (clause u) now refers to 'the abolition of all racial and gender-based restriction on ownership and use of land'. Frene Ginwala had earlier heralded this as a major breakthrough in the constitutional guidelines: 'land should belong to those who work it – which in most cases means women.'[7]

While the focus of the constitutional guidelines is still on repairing racism, which is not surprising in view of the fact that it is specifically apartheid legislation, and the concomitant class exploitation, which has been seen as the major antagonistic force in most people's lives, virtually every reference to race is accompanied by a reference to gender. Under the heading 'A Bill of Rights and affirmative action', the clause on the eradication of race discrimination (clause i) is now matched by a clause on the elimination of inequality based on gender (clause i *bis*). Interestingly, the wording is slightly different from one clause to the next; instead of 'a constitutional duty to eradicate sexist discrimination in all its forms', which would parallel the clause on racism, we have 'a constitutional duty to work towards the rapid elimination of inequality based on gender and to combat sexism in all its forms'. The wording suggests either that the ANC constitutional committee is not quite so optimistic about their powers to 'eradicate' gender inequality as they are regarding racism, or that they are not quite so committed. The distinction between 'inequality based on gender' and 'sexism' is puzzling; one hopes that it would not be possible to interpret the latter as, simply, ad hoc sexist behaviour, and 'inequality based on gender' as structural discrimination, which is not to be so aggressively fought. It may be that the phrase 'sexism in all its forms' would guard against this, however.

If this appreciation of the revised guidelines remains cautious, it is largely because of the continuing presence of the clause on the family (clause x). But before addressing the problems inherent in this clause, one needs, once again, to recognise the revisions that have been made. In the original constitutional guidelines, the clause on the family followed two clauses, the first on workers, the second on women. The original ordering had the effect of seeming to produce an associative movement from women to family, so that the original clause on the family – 'The family, parenthood and children's rights shall be protected' – readily implied that it was women, as always, who were to be regarded as custodians of the family. This implication was buttressed elsewhere in the guidelines through the constant suggestions that it was male economic rights that were being fought for. However, in the new phrasing, 'The family, parenthood, and equal rights within the family shall be protected', the words 'equal rights within the family' have been inserted (and children's rights given a separate clause), in an attempt to dispel earlier hints that the family would be protected at the cost of women's non-domestic aspirations. Moreover, the reference to women *and men* after workers deletes any impression regarding the exclusivity of women and workers. In conjunction with the earlier clause on gender rights 'in all spheres of public and private life' (clause w), the revision of clause x seems, then, to be a crucial one.

To step outside the constitutional guidelines for a moment, it is worth stressing that in the material world, too, women are being recognised as workers, and that the category 'workers' is accordingly no longer quite so dominated by men. Recent debate in the Congress of South African Trade Unions (Cosatu) on a workers' charter has extended the concept of labour protection to domestic workers (as well as farm workers and workers in the homelands) and proposes the negotiation of social security measures such as the provision of education, housing, child care and primary health facilities. Cosatu's draft proposals towards a workers' charter have also suggested that 'it is the duty of the state, employers, unions, workers and political parties and other organisations to ensure women's participation at all levels and to campaign against male chauvinism at home and outside'.[8] The South African Clothing and Textile Workers' Union (Sactwu), where women workers form the vast majority, recently elected two women onto its national executive committee, which is, says national treasurer Connie September, 'a move in the right direction'.[9]

Given this (gradual) social redefinition of women as more than simply mothers, it remains to be asked why one might feel suspicious about a clause on the family in the ANC constitutional guidelines. The fact is that the presence of this clause seems to speak rather more about entrenchment of existing attitudes than about social reform. Constitutions, like laws, are by their nature invariably open to interpretation, which means that unclear references to the family may open themselves, all too conveniently, to an occlusion of feminist readings. To look closely at its wording – 'The family, parenthood, and equal rights within the family shall be protected' – the organisation of the sentence, along with the word 'protected', offers a less than radical gesture: the clause reads, first of all, as if the family – as overarching structure – should be protected, and then, within that structure, as if those rights already established as familial ideals (the 'equal' but separate roles of husbands and wives) should be maintained.

One might argue that the word 'protect' is a legal term referring to the belief that all people are born equal, and that this fundamental equality should be protected against any subsequent social distortion. But in the sentence which, so to speak, fathers this clause, the word 'protect' has another meaning: the family, as social structure, is to be kept from harm, which means from change detrimental to it. Insofar as the family depends upon men and women taking up certain carefully defined positions within it, 'equal rights within the family' would thus either be protected from change, too, if the phrase recalls conventional positions, or else contradict the preservation of the family, its parent clause. As a whole, then, clause x might well be used to point back to the kind of patriarchal family, nuclear or extended, often eulogised in South African literary texts.[10]

It might be argued that the clause on the family exists for obvious reasons that have nothing to do with patriarchy. In a country whose economy has been underpinned by a radically underpaid labour force – reproduced by means of Population Registration, Pass Laws, Group Areas, the system of migrant labour, along with the general perpetuation of poverty – the family has been split apart, and traditional family principles have been disrupted. This damage needs to be repaired. Thus, for example, *South* interpreted the family clause in the original constitutional guidelines in the following way: 'Under an ANC government, migrant workers will be able to have their families live with them.'[11]

Suspicion about the family is part of what separates black South African feminism, as it is currently being formulated, from what is defined as western feminism, insofar as it is seen to be antagonistic to the (male-dominated) family: the orthodoxy appears to be that in western feminism the family is the site for struggle, whereas in South African feminism it is the site for resistance, offering a space from which the depredations of apartheid (or colonisation) might be refused.[12] Yet, despite the orthodoxy, one needs to ask which family principles are seen to have been disrupted, and which kind of family it is, precisely, that might offer resistance to western ideological impositions. Regarding the ANC guidelines, then, the following questions arise: Is the family that must be protected a nuclear or a polygynous family, and, if clause x includes reference to both, what does this mean in an urban setting? Thinking of situations where a male migrant worker forms a union with an urban woman as well as a rural woman, who might have borne his first but not his only children, what happens to these urban families if migrant workers now bring their wives with them? If one may speak of a nuclear family being disrupted, one may speak of the principle of polygyny under disruption, too: in an urban setting, the two women may not be able to establish a relationship within the social structure of the polygynous family but would be forced into overt competition with one another.[13] Whose family is to be protected here: the urban woman's or the rural woman's? In the *South* interpretation of the clause on the family, cited earlier, the family was simply seen in terms of a male migrant worker and 'his' wife and children. One needs to ask, instead, how women are positioned in polygynous structures, and, indeed, how they are positioned in nuclear families, urban and rural.

One also needs to ask whether the ideology of family is not a mask for the ideology of heterosexuality. The historical disproportion between the number of men and women in the cities, as well as the system of single-sex hostels, has meant a visible increase in homosexuality, which is, as is well known, treated with ambivalence in ANC thinking.[14] Or, is the major referent in the family clause the principle that the father and husband should function as the head of the household in a society where more and more women have become independent as urban dwellers, some even deciding not to marry the fathers of their children, perhaps on the principle that life may be simpler without a man to look after as well?[15]

Given these various disruptions to the family (and there are of course many others), the concept of 'protection' needs clarification: exactly what is to be protected, and why, and to whose benefit? Debate on the family is markedly absent from official ANC pronouncements,[16] an absence covered over by occasional statements and gestures that serve to authorise patriarchalism.[17] Assuming that the ANC's interest in the family is determined not only by a desire for the well-being of individual men, women and children, and for a stability offered to a destabilised community by means of secure family structures, but also by a commitment to nation-building (for nation-building depends largely on the existence of cohesive family and community structures), it is necessary to ask to what extent contemporary understandings of and aspirations towards 'nation' depend on *patriarchal* structures, and, if there *is* a dependence, to have the connections brought into the open for full and equal discussion by both women and men.[18]

To put all this another way, clause j reads: 'The state and all social institutions shall be under a constitutional duty to eradicate, speedily, the economic and social inequalities produced by racial discrimination.' Clause k reads: 'The advocacy or practice of racism, fascism, Nazism, or the incitement of ethnic or regional exclusiveness or hatred shall be outlawed.' Gender discrimination does not occasion so aggressive a stance. Clause s ('The state... shall take special steps to remove the barriers to women participating fully in economic life') and clause x ('The family, parenthood, and equal rights within the family shall be protected') take on a different tone from clauses j and k. Moreover, they do *not* combine to indicate that, as in the case of racism, 'the state shall take special steps to remove the barriers to equal rights within the family'; 'equal rights' will simply 'be protected', not promoted. Insofar as the orthodox distinction between 'economic' and 'domestic' goes, most women do participate in economic life, in the sense of working outside the home, and also participating in – that is, doing virtually all the work for – domestic life 'after hours'. So it is not simply that the barriers to *full and equal* participation in economic life should be removed; there is a fundamental need to have the relation between economic and domestic life scrutinised. Women should be quite unambiguously incorporated into an official discourse that does not need to establish any separation between domestic and economic spheres. This point will be returned to later.

If clause s does not, then, produce a feminist interpretation of clause x, and if the two clauses are kept separate by an implicit distinction between public and private life, the weight of any feminist orientation on the family in the constitutional guidelines falls squarely on the charter of gender rights proposed in clause w:

> A charter of gender rights shall be incorporated into the constitution guaranteeing equal rights between men and women in all spheres of public and private life and requiring the state and social institutions to take affirmative action to eliminate inequalities, discrimination, and abusive behaviour based on gender.

The presence of this clause may explain the absence of specific suggestions regarding 'equal rights within the family' (suggestions regarding paternal responsibility, state salaries and subsidies for women who have had to stay at home as childrearers, free and safe contraception and abortion, as well as the establishment of crèches), for these suggestions are presumably being left not to a *women's* charter, which would propagate the erroneous notion that they are specifically 'women's concerns', but to a charter of gender rights, which the women's branches currently being established will work on. It is not clear what relation a charter of gender rights will have to the clause on the family: whether the charter of gender rights will be used as a perspective from which to rethink the clause on the family, or whether the one will exist alongside the other, the radical moment jostling with the conservative one in an endless reminder of the fundamental ambivalence regarding the position of women.

The clause on a charter of gender rights raises an even more important and difficult question. Earlier in this chapter I suggested that the requirements posed by ANC feminists had not been met in the revised constitutional guidelines. According to Frene Ginwala, the ANC's national executive proposed that 'laws, customs, traditions and practices which discriminate against women' should be held to be 'unconstitutional'.[19] It also proposed that the constitutional guidelines' commitment to protect the family be *reconsidered*, calling for the establishment of women's rights over their own fertility, and for child care to be equally shared by fathers and mothers.[20] Furthermore, it proposed the *removal* of patriarchal rights over the family,[21] referring presumably to questions of guardianship, inheritance, and so-called illegitimacy. That these proposals are not reflected in the new guidelines but are, as already noted, deferred to a charter of gender rights brings one right up against the fundamental question regarding constitutions: whether they are to reflect the desires of the majority of the people or whether they are to cast forward to a harmonious future not necessarily yet articulated by the majority.

The truth is, of course, that while most people are agreed that racism must go, people by no means agree regarding the question of gender. The process of widespread negotiation is crucial, for a constitution cannot maintain itself without broad-based political support, nor can it in itself guarantee change. Sachs has said that 'the basic right underlying all other rights is the right of women to speak in their own voices, the right to determine their own priorities and strategies and the right to make their concerns felt'.[22] This sounds like an aim whose realisation would entail liberation, but in fact a profound difficulty starts here: the difficulty about women's 'own voices', which proceeds from the anxiety that one's 'own' voice is not necessarily readily available to a woman pushed and patted into shape not only by varieties of patriarchal decree[23] but also by a set of rigidly enforced political and ideological polarisations. How, to spell out the problem (and to shift it beyond the conventional domain of legal discourse), does one know when women are speaking in their 'own' voices rather than speaking from assigned subject-positions? It is to this difficult and important question that my essay will now turn.

In the contemporary reading of democracy, the ability to make a mark on a ballot paper is taken as a sign that one is speaking in one's own voice. And so of course it must be, for there is no politically decent alternative. Yet it is still the case, as Connie September says, according to her experience as chairperson of the Salt River committee of Sactwu as well as regional vice-chairperson and as treasurer of the national executive, that 'in elections you often see women pushing men for the positions. In discussions, women listen to the men rather than participate in debates'.[24] Political articulation has been male dominated because of an intricate combination of women's double role as working mothers and their conventional reluctance to fight against or even speak of this difficulty, coupled, of course, with sharp resistance from men to political participation by women. In trade unions, even in the predominantly female Sactwu, for instance, women shopstewards sometimes have to fight at home with their husbands for the right to assume a political role (the Sactwu legal department has had to deal with a number of divorces arising out of these differences).[25] Some women trade unionists talk about having to take up their conventional domestic duties as if they had no other role in the world.[26] In a recent interview, Boitumelo Mofokeng notes that politically vocal women are *redefined* by domesticity: 'Outside, we stand up on platforms, but at home, some of us go back to typical African tradition, we are submissive, passive, non-existent. I cannot relate to my husband or my brother the way I do to other men out there.'[27]

However, it is not easy to speak openly about such things. First of all, as a spokesperson for the Federation of Transvaal Women (Fedtraw) said: 'In South Africa there is a sensitivity in the area of asserting our rights for the emancipation of women because it forces us to challenge age-old customs which many women themselves respect.'[28] Secondly, as Boitumelo Mofokeng has said and what other women have confirmed: 'I can best describe the struggle of black women against their husbands as an internal one: against male domination, male exploitation. But to stand up on a platform – it would be like hanging your dirty linen in public.'[29] Open discussion of domestic strife transgresses conventional codes of behaviour, and is also felt to signal one's participation in the process of humiliation engendered within racism: men have a hard enough time without women adding their particular attack.[30] Moreover, black women who speak out against male domination are readily labelled 'white':

In South Africa the question of Western feminism, encroaching into the minds of the African women is a very, very sensitive question, particularly for the African man. Anytime you ask him to do something, to go and fetch the child today, or something like that he says, 'Look, you are already a feminist. You are a white woman and a feminist'. It is thrown in your face in the same way in which Communist is thrown into the face of the blacks in South Africa.[31]

Apartheid's oppositional categories – black versus white – are taken up as weapons by those eager to fuel anxieties that feminism *causes*, rather than results from, division. Under such conditions, then, by what process may such women come to speak in their own voices?

Feminist critics have argued that one achieves voice – or attains subjectivity as an individual – at the point where one recognises the ways in which one has been subordinated by a political system, and thus made to fit a political category at odds with one's own experience of and aspirations in the world.[32] In the South African context, the individual subject is organised by means of categories of race, class, gender and age, which are not experienced separately from one another: as different axes, they intersect in their constitutive capacities. For instance, just to speak of gender and race, a black woman's experience of racism is often different from a black man's, to the extent that the experience of sexism intertwines with, and adjusts, the experience of racism. Similarly, a black woman's experience of sexism is different from a white woman's.[33] This means that one's subjectivity, insofar as it is an articulation of one's social construction, is different depending upon one's particular race, class and gender position. Black men do not inhabit the same subject position as black women; nor, by the same token, do white women. When Emma Mashinini offers an oblique justification for identifying herself with a black South African working class rather than women in general, she is in fact clearing a space for the expression of problems unique to black working-class women: 'White mothers in this country do not have to suffer anxiety over what we call breadline problems... Breadline problems are [for example] questions of who will care for the children when their mother goes to work.'[34] Black women – mothers, in this case – experience a peculiar combination of racial and gender oppression: they go to work rather than stay at home because the fathers of their children are poorly paid; they cannot afford to pay home-help; they do not have easy access to créches; and they cannot expect their husbands to share child-rearing duties.

Yet Christine Qunta, for instance, says: 'I take the view that we are Africans before we are women.'[35] That the axis of race often or generally takes experiential priority over the axis of gender should not be disputed, but what should be addressed is the way the experience of racism is used to occlude the experience of sexism. In the case of black women, as Qunta's comment reveals, political necessity offers a choice: between being 'black' and 'feminist', being aware of one's social position as 'black' on the one hand and 'woman' on the other.[36] However, as Barbara Omolade has argued: 'Black women are not white women with color.'[37] Any call for a national struggle that excludes gender subordination, as well as the greater emphasis in the constitutional guidelines on reparations to do with race rather than gender, helps produce the self-denying choice being identified here, and propagates the erroneous and politically problematic notion that feminism is exotic to Africa.[38]

Nevertheless, it must be said that the assertion of subjectivity on the part of a black South African woman will often require her assertion of difference from the selfhood that has been constructed for her by 'western' feminism: if one or other form of patriarchy (black or white, urban or rural) functions as the dominating order against which a black South African woman wishes to define herself, so too can western feminism be seen as part of a dominating order or symbolic system against which self-assertion needs to be voiced.[39] In other words, it is not just with reference to racist and patriarchal structures that Trinh T Minh-ha is called upon to write:

> You who understand the dehumanization of forced removal- relocation-reeducation- redefinition, the humiliation of having to falsify your own reality your voice – you know. And often cannot *say* it. You try and keep on trying to unsay it, for if you don't, they will not fail to fill in the blanks on your behalf, and you will be said.[40]

Still, it seems crucial, as the existence of this paper suggests, that whatever contributions (white) feminist academics may be able to make should not be refused out of hand.[41] Feminist theory as it is currently being formulated in debate between 'third world' and 'first world', or 'east' and 'west', strives to break down the binary thinking on which systems of oppression and exploitation subsist. At the same time it recognises the historical complicity of white South African women with imperial power,[42] and what Gayatri Spivak calls the 'epistemic violence' perpetrated by western/white feminism's systems of 'information retrieval' and of classification, the term 'third world woman' being the prime example.[43] One possible contribution this theory-in-the-making can offer to the discussion of gender in South Africa is to encourage debate on the west's 'epistemic violence' in order to approach with greater sensitivity and honesty the question of the subjectivity of women in South Africa. This is in the face of the constitutive categories of race, class and gender (as well as age, marital status, and whatever others are felt to be important). It is a debate which should, finally, make it possible to speak of the black South African family as a site of resistance *as well as* a site of struggle.

Discussion about the family draws on *two* discourses, as already suggested: feminist discourse (which addresses the family as a site of struggle) and nationalist discourse (which addresses the family as a structure at risk under apartheid and its aftermath).[44] This essay has also suggested that subjectivity (or voice) depends on placing oneself as cognitive subject in language. This means recognising the ways in which one has been constituted in terms of specific discourses and thus dissociating oneself from them while at the same time claiming a particular and different place within language. Thus an overriding problem exists when black South African women feel they have to choose between one or the other discourse in terms of which to represent themselves: 'We are Africans [or] we are women.' In either case, one part of oneself is silenced – in the first case, one's status as a woman with a different set of experiences from black men, and in the second, one's status as a black South African, with a different set of experiences from white or western women. What is needed is a different discourse, in terms of which a different subject position is constructed, so that women may articulate themselves as, non-contradictorily, black women.[45]

It is of course true that many women may not feel themselves to be divided in the way being suggested: I am talking about the public articulation of self. However, if the discussion *is* to be about emancipation for women, and women's voices, it must be the argument of this paper, a) that women's voices cannot emerge as 'their own' without interrogating the various structures by which they have been defined, which includes interrogating the family itself, and b) that the continuing political enforcement of a link between women and the family militates against that interrogative process.

This is why the ANC position on the family poses a problem for women. The family is a signifying system *par excellence*,[46] for it defines 'men' and 'women' in specific ways. (The relative *positions* assigned to men and women are universal ones, while the precise *content* to these positions is historically and culturally specific.) The structure of the family depends on the simultaneous subordination and idealisation of women as mothers, and on a forced separation between the social/public/economic and private/domestic spheres. Men 'naturally' straddle the two spheres, but women must dash frantically from one to the other, pretending, all the while, that they are really 'domestic'. While the social construction of women starts with the family, women continue to be produced in one or other signifying system (newspaper reports, films, novels, letters to 'agony columns', political pamphlets and so on), in terms of their apparently fundamentally domestic nature. The ANC constitutional guidelines is itself a signifying system; its clause on the family threatens – by its very presence – to restore the division between the domestic and the social that women *in fact* are challenging, and to re-insert 'woman' in a signifying system which centres on the family and its conventionally gendered positions.

So, whatever adjustments need to be made in the guidelines to the position of women need to be made without protecting that primary context within which 'woman' has been socially defined. This does not mean that the family will or should dissolve; simply that the rights of men and women should be legislated for without recalling and dignifying the social institution by which the *sociologically* irrelevant fact of 'sex' has been transformed, and distorted, into 'gender'. The risk of entrenching or restoring patriarchal structures is simply too high.

People have argued, as for example has Ruth Mompati, that as women and men fight side by side in the struggle, men 'begin to lose sight of the fact that we are women'. After independence, they will not be able to turn round and say: 'Now you are a woman.'[47] But how far were we from independence, one wonders, at a recent ANC rally in Mitchell's Plain, when Nelson Mandela, Alfred Nzo, Joe Slovo and other men were introduced to the audience as 'comrade', while Ruth Mompati was called 'mother'. People have also argued that material changes to women's conditions will usher in their emancipation.[48] Yet material changes, although they are crucial to people's everyday survival and wellbeing, do not adjust the relative positions of women and men, as long as discourse (not only political discourse and legal discourse, but also the discourse of everyday life and the media) continues to define 'man' and 'woman' as *socially* significant distinctions (rather than neutral in the manner of, say, black-haired versus brown-haired people). Material changes do not shift existing social structures and processes of signification.

Nevertheless, on the topic of processes of signification, it should be noted that black South African women's discourse *has* defined the concept of 'mother' in such a way that it is forcefully distinguished from the meaning conventionally held in British and American culture.[49] I am not talking about, say, Ruth Mompati's definition of the role of a freedom fighter in motherly terms: 'Not only is she a soldier, she is also a mother – she brings soldiers into the world, she looks after these soldiers, she receives these soldiers, she is responsible for their maintenance and their welfare.'[50] This definition maintains a distinction between soldier and mother, and keeps the mother in the caretaking role that regulates her activities and stance throughout social and domestic life. I am talking instead about a tendency in recent writing by black South African women, one of whose particularly significant contributions has been to define the mother as an active, angry, political figure, in sharp contrast to the patriarchal representations of the mother handed down through a western, Christian tradition.[51]

Tapping into this thinking, over the last few years Shell has placed an advertisement (for petrol and service stations, presumably) in the *Weekly Mail* and *South* which masquerades as an advertisement for human rights – 'Everyone must enjoy human rights' – and figures the ideal of human rights by means of an image of mother-and-child, which contradicts the standard Christian iconography of the Madonna-and-child. While Shell's child sleeps peacefully, swathed against the mother's back, the mother looks determinedly into the future, looking away from the child and thus signifying herself as (cognitive and political) subject independently from the world of mother-and-child.[52] Although this advertisement inhabits a world which still places the burden of responsibility on the mother, and although the conjuncture of a human rights issue and capitalist advertising is a particularly unpalatable one, the representation of the mother as a figure not bound to her child in the meekness of self-sacrifice but as a figure *both there and elsewhere*, in both the domestic and the social, the private and the political, offers to South African feminism a potent figure for change, and a welcome relief from the representation of women handed down through a western tradition. Yet, while this difference is recognised and celebrated, even it must in turn open itself to scrutiny for the part it plays in positing the familial, however defined, as women's fundamental and original sphere.

Notes

I should like to acknowledge the financial assistance of the Human Sciences Research Council (HSRC) in the preparation of this essay. Opinions expressed and conclusions arrived at are not to be regarded as those of the HSRC. I should also like to thank Jenny McDonogh for her assistance in finding newspaper and magazine references.

1. Albie Sachs, *Protecting Human Rights in a New South Africa*, Cape Town: Oxford University Press, 1990, p53.
2. The text of the original constitutional guidelines may be seen in *Die Suid-Afrikaan*, 23, October 1989, pp16–17. For a feminist critique of these guidelines, see Dorothy Driver, 'Women and Language in the ANC Constitutional Guidelines', *Die Suid-Afrikaan*, 23, October 1989, pp15–18. The critique was first delivered at the Women's Constitutional Conference, Institute for a Democratic Alternative for South Africa, August 1989, and

was published, along with papers by Eleanor van der Horst and Sarah Christie, in *Towards a Non-Sexist Constitution: Women's Perspectives*, Cape Town: Idasa, 1990.
3. *South*, 9–15 August 1990, p17.
4. The text is to be found in Sachs, *Protecting Human Rights*, pp197–201.
5. Sachs stresses that his record of the proposed amendments should not be regarded as the official text, and at the ANC national workshop, 'Towards a Charter of Women's Rights', at the University of the Western Cape, November/December 1990, Frene Ginwala stressed, in private conversation, that the constitutional guidelines were still under debate, and had in certain respects progressed beyond Sachs's recorded version.
6. In a column entitled 'Missing the Point' in *Tribute* (August 1990, p12), Nokwanda Sithole argues as follows: 'In traditional African societies, that is *before* colonization, there is no evidence of a deliberate oppression of African women. They had respected socio-political and legal roles and rights… [and] were accorded the respect and position they deserved in their societies.' Christine Qunta refers to 'the contrast between the dignity and status of women in early African society and their degradation when slavery took on a racist character' and Dabi Nkululeko, in 'The Right to Self-Determination in Research: Azania and Azanian Women', says, 'The anti-apartheid movement… sees the oppression of women as the result of the deprivation of civil rights to African women, while the anti-colonial movement sees it as a consequence of the colonial expropriation of their livelihood and land, forcing them to sell their labour and bodies to their dispossessors, the settler-colonial capitalists' (both in Christine Qunta (ed), *Women in Southern Africa*, Johannesburg: Skotaville, 1987, p12 and 98). In a review of Ifi Amadiume's *Male Daughters, Female Husbands: Gender and Sex in an African Society* (London: Zed Press, 1987) Patti Henderson notes that 'women in Nnobi [in south eastern Nigeria] are much more constrained, less mobile and poorer than were their sisters of previous generations' and that 'motherhood was highly regarded and yet did not prevent women from attaining positions of economic, ritual and political power', and implies that a similar situation exists in South Africa (*Agenda*, 3, 1988, pp48 and 43). See also Boitumelo Mofokeng, 'Breaking the Silence', in *Buang Basadi: Khulumani Makhosikazi: Women Speak* (Johannesburg: Cosaw, 1988, p8): '[woman's] role as the first teacher in the home, the mentor and custodian of our culture, was not just forgotten but completely destroyed.' I would not wish to dismiss these arguments out of hand, yet each one shows an unwillingness to confront the patriarchalism of the past. For other useful studies of this question, see Belinda Bozzoli, 'Marxism, Feminism and South African Studies', *Journal of Southern African Studies*, 9(2), 1983, pp139–71; Jeff Guy, 'Analyzing Pre-Capitalist Societies in Southern Africa', *Journal of Southern African Studies*, 14(1), 1987, pp18–37; and Cherryl Walker, 'Women and Gender in Southern Africa to 1945: An Overview' in Walker (ed), *Women and Gender in Southern Africa to 1945*, Cape Town: David Philip, 1990, pp1–32.
7. *South*, 30 August–5 September 1990, p19.
8. *South*, 14–20 June 1990, p19.

9.   *South*, 9–15 August 1990, p8.
10. For some literary idealisations of the patriarchal family, see Noni Jabavu's *The Ochre People*, 1963, reprinted Johannesburg: Ravan, 1982; Bessie Head's title story in *The Collector of Treasures*, London: Heinemann, 1977; Njabulo Ndebele's *Fools and Other Stories*, Johannesburg: Ravan, 1983; and Ellen Kuzwayo's *Call Me Woman*, Johannesburg: Ravan, 1985. Despite Head's and Kuzwayo's critiques of male abuse, Kuzwayo's text shows nostalgia for the apparently benevolent patriarchal structures of the past, and Head's story constructs one for the future.
11. *South*, 5–14 February 1990, p9.
12. Miriam Tlali says that she would call herself a feminist 'but not in the narrow, Western kind of way of speaking about a feminist. Black women are very much conscious of the fact that they are in fact the very people to make the home and very little credit is given to their efforts – which are so much crucial to the running of the home and the society. And I think the South African black women are very strong' (Craig McKenzie and Cherry Clayton (eds), *Between the Lines: Interviews with Bessie Head, Sheila Roberts, Ellen Kuzwayo, Miriam Tlali*, Grahamstown: NELM, 1989, p74). Phina Letsoalo adds: 'we are not seeking to overthrow tradition... We do not want to take away the men's authority and power' (*Tribune*, August 1990, p91). The distinction being made here receives its parallel in the American context, about which Elizabeth V Spelman writes in *Inessential Woman* (London: The Women's Press, 1988, p132): 'The family may be the locus of oppression for white middle-class women, but to claim that it is the locus of oppression for all women is to ignore the fact that for Blacks in American life the family has been a source of resistance against white oppression.' In her essay 'The Township Family and Women's Struggles', Catherine Campbell makes the pragmatic suggestion that any local struggle for women's rights should not attempt to interrogate patriarchy, since African women's struggles have thus far been precipitated by threats to the family (*Agenda*, 6, 1990, pp19–20).
13. For discussion of this in a Nigerian setting, see Buchi Emecheta, *The Joys of Motherhood*, London: Heinemann Educational Books, 1979. Emecheta is protective towards polygyny as an institution, but shows that pre-colonial patriarchal figures were often free to abuse it, and that it does not function for the family in an urban, working-class environment.
14. 'The common assertion is that such deviant behaviour... is not part of our culture' (*True Love*, September 1990, p18). Some of this prejudice came to the surface in the Winnie Mandela/Paul Verryn case. Again, however, it should be noted that the ANC is the only political party to have shown their support for gay liberation.
15. Recent figures suggest that up to 57 per cent of black households are headed by women (*Fair Lady*, 14 March 1990, p193); that 70 per cent of small businesses owned by black South Africans are run by women (*Femina*, November 1989, p59); and that two thirds of all black professionals in the country are women (*Femina*, February 1990, p28). S'bongile Nene, a sociologist at University of the North, has said: 'The black male is in a state of frequent crisis with his woman... This is because

his mother was a totally traditional woman in the tribal sense, whereas his wife is a woman of the new generation: A woman who is prepared to challenge traditional roles. Thus the black man experiences a severe conflict of expectations. He also has another distinct problem: Sons have to grow up without their fathers acting as role models. So often, the fathers are migrant workers far away from home; in the cities. Rural boys are brought up almost exclusively by women. Even the scoutmaster has become a scoutmistress! The fathers are just missing' (*Tribute*, December 1988, p54). For a historical precedent to what I am suggesting, see Kathy Eales, who reads the pass law campaign as a struggle over (black versus white) patriarchal control of black women: the campaign was motivated primarily by women and men who felt that the 'dignity' of women was at stake ('Patriarchs, Passes and Privilege: Johannesburg's African Middle Classes and the Question of Night Passes for African Women, 1920–1931', in Philip Bonner, et al (eds), *Holding Their Ground: Class, Locality and Culture in Nineteenth-and Twentieth-Century South Africa*, Johannesburg: Ravan, 1989). Thus, at an ideological level, the pass law campaign reinserted women into existing patriarchal definitions, even while the energy, activity and variety of motivations of individual women threatened to explode these definitions. This historical precedent would extend into the late fifties and early sixties, a period when – as *Drum* magazine reveals – male writers and readers experienced considerable anxiety over the relative freedom of urban women, whether wives or 'good-time girls'.

16. It is true that in his book, *Protecting Human Rights* (p65), Sachs has a chapter on the family which opens with the question, 'How can a society strengthen the family and at the same time weaken patriarchy?' This may well initiate official debate, but does not at the present time constitute it.

17. Nelson Mandela, for example, said on coming out of Paarl prison, 'It is not a nice feeling for a man to see his family struggling, without security, without the dignity of the head of the family around' (*Argus*, 13 February 1990, p13); and Ruth Mompati, in an interview presumably partly aimed at women who are not (yet/only) mothers, conflates the two, 'We, as women... should begin to teach our children', and adds, 'When I married and had two children, I felt I was fulfilled as a woman' (*True Love*, July 1990, p16). Patriarchalism was recalled even at the launching of various branches of the women's league: in Durban, for instance, which was attended by 10 000 women, only two of the keynote speakers were women, and when it was the turn of one of them, Adelaide Tambo, to speak, she read out a message from the ANC president, her husband.

18. See Cherryl Walker's review in *Agenda*, 6, 1990, of an essay by Deborah Gaitskell and Elaine Unterhalter in *Woman–Nation–State* (edited by Nira Yuval-Davis and Floya Anthias, London: Macmillan, 1989, p48): 'Commitment to the nation-building goals of the ANC has clouded the analysis of gender'; 'It is not clear why a more progressive conception of "the nation" should necessarily translate into a more progressive conceptualization of "woman"' (p47).

19. *South*, 7–13 June 1990, p5.

20. *South*, 7–13 June 1990, p5.

21. *South*, 30 August–5 September 1990, p19.
22. Sachs, *Protecting Human Rights*, p57.
23. Tsitsi Dangarembga's Zimbabwean novel, *Nervous Conditions* (London: The Women's Press, 1989), provides a path-breaking investigation into the difficulties of speaking in one's own voice, given women's subordination under colonialism, Christian mission education and rural patriarchalism.
24. *South*, 9–15 August 1990, p8.
25. *South*, 9–15 August 1990, p8. In Beata Lipman (ed), *We Make Freedom: Women in South Africa* (London: Pandora, 1984, p81), Rita Ndzanga, who was secretary of the Toy Workers' Union, and active within the South African Railways and Harbour Workers' Union before her banning, said: 'We find when new members come in to the union from the rural areas they take a bit of time to get used to a woman trade union organiser – at first they won't listen to us!'
26. Mary Ntseke, organiser for the General and Allied Workers' Union, said: 'At home I must be a woman according to African custom. I must be under my husband's control all the time' (Lipman (ed), *We Make Freedom*, p86). And Liz Abrahams, secretary of the Food and Canning Workers' Union in Paarl, reports that one of the men in the union said to her about his wife: 'If she's going to be so active in the union then she's not going to listen to me any more' (Lipman (ed), *We Make Freedom*, p91). There are always exceptions. Speaking about her and her husband's banning orders before the Rivonia Trial, Albertina Sisulu says, 'When I was at work Walter... did all the housework, the washing and the bathing of the children. Ideas of feminism are not new to us' (*Fair Lady*, 11 April 1990, p68).
27. 'Workshop on Black Women's Writing and Reading', including Boitumelo Mofokeng, Thandi Moses, Sanna Naidoo, Lebohang Sikwe, Veni Soobrayan, and Nomhle Tokwe, with Margaret Lenta and Margaret Daymond, *Current Writing*, 2, 1990, p82.
28. *True Love*, January 1990, p12.
29. 'Workshop', p83. Emma Mashinini in *Strikes Have Followed Me All My Life* (London: The Women's Press, 1989, p12) also refers to the taboo on discussing domestic problems in public, using the same metaphor of not exposing 'the dirty linen in public'. However, she notes that wife-battering is starting to be discussed in local clinics in the black community at least.
30. A rural woman called Nomasonta Mkize tells the following story: because of the loss of a leg in an accident 15 years ago, she must pay children to fetch water for her, 3 km from their home, using roughly 10 per cent of her earnings to do so. Her husband, 'like most men in the village', calls this 'woman's work', and refuses to help, although he does not have a job – or perhaps *because* he does not, suggests the local community worker Gay Maphumulo: 'It would be like undermining him because he is not working' (*Femina*, February 1990, p24).
31. Quoted in Kirsten Holt Peterson (ed), *Criticism and Ideology: Second African Writers' Conference, Stockholm 1986*, Uppsala: Scandinavian Institute of African Studies, 1988, p185. Interestingly, Emma Mashinini identifies her first husband with a 'white boss' for sitting around reading a

newspaper while she works (Mashinini, *Strikes Have Followed Me All My Life*, p15).

32. See, for example, Monique Wittig, 'One Is Not Born A Woman' (*Feminist Issues*, 1(2), 1981, p52): 'When we discover that women are the objects of oppression and appropriation, at the very moment that we become able to perceive this, we become subjects in the sense of cognitive subjects, through a process of abstraction.'

33. This is argued by Teresa de Lauretis, 'Displacing Hegemonic Discourses: Reflections on Feminist Theory in the 1980s', in Deborah Gordon (ed), *Feminism and the Critique of Colonial Discourse* (Santa Cruz: University of California at Santa Cruz, 1988, pp127–44). See also Spelman's *Inessential Woman* (p15): 'One's gender identity is not related to one's racial and class identity as the parts of pop-bead necklaces are related, separable and insertable in other "strands" with different racial and class "parts".'

34. Mashinini, *Strikes Have Followed Me All My Life*, p40.

35. *Tribute*, August 1990, p44.

36. This 'choice' between being an 'African' and a 'feminist' becomes an interesting problem in Ellen Kuzwayo's *Call Me Woman*. For a preliminary examination of this, see Dorothy Driver, 'M'a-Ngoana O Tsoare Thipa ka Bohaleng – The Child's Mother Grabs the Sharp End of the Knife: Women as Mothers, Women as Writers', in *Rendering Things Visible: Essays in South African Literary Culture* (Johannesburg: Ravan, 1990). White women have also made such choices, with disastrous historical effects. See Cherryl Walker, *Women and Resistance in South Africa* (London: Onyx Press, 1982) for discussion of this. For example, one of the early South African suffragists, Aletta Nel, made the following response when she was asked if she favoured extending the vote to black women: 'As a woman, sir, yes… but as a South African born person, I feel that it would be wiser if we gave the vote to the European women only' (Walker, *Women and Resistance*, p24).

37. Quoted in Spelman, *Inessential Woman*, p13.

38. See, for example, Kumari Jayawardena, *Feminism and Nationalism in the Third World* (London and New Jersey:.Zed Books, 1986, p3), who argues that feminism is indigenous to the 'third world': 'The fact that such movements for emancipation and feminism flourished in several non-European countries [in the eighteenth and nineteenth centuries] has been "hidden from history".'

39. In 'Three Women's Texts and a Critique of Imperialism', (*Critical Inquiry*, 12, 1985, p245), Gayatri Chakravorty Spivak argues that western feminism is characterised by the 'mesmerizing focus' of the 'female individualist'. See also her *In Other Worlds: Essays in Cultural Politics* (New York and London: Methuen, 1987). Chandra Mohanty, 'Under Western Eyes: Feminist Scholarship and Colonial Discourses', (*Feminist Review*, 30, 1988, p62), also offers a particularly useful critique of western feminism, and includes in this category the methods of analysis followed by middle-class, urban African and Asian scholars producing scholarship 'which assumes their own middle-class as the norm'.

40. Trinh T Minh-ha, *Woman, Native, Other: Writing Postcoloniality and Feminism*, Bloomington, Ind.: Indiana University Press, 1989, p80.

41. Frene Ginwala has hinted that white women academics should look at male domination in white South Africa, rather than focus solely on the ANC (*South*, 30 August–5 September 1990, p19). In 'Arab Women and Western Feminism: An Interview' (*Race and Class*, 22(2), 1980, pp178–9), Nawal El Sa'adawi also argues, quite rightly, that it is important for middle-class women to recognise their own entrapment in patriarchal structures rather than simply directing their feminism to women of other countries. A particularly crude rendition of this position manifested itself when a version of this paper, delivered at a recent conference, received the following objections by two black South African men: a) you forget that white women have also oppressed black men; b) you are speaking *for* black women. In both cases the men came up to the microphone to express their objections and then left the microphone immediately: these were not points for discussion. The effect of such remarks (and perhaps the intention) was to position me as white, and thus as not authorised to speak about black women, or even black South Africans more generally, or even the ANC constitutional guidelines (as if they and I were from different countries). And at the *Weekly Mail* Book Week in November 1989, where I was the only white woman on a panel including four black women, it was again suggested that my discussion of gender problems experienced by black South African women was out of place. My rejection of this (im)position does not mean I oppose the arguments regarding western feminism, as cited above. The ANC constitutional guidelines have important implications for all South African women.

42. See Dorothy Driver, '"Woman" as Sign in the South African Colonial Enterprise', *Journal of Literary Studies*, 4(1), 1988, pp3–20.

43. See Spivak, 'Three Women's Texts' for this discussion.

44. This reference to the family in terms of two discourses is indebted to El Sa'adawi's discussion of the veil in 'Arab Women and Western Feminism' (p181) and Spivak's discussion of *sati* (the self-immolation of widows) in 'Can the Subaltern Speak', in Carey Nelson and Lawrence Grossberg (eds), *Marxism and the Interpretation of Culture*, London: Macmillan, 1988. Spivak notes that *sati* has been defined as, contradictorily, (i) a signifier of national identity, which is also read as a 'nationalistic romanticization of the purity, strength, and love of… self-sacrificing women' (p301), and (ii) a signifier of Hindu patriarchalism. Her major point is that both definitions of *sati*, the first from Hindu nationals, the second from British colonials, deny Indian women a place from which to speak: they are fixed by the subject positions assigned to them.

45. It is presumably for such reasons that Lauretta Ngcobo uses the term 'blackwoman' in her introduction to *Let It Be Told: Essays by Black Women in Britain*, London: Pluto, 1987.

46. See Elizabeth Cowie, '"Woman" as Sign', *m/f*, 1, 1978, pp49–62, for a discussion of kinship structures as a signifying system in which women are defined.

47. *Femina*, June 1990, p108.

48. See Catherine Campbell, 'The Township Family and Women's Struggles'. Although I take a different view from hers, I respect the pragmatism of her decision.

49. See, in particular, Ellen Kuzwayo, *Call Me Woman*, Emma Mashinini, *Strikes Have Followed Me All My Life*, and Lauretta Ngcobo, *Cross of Gold*, London: Longman, 1981.

50. *Tribute*, May 1990, p21.

51. In Tsitsi Dangarembga's *Nervous Conditions*, the figure of Lucia represents the woman not yet tamed by Christianity. And in *The Joys of Motherhood* (p10), Buchi Emecheta has Nwokocha Agbadi reflect: 'To regard a woman who is quiet and timid as desirable was something that came after his time, with Christianity and other changes.' Nevertheless, it is important to see that, at least in the second instance, the characterisation of women is still mediated through patriarchy, as the word 'desirable' reminds us.

52. See, for example, *South*, 14–20 June 1990, p6.

Capitalising on African Strengths

Women, welfare and the law

Sandra Burman

*T*he family is in a state of change in South Africa, particularly in the urban areas. In all sections of the population, women are providing for the upbringing of children to a far greater extent than ever before. However, apartheid legislation has reinforced – or recreated – different patterns in different population groups, making it difficult to generalise across the whole population on the more detailed patterns of causation and practice. Given limitations of space, this paper will therefore concentrate on the largest section of the population – the African family.

Since many people do not bother to obtain a formal divorce, accurate figures for marriage break-up are difficult to come by, especially if customary law unions are included. However, research at the Socio-Legal Unit of the University of Cape Town indicates that in Cape Town probably considerably over 50 per cent of African marriages, contracted by either civil or customary law, end in *de facto* divorce. In at least two-thirds of these cases, there are children from the marriage. In the case of civil law divorces, the custody of the vast majority of these children will be given to their mothers, although some mothers will send them to live with the mother's family for at least part of their childhoods.[1] There is no hard evidence on what percentage of children from customary law marriages will in fact remain in their mother's custody.

In addition, according to the latest figures available for Cape Town, 68,2 per cent of all African children born in 1988/89 were born outside any form of marriage.[2] Although some of these women may subsequently marry, current research indicates that such a woman is unlikely to take her illegitimate child into the new marriage unless the husband is the child's father. Failing that, the child will probably be left with the woman's family, often her single or divorced mother. Thus, while it is currently impossible to quantify the number of children being brought up in female-headed households in Cape Town, it seems likely that the vast majority of children will spend at least part of their growing years in one.

The expenses of such children must be paid for. But women's pay in South Africa is substantially lower than men's (particularly in the unskilled category, including domestic work), and unemployment is high, even for those free to seek jobs and desperate to work. Moreover, to earn such wages, a woman must arrange child care (for which she may have to pay substantially) or leave her children unsupervised, with all the attendant dangers. Although the law stipulates that fathers should pay *pro rata* for the upkeep of their children, whether born in or out of marriage, research on Cape Town has shown that over 85 per cent of African fathers against whom there is a maintenance order default at some stage during the subsistence of the order. Moreover, interviews indicate that many women do not apply for an order even when the fathers of their children are not making informal payments regularly or at all. Where an order exists, research shows that most are substantially lower than the man's pro rata share of the costs of the child, and over 30 per cent of orders, even if doubled to allow for an equal contribution paid by the woman, result in a total sum for the child's expenses which is below the PHSL poverty datum line maximum for a child of that age range.[3] Part of the problem is that the lowest-paid sections of the population have the largest families and by far the highest illegitimacy rates, resulting in the poorest people having the highest maintenance obligations. Although it has recently become illegal for Africans to acquire a civil law wife in addition to a customary law wife, the legislation (Act 3 of 1988) was not retroactive and the practice of marrying first by customary law and then marrying another woman by civil law was common among temporary migrants to the cities until December 1988. It resulted in many men having maintenance obligations to even more families than merely successive marriages would produce. Men are either loath to pay a higher amount, or state officials are loath to award higher amounts, believing that men are more likely to default if ordered to pay more, although this is not proven.

Where payment by fathers cannot be obtained, state maintenance grants are meant to provide a safety net for mothers. However, both amounts and conditions differ for different population groups and are very difficult to obtain, especially by Africans. Moreover, maintenance grants are available for a maximum of four children, whether legitimated by some form of marriage or not, and are obtainable for only *one* child born of an irregular union. Grants are available only if the man is dead, disabled, a pensioner, in prison for more than a year, or has vanished – and there is a police certificate to verify this point. Failing this, assistance from family and friends, charity, or resort to assorted means of obtaining funds in the informal sector are the main – and usually inadequate – means of survival.[4] Thus, a high proportion of mothers must provide for their children out of uncertain and, frequently, grossly inadequate, incomes.[5]

Solutions?

What solutions are possible? One with an obvious appeal is to tighten the law to make a father pay his share of the child's expenses. However, recent international research indicates that, even in much wealthier countries than South Africa, the default rate on maintenance payments by fathers is unacceptably high. The only two countries where this is not the case – Germany and Sweden – have a range of state benefits at every stage of a person's life so generous as to outweigh the cost to a man of child maintenance. Moreover, in both countries the populations are so well documented and the enforcement systems so efficient that it is extremely difficult for defaulters to 'vanish'. None of these conditions apply in South Africa, and although the present South African system of obtaining maintenance from fathers could be substantially improved, the default rate is likely to remain high. Moreover, with increasing unemployment, many men are unable to pay and cannot be ordered to do so until they obtain a job in the formal sector of the economy for which the payment of wages can be proved. Yet a high proportion of 'unemployed' men live on 'invisible' earnings from the informal sector, sometimes in considerable style.

It could well be argued that the system of obtaining maintenance from fathers is patently not working and that therefore it would make more sense to abolish it. While people tend to object to allowing men 'to have their fun without paying for it', there is very little evidence that most are paying for it under the present system anyway. Yet, while support by non-custodial parents continues to be regarded as the basic source of child support, the state is inclined to rely on such private support to pay for children even when it is blatantly not doing so. Were it to be abolished, some savings would be made on the present enforcement machinery of maintenance officers, court and police time, and this could be put towards a state system.

However, the South African state is far from wealthy enough to institute an alternative system of child allowances. The savings from the abolition of the current enforcement system of support from fathers would be only a drop in a very large bucket of claims. 'When apartheid goes, the state will take care of us' is a sentiment frequently voiced at present. Underlying this sentiment is an expectation that, once apartheid is abolished, it will be possible to share out the income from the economy more equally, so that the deprived majority of the population will receive its fair share *and that its fair share will be big enough to provide individuals with as much as they need* – for education, pensions, sick care, child care, and all the other things that people expect that the state will provide. Unfortunately, the facts do not support this.

The South African economy may be viewed as a cake which has been very unevenly divided to date, with a few people getting most of it. Part of it was shared out through the budgets of departments that provided services, such as education, health, and welfare, and in each case whites received more per head than did people with other 'race' classifications. But if the cake were now to be redivided equally between all the people entitled to a share, the current arithmetic indicates that such shares would still leave many basic needs unsatisfied. Admittedly, the cake is not a completely fixed size. It may get bigger, and the amount available for welfare, education, and health payments may also be increased by cutting other items, such as military expenditure. But the welfare budget would have to grow considerably to be able to provide all the benefits at the rate whites have enjoyed to date,[6] and much the same applies to other budgets.

And the cake may also shrink. There are various factors which, it must be faced, could well have this effect in the last decade of the twentieth century, such as political unrest, emigration of skilled manpower, shrinking investment, and the effect of AIDS on the economy. It is therefore necessary to examine what can be learnt from current models of family assistance provided by other countries, to adopt what is useful for South Africa and then to provide for those items not covered – by rethinking solutions from the beginning.

One possibility which should be considered is a system of automatic taxation of every man with a child, and the payment of a child allowance for every child to the mothers of children. This would be more reliable than the present system of tax allowances for children and court orders against fathers. There may be pitfalls in such a system, but lessons could be learnt from a study of those countries which already operate similar arrangements.[7]

However, low wages and high unemployment rates are likely to render such payments inadequate to meet all the expenses of children, even if the problems of tax enforcement were overcome. If the state cannot make up the shortfall by providing an adequate system of cash payments to individuals, perhaps state funds, either as well as or instead of child allowance, should rather be concentrated on services where economies of scale could be used and the still-existing strengths of the society built upon. In South Africa, even though the family is much weakened as a unit, there is still considerable community cohesion in both rural and urban settlements of all sizes. It may be possible to utilise this strength. Child care, for example, is currently performed in poorer households by individuals in the family, usually elderly relatives, who are often unpaid, in need of adult company, and sometimes unable to control the children. Payments to créches and child care centres run by the community and staffed by its members, who would be paid for their services, might be both cheaper than child support grants and productive of better child care. As many of the staff would probably be the same women who would otherwise be struggling with child care in isolation, it would also meet many needs of the elderly. A scheme of this kind has been very successful in a rural community in Gazankulu. In more industrialised areas additional funding might also be obtained by selling places in such créches to local industrialists for their workers. On the same lines, subsidised schemes for school feeding from central kitchens, where they have existed, have till now been run by charities in the townships but are beginning to be taken over by communities in some areas, staffed in rotation by members of the community, who are paid. Subsidised and assisted across the country, they might similarly give better value for money than child care allowances, and facilitate more community, as opposed to centralised state control. It may be possible to redesign a social welfare system on these lines, though care would have to be taken that it did not degenerate into increasing the workload of women of the community, rather than providing them with sought-after jobs at a suitable level of remuneration.[8]

There is another possible source of funding which might be investigated. Bridewealth (the payment by the groom's family to the bride's, on the marriage), whether known as lobola, lobolo, bohadi, or any other of its many names, shows no sign of disappearing. On the contrary, its value is increasing, and in all sections of African society. Currently, the payment for a well-educated girl is several thousand rand. One of the main purposes of this institution originally was to provide a form of insurance for a woman and her children should the marriage end through no fault of her own. If her husband's behaviour forced her to leave his homestead and return to her family, who had received payment for her, then there would be means to provide for her and her children, if she brought them with her. Nor did it matter if the marriage ended only after many years of existence: since the payment was made in cows which were never sold, and cows have calves, the means to provide for her would still be there. But since payment is now almost always in money which is usually spent immediately, if the marriage ends and the wife returns to her family, there is no ready-made source of food and clothing for her and the children, who are a burden on her family of origin. Even if the bridewealth had been spent on such items as a kitchen suite and bedroom suite for the young couple, as is increasingly the case, she probably could not bring it with her if she left the marital home, and even if she could, it would be second-hand furniture and not of much value. But if the institution of bridewealth could be updated, so that it served its original purpose of providing a safety net for the woman and her children if in need, then a source of funds universal throughout the African community could be tapped for the future of the new South Africa.

For this, a new structure would probably be necessary.[9] Existing financial instruments or arrangements which are available on an individual basis are not satisfactory. As the insurance of a marriage is held to be contrary to public morals and therefore illegal, the bridewealth could be invested only in a life assurance investment or a unit trust account to obtain exposure to growth assets. (Savings accounts or fixed deposits would also be alternatives, but historically interest yields have not kept pace with inflation.) However, individual instruments remain the legal property of the owner, and whether this were the woman's parents or the young couple, there would be a standing temptation to access the funds when cash was required.

For any new structure to work, however, community acceptance would be essential, as well as legislative change, and this would require considerable national discussion, as people are likely to resist forfeiting the cash bonanza bridewealth currently represents to a woman's parents.[10] A possible approach might be to constitute a 'bridewealth fund'. Contributions (either a single lump sum or regular monthly or annual amounts over a few years) would be made to the fund by the suitor or groom or his family. Certificates would be issued to him, the bride, and to the bride's parents, detailing the payments.

The fund could be constituted in a similar manner to a retirement annuity fund, or as a trust fund. The key aspect would be the powers conferred on the trustees in terms of investment and disbursement of money from the fund. Rules would need to exist which would ensure that:

- Investments were managed in a prudent manner by suitably qualified portfolio managers with due regard to the liabilities of the fund.
- Proper records were kept of the assets and liabilities, and of the individual members' interest in the fund.
- The trustees would be empowered to disburse all or part of the members' interest upon evidence of the occurrence of the contingencies covered. These might be events such as:
  a) termination of the marriage
  b) death of either spouse
  c) expiry of a specific term
  d) attainment of a particular age by the members.

Issues which would need to be addressed in creating such a fund would be the tax status of such a fund, supervision and controls, and the cost of setting it up and continuing administration. One possible problem which would need to be considered is that in the lowest income group, where bridewealth payments are small, the amounts involved would yield very low pay-outs and might not be commercially viable.

It is essential, however, that such a bridewealth fund should not be regarded as more than a source of funds in the emergency of the marriage ending, or a lump sum saving to help in old age if the marriage survived. Given the probable inability of the state to make full cradle-to-grave welfare provision for its citizens, there should also be encouragement for individuals to take responsibility for their future financial security. The emphasis in this should not *focus* on the application of what has already been saved – such as bridewealth – but on current saving, together with the use of life and disability insurance to protect against other contingencies.

[This paper is also published in the *South African Journal of Human Rights*, 7, 1991.]

Notes

1. S Burman and R Fuchs, 'When Families Split: Custody on Divorce in South Africa' in S Burman and P Reynolds (eds), *Growing up in a Divided Society: The Contexts of Childhood in South Africa*, Johannesburg: Ravan, 1986, pp115–38; S Burman, 'Law versus Reality: The Interaction of Community Obligations to and by the Black Elderly in South Africa' in

J Eekelaar and D Pearl (eds), *An Aging World: Dilemmas and Challenges for Law and Social Policy*, Oxford: Clarendon Press, 1989, pp211–25.

2. Medical Officer of Health, *1988/89 Annual Report of the Medical Officer of Health*, 2, City of Cape Town, 1990, Table III.14.

3. The Primary Household Subsistence Level (PHSL) is a poverty data measure calculated by the Institute for Planning Research, University of Port Elizabeth, inter alia for a four-child household in Cape Town of those classified as black. The PHSL is a particularly low poverty data measure, as it does not include rent and transport expenses.

4. S Burman, 'Marriage Break-Up in South Africa: Holding Want at Bay?', *International Journal of Law and the Family*, 1(2), 1987, pp206–47.

5. S Burman and S Berger, 'When Family Support Fails: The Problems of Maintenance Payments in Apartheid South Africa', in *South African Journal on Human Rights*, 4, 1988, pp194–203, pp344–54.

6. P le Roux, 'Whither with Pensions in Post-Apartheid South Africa?', *Monitor*, December 1990, pp90–6.

7. While such a policy may theoretically encourage a higher birth rate, historical evidence, such as France in the inter-war period, does not support this. In fact, tax rebates are never large enough to act as an incentive to have children.

8. F Lund, 'Women, Welfare, and "The Community"', paper presented at the conference on *Women and Gender in Southern Africa*, Durban, 1991.

9. I am indebted to Peter de Beyer for giving his time and actuarial skills to produce the following outline.

10. The other objections frequently advanced to changes in bridewealth arrangements are that bridewealth binds the bride's and groom's families in striving to preserve the marriage, and that men do not value women for whom they have not paid. It might be argued that, since it is rare nowadays for bridewealth to be reclaimed on the breakup of the marriage, unless that occurs within months of the wedding, the binding of the families is now more token than real and could be served by a token payment. As regards the second objection, the man *would* have paid for his wife – and also saved himself some of the family insurance that a prudent man of means would aim to take out for his family.

Women's Rights and the Family in Traditional and Customary Law

Thandabantu Nhlapo

*T*his paper attempts to look at the position of the family in customary law in South Africa. It adopts a theoretical and general approach, the aim of which is to contribute to the debate on the constitutional protection of women's rights in a future South African constitution. Believing that issues of family law cannot be separated from issues of women's law, this paper will have fulfilled its function if it manages to sketch out the nature and scope of the problems that will be encountered on the road towards modernising the African family.

In particular, I wish to suggest an answer to a question that is often asked: 'Are African customary law and tradition really inimical to women's rights and, if so, in what way(s)?' The answer will take the somewhat unusual form of avoiding all attempts to compile a 'hit list'[1] of customs considered to be oppressive to women. Instead I will propose an explanatory theory which improves our understanding of *why* sex discrimination appears to be such an enduring feature of African traditional systems. Hopefully, in the process the thinking that lies behind individual customs will find explanation.

It will be seen that such explanations hinge critically on an understanding of the *values* underlying the African family. This paper is therefore largely about values in customary family law and how these affect the position of women within the family.

Problems of definition

It is useful at this stage to set out the meanings that will be ascribed to the two central concepts in this chapter: the family, and customary law.

The family

In both Roman-Dutch law and African customary law the family is defined in terms of a relationship that arises from marriage. This approach is not without its critics. Alternative theories of the family, especially those found in feminist writing, call for a broader definition – one that removes the family's association with marriage. Such definitions would conceive of the family in terms which accommodate various permanent or semi-permanent groupings, ranging from the situation of the single, never-married parent, to that of the informal household (whether or not centred around a married couple) comprising in-laws and other relatives and dependents. Within this range would be found groupings involving unmarried parties, heterosexual or homosexual, with or without children.

Debate over the concept of family will no doubt continue well into the foreseeable future, and will assume increasing importance as the impact of changes in contemporary lifestyles begins to be felt in South Africa. For our purposes, however, it is possible to sidestep the debate by recognising that, as a social fact, marriage and family are inseparable in African customary law.[2]

Customary law

It is now fairly well documented that what is applied in many African countries as customary law is – in Martin Chanock's popular phrase – 'neither customary nor law'.[3] In this paper I adopt a view of customary law which is influenced by recent accounts of the interaction between African custom and colonial rule.[4] These accounts describe the shift from 'custom' to customary law which took place most prominently in the sphere of the family during the colonial period. In most of Africa the process consistently involved an alliance between the colonial administration and African male elders. The latter, as the traditional holders of power over 'strategic resources' – namely land, cattle, women and children[5] – saw this power dwindling[6] and sought to regain it by manipulating institutions such as lobolo and guardianship.

The colonial administration, for its part, either misunderstood the nature of African institutions or held a view of African society which saw women as rightless entities under the authority of men. Whatever their different motivations, these forces between them promoted, in the name of tradition, the emergence of rigid rules of 'customary law' in place of custom.[7] Since then, urbanisation, influx control and the continued creation of customary law through the medium of western-style courts have all affected the final product.

Further mention of values in customary family law will be against the background of the understanding outlined above. That is to say, we will deal with fundamental African thinking on the subject of the family, whether or not such thinking coincides with what the courts will apply as customary law.

Traditional values in African family law

It was suggested earlier that in customary law, marriage and family are inseparable. And it is in marriage that the position of women is defined in terms that may prove problematic. The statement made earlier about the link between marriage and family should thus read: 'African values towards women and the family are closely tied up with the African view of marriage.'

In my view, the overriding value in the African family is reflected in the *non-individual nature of marriage*, sometimes called the collective or communal aspect of the marriage relationship.[8] This notion embodies the idea of marriage as an alliance between two kinship groups for purposes of realising goals beyond the immediate interests of the particular husband and wife.[9] This does not mean that the two parties are unimportant – they are, but only as the point at which the two families, lineages or clans are joined for purposes which have community-wide significance.[10]

The goals aimed at by this type of marriage can be summarised as procreation and survival. Both of these goals can be seen to have been essential for the wellbeing of the larger group in pre-industrial society: wives and children were an economic asset, and the rules that developed around them were part of a survival strategy. But we must be aware that to say the interests of the group are more important than those of the individual is to say something else: in patriarchal societies group interests are framed in favour of men.

And here we get the first indication of why inequality is such an enduring part of African customary systems. The field of family relations is one in which Africans construct the foundations of the rest of their social lives. Radcliffe-Brown's statement is as valid today as it was when he wrote it: 'For the understanding of any aspect of the social life of an African people – economic, political or religious – it is essential to have a thorough knowledge of their system of kinship and marriage.'[11] If that system masks inequality under the guise of group interests, women and children (lacking a say in the articulation of those interests) are certain to be disadvantaged.

We can illustrate this with some examples. Having determined that marriage is a tool in service of purposes much broader than the immediate interests of the couple, we find that there are certain consequences that flow from such a stance.

- The need to procreate leads to a complex of rules relating to barrenness. The sororate, for instance, covers the situation where a younger sister is required to take the place of a wife who is unable to produce children. The levirate may be invoked in the case where a man dies before he has fully exploited the procreative capacities of his wife: he can have children fathered for him (more properly, for his family) by a relative.

- The same view of marriage countenances child betrothal and 'forced marriage'.[12] Even more unfortunately, it countenances attitudes towards nubility which sometimes clothe the taking of sexual liberties with the very young with some measure of acceptability.[13] The respect-for-elders ethic and the ability of the perpetrator to plead customary rights such as his preferential claim to young sisters and cousins of his wife, combine to render this area notoriously resistant to penetration by the 'white man's laws' of sexual impropriety.

- It may also be plausibly argued that a marriage where the most important aims are external to the parties involved, where men acquire rights over women and children but not vice versa, and where these rights are secured by the movement of cattle, has a direct bearing on the perpetual minority of women. This in turn surely has a bearing on chastisement and physical violence in general, not to mention the position of widows and the dehumanising bereavement rituals and mourning taboos to which they are sometimes subjected.

Many of the items on the 'hit list' would thus find explanation in the very nature of marriage and the family as conceived by the African value system. We can now hazard an answer to the question: 'What is it about custom that is inimical to women's rights?' It is everything that emanates from an attitude to women in marriage and in the family which sees them solely as adjuncts to the group, a means to the anachronistic end of clan survival, rather than as valuable in themselves and deserving of recognition for their human worth on the same terms as men.[14]

Culture and human rights

No attempt to analyse the position of women in African customary law from the standpoint of rights is immune from the suggestion that the whole process is a 'western-inspired' exercise and therefore irrelevant at best and, at worst, traitorous. In this connection it is often argued that the whole notion of human rights is foreign to Africa and is an inappropriate standard against which to judge political and social arrangements on the continent.[15] At a general level the argument, based as it is on cultural relativism, objects to the imposition of western ideological and cultural values on third world societies.

This argument can be rejected on several grounds, two of which will suffice here. In the first place, one's membership of a particular group or community is not a *morally* relevant circumstance, and human rights discourse is pre-eminently a moral enterprise. To argue that if a particular society has always had authoritarian practices it is morally defensible that it continues to have them, is to accept an extreme form of moral and legal positivism. The assertion that the rules enacted by the group are necessarily correct as a matter of critical morality is of dubious validity at best.[16]

Secondly, and much more practically, the idea that 'human rights' is a western construct with limited applicability to the African reality is misleading for the simple reason that traditional African society recognised human rights norms of many types, some of which coincide squarely with the internationalised modern ones.[17] Even where a particular norm has no counterpart in modern terminology this is not necessarily to its disadvantage. For example, the right to life appears to have been much wider in traditional culture: it included not only a prohibition against killing but also the obligation to assist in providing means of subsistence to needy members of the community. To argue that a rights-based critique of customary practices is foreign ignores the facts.

Indeed, recent developments may have rendered refutations of the anti-human rights argument superfluous. On 21 October 1986 the African Charter on Human and Peoples' Rights came into force with the attainment of 31 ratifications from among the 50 member states of the Organisation of African Unity. The charter is important as an attempt to provide some rethinking on human rights in an African context and constitutes the first body of norms that cannot be criticised in Africa for its alien origins. It thus goes a long way towards undermining some of the objections set out in the foregoing discussion. It also offers an indication of how far international mores have influenced the African human rights debate.

This document, which may have relevance in a new South Africa, attempts to be culturally relevant by insisting that its provisions should be read with African traditions in mind, and that our reflections on the concept of human and peoples' rights should take into account the 'virtues of... [our] historical tradition and the values of African civilization'.[18]

When, in Article 18(3) the charter calls on states to ensure 'the elimination of every form of discrimination against women', it is difficult to see how that call can be reconciled with the duty placed on the same states to be 'conscious of the values of African civilization'.[19] On the face of it, given the way we have seen these values operate in family law with respect to women, there is an obvious potential for conflict between the charter's objectives.

This tension lies at the heart of any attempt to modernise customary family law so that it has a positive, rather than negative, impact on women's rights. What follows is a proposal for a theoretical resolution of this tension.

Traditional values and discrimination

The values underlying some African cultural practices in the family sphere can be explained and understood in terms of the needs of the larger group in days gone by. The most striking way in which African society expresses its panic at the march of change is its attempt to preserve or revive these practices, long rendered inappropriate by today's social, political and economic context. Anachronistic adherence to so-called 'African ways' poses obvious problems for the cause of women's rights. Yet total abandonment of these values may pose an even greater threat to social cohesion by creating a cultural vacuum in circumstances where there are no ready substitutes.[20]

I believe that if enough understanding of these values is acquired (for example, their nature, origin and function), it ought to be possible to salvage from them a 'usable residue' of Africanness which enhances rather than diminishes the human rights ideal in family law. In other words, a clear distinction must be drawn between the *substance* (or function) of the value and the *form* of its expression.

This distinction can be illustrated by focusing on three categories of actors in family law: the elderly, children and women (wives and mothers).

The elderly

Respect for elders is a cherished value in perhaps all African societies but by definition it is a notion that discriminates against the young in favour of the old.[21] On the one hand, respect for elders as a philosophy continues to be an effective way of inculcating habits of humility, courtesy, consideration and decency in the young: on the other, it institutionalises relationships of inequality and, for women, even hardship in society.

Quite apart from the notion of respect for elders as a social obligation on the young stemming from the demands of etiquette, the question of the elderly in African society has much more serious *economic* implications. In traditional Africa elderhood was a status position which ensured wealth, power, authority, privilege and leadership. These accrued to the elderly, largely because of the latter's control over 'strategic resources'. Within the family elders were able to make demands on junior relatives in terms of labour or property and in this way the old-age security of the former was assured.

There was thus a clear link between institutionalised inequality and the security of the elderly. For example, control by elders of marriageable women and their easy access to younger mates, though apparently objectionable to the modern mind, were in fact central to the provision of old-age security in an agrarian society.[22]

Thus a man might take a succession of young wives (sometimes at the urging of his first wife), with cattle he has amassed over the years from the marriages of his daughters, or fines for their seduction (or for the occasional infidelities of their mothers). Such a monopoly over resources is clearly discriminatory, yet, as Eekelaar[23] observes, these practices mark 'the manipulation, by a society, through an ideology of deference to the elderly, of its human resources in such a way as to sustain its aging generation'. The substance or function of the value of granting pre-eminence to age was, among other things, to ensure the subsistence of older people in societies where social welfare was unknown. There thus remains much positive content in this norm which can be maintained even if its negative aspects – the inegalitarian and sometimes despotic form in which it is expressed – disappear.

Alternatives may not be easy to find in all cases. As the elders lose control over the young they tend to fall back on neo-traditionalism which usually aims at regaining power over women and children, thus creating tension between the claims of the former to old-age support and those of the latter to independence. In addition many African states are severely restricted by poverty in providing adequate social security for the elderly.[24] Just as clearly, however, a norm expressed in a manner that has a negative impact on large sections of the community can benefit from some re-adjustment. Perhaps greater state intervention in some form can provide such re-adjustment.

Children

Children are at the centre of the African conception of marriage as an arrangement serving interests wider than the immediate needs of the spouses. A man needed many sons to ensure the survival of the lineage and to increase his power within the clan, and daughters who by their marriages would swell his herds and create beneficial alliances with other clans. As members of the family, children were also important participants in the household economy. The whole clan thus had an interest in the children of its members, their upbringing, socialisation and eventually, marriage.

The value of the extended family, ensuring stability and providing an emotional, economic and political support system for its members, had perfectly rational origins and expresses important modern norms. It is accepted that in the debate over the extended family and the nuclear family the former exhibits many positive characteristics.[25]

It would be perverse to argue for the abolition in Africa of the role of the wider family and the community in marriage. The positive aspects of this communal value are too clearly demonstrated. It is the forms in which this value is expressed which can be adjusted to rid it of its discriminatory content. In this area the conflicting interests are those of fathers and their lineages on the one hand, and mothers and their children on the other. (The case of mothers is discussed in more detail below.)

Here it should suffice to emphasise that the value of the extended family is worth retaining; alternative formulas may, however, have to be found to express it in ways that are non-discriminatory. In matters of child custody and other rights over children, for example, the compelling justification for preferring fathers (and even grandfathers) to the exclusion of the mothers[26] has been considerably weakened by changed economic and social conditions. The pointed de-personalisation of mothers is not logically necessary for the *function* of the extended family to be fulfilled.

Women/wives/mothers

African women are expected to become wives at some stage in their lives and as wives they are required to be, first and foremost, mothers. It is only in a minority of cases that issues of womanhood are relevant in isolation from those of wifehood (or widowhood) and motherhood. It can be said that as wives African women do not enjoy a great deal of freedom of choice. Their lives, particularly in terms of personal independence and equality of decision making, are subjected to the needs of the family. Family ties serve to subordinate the interests of women as persons to the interests of the wider group.

However, in the context of a subsistence economy the very rules that appeared designed for the subjection of women often operated to ensure their security. The economic priorities underlying the pre-eminence of marriage and large families produced practices which worked in part to ensure that no woman was left without someone directly responsible for her maintenance.[27] This positive core in the African concept of marriage is of great merit: indeed to abandon it would immediately be to raise the question of alternatives.

The role of women as mothers, too, has a great impact on their lives. African marriage has its most telling consequences on women as mothers, mothers-to-be or potential mothers. This type of marriage – expressed in the extended family and their strong role in the lives of the married couple, guiding, directing and sometimes compelling their compliance in the protection of interests deemed superior to those of the partners – may be summed up as survival-through-procreation. Its origins lie in the overriding need for the family, the lineage and the clan to reproduce themselves and ensure their survival. Procreation was necessary primarily for economic reasons, a value which was fundamental in a system of subsistence agriculture.

As presently constituted, however, this value operates to deny women equality *precisely because they are the means by which the overriding goals of the wider group are achieved.* The motherhood role makes possible the paradox of women in African society: revered for their fertility and restricted because of it.[28] Motherhood lies at the root of the community's survival and, as we pointed out earlier in patriarchal societies, group interests are often synonymous with male interests. A male-dominant society perceives no contradiction in practices which discriminate against women for the very reason of their great importance to the group's survival. It is this type of thinking which also explains the one-sided sexual morality for which African societies are known, which imposes almost monastic rules of behaviour on women but not on men in similar circumstances.[29]

Today there exist other options for ensuring economic security and survival. Value judgments will have to be made in choosing possible approaches. In this Africa is not unique. Controversy has raged in England for many years over the choice of policy towards spouse maintenance after dissolution of marriage. The well-known debate between Ruth L Deech and Katherine O'Donovan has demonstrated the problems encountered whenever the formal method of expressing a particular value comes into conflict with other, emerging, values.[30]

In Africa, too, the search for alternatives is not expected to be easy. There may be competing theories as to the proper basis for policy on such matters as family security and maintenance. What is clear is that economic security means the material wellbeing of citizens of nation-states, based on policies adopted and pursued by national governments. It is no longer a matter of survival in families, roving bands or small village units cut off from the effects of the international system of capital. Many of the practices which may have made sense in pre-colonial times are dysfunctional in today's formal society.

Procreation in particular can no longer be considered the only means by which society ensures its economic survival. Indeed, there are senses in which a strongly pro-natalist culture effectively diminishes the chances of economic progress. Black South Africa's high birth rate is itself a significant factor to be taken into account in rethinking marriage values. When these values are reassessed it should be possible to free women from many of the conventions which contribute to their subjection. Many practices and regulations involving women would fall to be re-examined: the levirate, the sororate and social disapproval of childlessness, and the rules relating to widows.

Conclusion

It must be noted that the fundamental value of strong kinship ties and collective responsibility for the welfare of the group enriches African communities: these communities would benefit further if, by the removal of inequalities, they were rendered more balanced. What has emerged from the foregoing is a clear indication that the African value system does not perceive women as separate entities but always as adjuncts to the family. A woman's personhood is lost in the group much more than a man's is subsumed under the so-called community principle. Removing inequalities will thus crucially involve the discovery of ways of ensuring that cherished African values are not expressed in a form that de-person-alises women. This is not an argument for western-style individualism: it is an argument for individualisation. It is premised on the belief that it is unintelligible to speak of human rights if one is not speaking also of a certain level of concern with the wellbeing of each and every individual. The African woman's ability to procreate does not appear to be a sound reason to deny her the enjoyment of ordinary rights as a human being.

Notes

1.   In the minds of many people there does exist such a list. Certain to be
     included in it would be polygamy, lobolo, the levirate, the sororate, child
     betrothal and mourning taboos. For lawyers the focus would also be on

women's proprietary incapacity, perpetual minority and inequality in grounds for divorce.

2. This is not to say that informal arrangements are unknown in traditional life. Nor is it being asserted that the traditional concept of marriage is itself unproblematic. What is meant is that in traditional society a family is a unit that has its origins in marriage. Disputes over family-like relationships revolve around marriage: its validity, and whether it was attempted, completed, etc.

3. M Chanock, 'Neither Customary Nor Law: A Case of Mistaken Identity', unpublished paper delivered at the *Regional Conference on Social Change and Legal Reform in East, Central and Southern Africa*, Harare, 13–16 January 1987.

4. Chanock, 'Neither Customary Nor Law'; M Chanock, *Law, Custom and Social Order: The Colonial Experience in Malawi and Zambia*, Cambridge: Cambridge University Press, 1985; B Rwezaura, *Traditionalism and Law Reform in Africa*, Saarbrücken: Europa–Instituut, Nr 17, 1983; TW Bennett, *Application of Customary Law in Southern Africa*, Cape Town: Juta, 1985, Chapter II; AJGM Sanders, 'How Customary is African Customary Law?', *Comparative and International Law Journal of Southern Africa*, 20, 1987, p405.

5. B Rwezaura, 'Rural Women and the Law in Contemporary Africa', unpublished paper prepared for the fourth *International Women's Rights Action Watch (IWRAW) International Conference*, Vienna, 20–22 February 1989.

6. How do you command your daughter to marry a man of your choice when a missionary education has exposed her to reading and writing, and courtship by letter – not to mention financial independence through wage labour?

7. See Chanock, *Law, Custom and Social Order*, who makes it clear that there is doubt as to whether there existed anything like 'pure' and settled custom even in pre-colonial times.

8. In conformity with the generality of the tone of this paper, the word 'African' will be used throughout. There is thus no attempt to identify any traditional societies by name, an approach which allows for freer discussion of the theoretical questions the paper seeks to explore. See RT Nhlapo, 'Family Law and Traditional Values: A Study of the Legal Position of Women in Swaziland with selected references to developments in Zimbabwe', unpublished DPhil thesis, Oxford University, 1990.

9. A Phillips (ed), *A Survey of African Marriage and Family Life*, London: Oxford University Press, 1953; H Kuper, *The Swazi: A South African Kingdom*, New York: Holt, Rhinehart and Winston, 1963.

10. See JF Holleman, *Shona Customary Law, With Reference to Kinship, Marriage, the Family and the Estate*, Manchester, 1969.

11. AR Radcliffe-Brown, 'Introduction' in AR Radcliffe-Brown and D Forde (eds), *African Systems of Kinship and Marriage*, London: Oxford University Press, 1950, p1.

12. Among those groups where these customs still persist. The statement can be validated quite separately from the question of the existence or otherwise of any statutory prohibitions against these practices.
13. On the effects of 'respect for elders' on consent to sexual intercourse, see AKA Armstrong, 'A Note on Several Aspects of Rape in Swaziland', *Comparative and International Law Journal of Southern Africa*, 19, 1986, p474.
14. Putting it this way makes it unnecessary to embark upon the, often tedious, inquiry into individual customs and practices. The assertion is simply that as long as customary family law aims at preserving the view of marriage outlined above, the rights of women as a specific group in society are not yet being seriously considered.
15. To my mind this is the argument implied whenever a speaker says – as happened on a Sunday programme on TV2 recently: 'We don't need a white woman from England to tell us that we are oppressed. God created the family and gave the people within it different duties and roles, in accordance with the different cultures he created for them.' See RT Nhlapo, 'International Protection of Human Rights and the Family: African Variations on a Common Theme', *International Journal of Law and the Family*, 3(1), Oxford, 1989, pp1–20.
16. See generally FR Teson, 'International Human Rights and Cultural Relativism', *Virginia Journal of International Law*, 25(4), 1985, pp890–4.
17. B Hannum, 'The Butare Colloquium on Human Rights and Economic Development in Francophone Africa', *Universal Human Rights*, 1, 1979, p65.
18. African Charter on Human and Peoples' Rights, Preamble, Paragraph 4.
19. African Charter on Human and Peoples' Rights, Preamble, Paragraph 4. Compare Article 7 of the constitutional guidelines proposed by the African National Congress, *A Bill of Rights for a New South Africa*, University of the Western Cape: Centre for Development Studies, 1990, p15. ('Men and women shall enjoy equal rights in all areas of public and private life, including employment, education and within the family.')
20. We might note also that constitution-building for a new South Africa will be above all an exercise in negotiation and consensus-seeking. The avoidance of cultural shocks to the majority of the population may not be an unimportant consideration in this process.
21. See BA Rwezaura, 'Changing Community Obligations to the Elderly in Contemporary Africa', in Eekelaar and Pearl (eds), *An Aging World: Dilemmas and Challenges for Law and Social Policy*, Oxford: Clarendon Press, 1989.
22. Rwezaura, 'Changing Community Obligations'.
23. J Eekelaar, 'Introduction', in Eekelaar and Pearl (eds), *An Aging World*, p180.
24. See generally S Burman, 'Law versus Reality: The Interaction of Community Obligations to and by the Black Elderly in South Africa', in Eekelaar and Pearl (eds), *An Aging World*.
25. Recent writings in Britain, Europe and the United States have opened up the question of the nuclear family and its future. There is greater awareness

of the positive role of grandparents, uncles and aunts within the family. See Kaganas and Piper, 'Grandparents and the Limits of Law', *International Journal of Law and the Family*, 5(2), 1990; Lowe and Douglas, 'The Grandparent-Grandchild Relationship in English Law', in Eekelaar and Pearl (eds), *An Aging World*.

26. Based on the concept of lobolo as 'child price'.
27. See A Phillips, *A Survey of African Marriage and Family Life*, pxvi, who points to the 'social security' value of such apparently obnoxious practices as polygamy and the levirate.
28. There are many examples of this paradox. Responses from interviewees show strong support for equality, in theory. But specific restrictions on women's lives are invariably defended on the grounds that it is precisely women's importance in the scheme of things which makes her behaviour subject to controls. For instance, it is argued that the breaking of taboos by widows, pregnant women, nursing mothers, etc, could bring down the wrath of the ancestors upon the whole community, while men's actions were hardly ever significant enough to merit the attention of the ancestors.
29. African society – though by no means unique in this respect – exhibits many contradictions on the subject of nudity, for instance. On the whole, attitudes to the naked body are far less self-conscious than in the west: mixed bathing at the river is a common sight. Yet there is a plethora of rules and taboos governing only women: how they sit, what they wear, when they should not appear without headgear and so on.
30. RL Deech, 'The Principles of Maintenance', *Family Law*, 7, 1977, p229; K O'Donovan, 'The Principles of Maintenance: An Alternative View', *Family Law*, 8, 1978, p180.

The Family in South African Politics

Conceptualising progressive change

Nolulamo N Gwagwa

*T*he paper begins by briefly pointing out why analysis of the family is important in the South African context.[1] This will be followed with an examination of the concept of the family, which will take two forms. Firstly, a presentation of a broad comparison of the treatment of the family concept by the current South African regime, with the African National Congress. Secondly, a brief perusal of literature on the same concept will be done. The aim is not to establish 'the' definition of the family, but rather to concentrate on identifying the key issues, thus suggesting a broad conceptual framework for analysis of the family in South Africa.

It will be argued that the dearth of analyses of the family will prove detrimental to the process of redefining social relations in general, and gender relations in particular. If our struggle for such a redefinition is misdirected, then so will the criteria used to measure progressive change (both nominal and fundamental). The case of the growing number of women-headed families will be used to illustrate this point.

Why an analysis of the family?

In the South African context, there are very valid reasons why analysis of the family should be undertaken. Firstly, analysing the family is a planning task. Many planners adopt 'the family' as the smallest planning unit without examining what they mean by 'the family'. This is pertinent for all areas of policy: housing, health, social services, and so on. 'The family' is usually based on two assumptions: a nuclear family with two children; a clear and benign sexual division of labour.[2] For example, where planners attempt to address the housing problem, the crisis is usually expressed in numerical terms and as such solutions end at the level of the ability and inability to provide x number of units. The very real negotiations that occur within each family in an attempt to gain access to and sustain that housing is considered outside planning boundaries. On the contrary, for housing solutions to have any meaning to the user it is necessary for planners to examine what occurs within the family, and how the family defines itself.

Secondly, analysing the family is also a political task. Gender oppression has been identified within the South African struggle as a political problem. The family is a very central site where all forms of oppression (national, economic and gender) are acted out, as well as where struggles are waged against these same forms of oppression. The family is both a site of oppression and a site of resistance. It is a political task to analyse how these contradictions are articulated at family level. It is at a family level that one can begin to understand the true meaning of 'triple oppression', that oft-used term to describe the levels of oppression of black women in South Africa.

The central feature of apartheid has been 'separate development' according to race and ethnicity. The manipulation of the family through migrant labour and the homeland system played an important role in achieving apartheid policies. The family, therefore should be one of the key areas targeted by the progressive forces, in an attempt to reach a non-racial and unitary South Africa. Electoral systems (one person one vote in a common voters roll) and redrawing of boundaries (municipal, etc) in themselves may not necessarily articulate a single nation. Indoctrination through socialisation has been a powerful apartheid weapon. While also acknowledging the role of the apartheid education system, indoctrination still happens first and foremost at family level. Progressive political theorists grappling with the national question[3] need to seriously consider analysis of the family and its progressive and regressive roles towards nation-building. An analysis of the concept of the family as expressed by two different political views in South Africa shows how the family has been 'used' to achieve political ends. Of particular concern is how far such a treatment of the family takes us towards reaching 'a new South Africa', as broadly defined in terms of transformed racial, economic and gender relations.

The concept of the family

The need for a 'stable family' in South Africa would seem to be one area of 'consensus' across the political spectrum. Probing further, however, it becomes clear that this seeming 'consensus' marks the family as a site of ideological battle, hence the irreconcilable reasons for calls for its 'protection'. A brief comparison of the current South African regime (the state), and the African National Congress, bears this argument out.

In its National Family Programme, the state expresses 'considerable concern about the state of marriage and family life in the RSA'.[4] The reason is that 'a healthy family life is fundamental to social stability because the family functioning on a sound level plays a vital role in the establishment and propagation of religious values, cultural values, norms, own identity and national pride'.[5] In this context the family is defined 'as a social arrangement based on marriage and a marriage contract including recognition of rights and duties of parenthood, common residence of husband and wife and children and reciprocal economic obligations between husband and wife'.[6] The programme's aims, principles and objectives almost exclusively emphasise the 'preparation of the future mothers of our country for their particular maternal responsibilities towards the newborn infant, the family and society in general'.[7]

The state's definition of the family assumes a nuclear family form, while situating the family ahistorically and assuming uniformity across race and class. On the other hand, emphasis on 'cultural values, norms and own identity' highlights an interesting ideological attempt to reassert racial segregation.[8] The proposed focus on the family as a natural and fundamental social unit is certainly an attempt to almost enforce family members to 'fulfill their natural roles', including the ability to provide for their own needs. The role of the family as the site for reproduction, physical caring, homemaking and socialisation of children gives it ideological, economic and social responsibilities.

While acknowledging critiques of functionalist approaches to the family (that is, seeing the family as functional to apartheid and capitalism), it is important to contextualise the origins of this programme within the state's economic and political crises of the 1980s. Wolpe[9] submits that it was the deepening political and economic crises that facilitated a 'defensive and offensive restructuring of the state' in the early 1980s. It is within this restructuring of institutions of black representation and the apparatuses of control of blacks (particularly the youth) both within and outside the bantustans, that the National Family Programme should be located. The programme was commissioned in 1982 in the Department of Constitutional Development to formulate 'a programme for the enrichment of family life'.[10]

The programme deliberately aims to combine the 'traditional African' and 'western capitalist' family concepts in an attempt to, on one hand, reconstruct 'discipline' based on cultural values and norms, and on the other, individualise and privatise the family based on western capitalist values. The state is seeking a political solution within the boundaries of discipline ('law and order') and racial segregation, with the family being asked to perform this task. Calling for the family to 'regulate its size in accordance with its means', while stressing 'reciprocal economic obligations' between members, is an attempt by the state to exonerate itself from economic responsibility towards the black populace. Falling back onto religious definitions of marriage implies a nuclear family, femininity and its related gender relations, particularly its impact on women.

The state atomises the family from society, that is, the social, political and economic conditions within which it is located. The family concept itself is treated as static and immune to changing material conditions. The state's 'reconstruction' of the traditional family, with it roles of motherhood and wifehood, deserves a closer look. What is the significance of the state's retrieval of the traditional family, motherhood and wifehood in an attempt to mobilise support for its policies? Why is it always these three (traditional family, motherhood and wifehood) that get called upon in times of crises?[11] It seems that there is an urgent need to understand these concepts both in their historical and contemporary meanings, if one is to work towards building a progressive future South Africa. It is at this point that it becomes instructive to examine the ANC's conception of the family.

An interpretation of some of the ANC's political statements portrays the organisation as having a static view of this dynamic institution. This flaw originates from the organisation's use of the family as a mobilising tool, which leaves no space for a consistent analysis of the family.[12] The family gets subsumed within the wider struggle against apartheid and capitalism. For example, condemning pass laws being introduced for women in the Orange Free State in 1913, the ANC argued that 'the family was sacred – the jail would separate [women] from their families – [whilst] women had a special role in maintaining [the family's] integrity'.[13]

Later on in the 1940s, one saw a politicisation of motherhood by the ANC around issues such as better wages, pass laws, housing, etc. It is, however, interesting that these are all practical gender needs. While there was an attempt to politicise motherhood, its actual location, the family, was not being discussed. Politicising motherhood only, without a politicisation of the family, particularly relations within it, is of little consequence as far as social relations are concerned.

At the Luanda second ANC women's conference in 1987, one of the papers reads:

> The most important unit of society, the family, is shaken. The African family cannot be properly located in the social structure of South African society. The separation of men from their families by migrancy has broken families. The instability becomes fertile grounds for the mushrooming of new family forms.[14]

The ANC's proposed constitutional guidelines call for the family to be protected.[15] However, nowhere has this been elaborated. Does this mean support for an unpoliticised family? An unambiguous elaboration on this by the ANC is crucial. For example, Inkatha's philosophy is based on this notion of protecting the family. But what is different is that it appeals to 'tribal chauvinism' and gender subordination.[16] On the other hand, the state's concern in protecting the family is in fact with the management of political and economic crises through a depoliticisation of conflicts.

In suggesting a way forward, two interrelated flaws in the ANC/MDM treatment of the family emerge.[17] Firstly, in using the family as a mobilising tool, the progressive movement generally has failed to analyse and theorise the family. Wider political reasons for the urgency of such a task were advanced earlier in this paper. Secondly, and perhaps as a consequence of the above failure, concentration has been on the family form that has been 'destroyed by apartheid'. Further, 'these policies – "influx control" and "resettlement" in particular – have had a devastating effect on the black family... In the bantustans as many as 60% of the households are headed by women.'[18]

Thus debate on the family tends to be shifted to a narrow concern with family form. At one level there is preoccupation with marriage regime, hence family law, in as far as it will and will not support this or that family form. At another level there is a preoccupation with pros and cons of particular family forms, for example, a female-headed family. While not belittling the importance of such work, this paper is concerned with the lack of a clear (even if broad) conceptual framework on the part of the progressive movement in its treatment of the family. An examination of some of the rhetoric on women-headed families bears this out.

There is general consensus on the growing number of women-headed families in South Africa. However, failure to distinguish between different types of such households, for example, matrifocal and consanguinity models,[19] is a serious omission. Furthermore, the tendency to lump together *de jure* and *de facto* matrifocal families (as in most figures on homelands, for example) is highly problematic. Such an approach stems partly from the general hypothesis that 'women-headed house-holds' are both a choice on the part of women and also an assertion by women to register their independence.[20] While not totally destroying this hypothesis, this paper cautions against a superficial treatment of these issues. Complex questions should be raised from such an hypothesis.

In women-headed families women remain as a pivot. It is to the 'mother', as in conjugal families, that children look. Women's main roles in female-headed families still centre on reproductive work. There is thus a need to examine empirically to what extent women 'choose' to enter into matrifocal and/or consanguinity family forms as a 'survival strategy' to enable themselves better to perform their reproductive role; or as an attempt to question issues of sexual division of labour and their lack of economic and social independence.

Amongst low income families, women-headed families tend to be the poorest, which points to the fact that by heading households, these women's position in the production sphere does not necessarily change in any significant manner. If that is the case, then to what extent and under what circumstances can 'women-headed families' be considered progressive? This can only be established if a conceptual framework for analysing the family is drawn not just on the basis of family form, but taking gender relations as its central focus.

In South Africa the mission and goal of progressive forces is to achieve social change. Social relations are fundamental to the analysis of social change. Therefore one of the central features of women-headed households that needs to be established is the extent to which they re-define social relations, and hence roles performed by both men and women within the family and in society at large. In this way one draws a link between institutional form, roles and relations. Social change in this case would be defined as a total change in how society is organised (transformation of social relations), as opposed to just a change in the structure of domination.[21]

Towards a conceptual framework of the family

In an attempt to develop a conceptual framework of the family in a South African context, it is useful to list briefly some of the definitions of the family in the literature. This is not to suggest that a conceptual framework is in effect a definition.

Flax usefully reviews feminist debates on the family as follows:

- The sexual division of labour, especially women's exclusive responsibility for young children, which is a persistent feature of history, is a crucial factor in women's oppression and the analysis of it.

- Understanding the family, its history, psychodynamics, and relation to other social structures is a central task of feminist theory.

- The family is a complex structure composed of many elements: the sex/gender system, the varying relations to production and to other social structures, ideology, and power relations.

- The family is oppressive to women and is a primary source of the maintenance and replication of both gender and identity...

- The family as it is currently constituted must be changed. At minimum this requires the equal involvement of men and women in the care of young children.

- Gender is created by social relations experienced first in the family...

- The different roles women and men play both inside and outside the family are not natural but grow out of and are the expression of a complex series of social relations: patriarchy, economic systems, legal and ideological structures, and early childhood experiences and their unconscious residues...

- Nothing human is unchanging or absolutely unchangeable. This includes the character of childhood, the family and human nature...[22]

Pascal defines the family as a site where sex is translated into gender.[23] Barrett and McIntosh argue that it is a slippery phenomenon that is not only a social and economic institution but also an ideological construct.[24] Preston-Whyte submits that a family is a domestic unit where there was and is at least one conjugal pair – husband and wife.[25] Chant adopts Gonzalez's suggestion that it is a wide concept embracing the network of relationships maintained with kin and friends living outside the domestic unit.[26] Finally, Campbell insists that a family is a dynamic institution at the intersection of a very historically specific and complex network of social relations.[27]

Bearing in mind the above, it is worth considering a broad conceptual framework for analysing the family that takes gender relations as its focus, and then moves from that to understand gender roles and family form.[28] It has been argued that social relations are fundamental to the analysis of the concept of social change. For purposes of analysis, a further distinction needs to be made between three crucial levels of relations. Firstly, are gender relations within the family itself, that is relations between men and women? Secondly, are relations that the family enters into within its broad context (with production and with other social and political institutions)? Thirdly, are relations that men and women (as gendered species) enter into within this broad context?

An examination of this complex network or set of relations should of necessity take an historical nature. The fact that both external and internal relations need to be examined simultaneously is supported by the

Cuban experience. Concentration was put on external relations, that is, relations of production, with the hope that by drawing women into production, internal family relations would be transformed. However, because women remained immersed in reproductive work, their productive capacity was not fully utilised. The introduction of the Family Code as a legal solution to domestic work and gender relations failed because of a disjuncture between the external and internal solutions. Furthermore the role of machismo and tradition was overlooked.[29] As a result unequal gender relations persisted in Cuba.

People are socialised into specific gender roles. They enter into relationships largely on the basis of roles they can perform as their contribution within the family. In addressing gender relations, it is self-defeating to address women's roles without simultaneously addressing men's roles, both within and outside the family. This is where 'the women-headed households debate' narrows. Adding onto a woman's socially defined role some of the man's cannot be a transformation of a woman's position.

Finally, any debate on family form should fall within broader discussions of gender relations and roles. Family form in itself is not necessarily a sign of progress or regression. Therefore, reform of family law, for example, can only provide a useful institutional framework, but will not on its own produce equal gender relations. A broad conceptual framework of the family that takes as its focus gender relations, whilst simultaneously taking on board gender roles and family form, is both a planning and political task in South Africa.

Notes

1. I am indebted to Susan Bazilli for her assistance in editing this paper. Most important to me was her support and encouragement without which this work would not have been published. Secondly, I would like to thank Caroline Moser under whose supervision this work was originally done at the London School of Economics and Political Science. Last but not least is Ayanda who has always taken it upon himself to push me.
2. C Moser and L Peake, *Women, Human Settlements and Housing*, London: Tavistock, 1987.
3. See for example the articles in M van Diepen (ed), *The National Question in South Africa*, London: Zed Books, 1988.
4. Government of South Africa, 'The National Family Programme', 1988, p58.
5. Government of South Africa, 'The National Family Programme', p58.
6. Government of South Africa, 'The National Family Programme', p3.
7. Government of South Africa, 'The National Family Programme', p3.

8.   N Gwagwa, 'The Relationship between the State, the Family, and African
     Women: Towards a Post Apartheid South Africa', unpublished MSc
     dissertation, London School of Economics and Political Science, 1989.
9.   H Wolpe, *Race, Class and the Apartheid State*, Paris: Unesco, 1988.
10. Government of South Africa, 'The National Family Programme', p1.
11. See Gwagwa, 'The Relationship between the State, the Family and African
     Women', note 8 for an historical examination of this phenomenon.
12. Gwagwa, 'The Relationship between the State, the Family and African
     Women'.
13. African National Congress, *Women March to Freedom*, ANC: Lusaka, 1987.
14. African National Congress, 'ANC Second Women's Conference'
     unpublished papers, Angola, 1–6 September 1987. For an analysis of this as
     well as the concept of 'motherism' in ANC politics and the 'collusion'
     between the male leadership of the ANC with the state, see Julia Wells,
     'The Rise and Fall of Motherism as a Force in Black Women's Resistance
     Movements', *Women and Gender in Southern Africa* conference, Durban,
     1991.
15. African National Congress, *Proposed Constitutional Guidelines for a
     Democratic South Africa*, Lusaka: ANC, 1988. See also C O'Regan and C
     Murray in this volume for further comment.
16. S Hassim, 'Inkatha's Backbone: An Analysis of the Women's Brigade and
     its Role in Inkatha's Politics', paper no 23, *Workshop on Regionalism and
     Restructuring in Natal*, Durban, 1988.
17. I am referring here to the African National Congress and the affiliates
     commonly referred to as the 'Mass Democratic Movement' or MDM.
18. African National Congress, *Women March To Freedom*, note 13, p10.
19. See E Preston-Whyte, 'Women-headed Households and Development: The
     Relevance of Cross Cultural Models for Research on Black Women in
     Southern Africa', *Africanus*, 18(1/2), 1988.
20. S Hassim, J Metelerkamp and A Todes, '"A Bit on the Side?" Gender
     Struggles in the Politics of Transformation in South Africa', *Transformation*,
     5, 1987; and V van der Vliet 'Staying Single: A Strategy Against Poverty?',
     Report for the Second Carnegie Inquiry into Poverty and Development in
     Southern Africa, 1984.
21. R Ramirez, MSc Lectures, Development Planning Unit, University of
     London, 1989/90.
22. J Flax, 'The Family in Contemporary Feminist Thought: A Critical
     Review', in J Elashtain (ed), *The Family in Political Thought*, Brighton:
     Harvester, 1982, pp250–1.
23. G Pascall, *Social Policy: A Feminist Analysis*, London: Tavistock, 1986.
24. M Barrett and M McIntosh, 'The Family Wage: Some Problems for
     Socialists and Feminists', *Capital and Class*, 11, 1980.
25. Preston-Whyte, 'Women-headed Households and Development'.
26. S Chant, 'Single-parent Families: Choice or Constraint? The Formation of
     Female-headed Households in Mexican Shanty Towns', *Development and
     Change*, 16, 1985.

27. C Campbell, 'Township Families and Social Change: Towards a Working Conceptualisation of the Family for Township Research', unpublished MA dissertation, University of Natal, 1989.
28. See Campbell, 'Township Families and Social Change', for an extended discussion.
29. M Nazzari, 'The Women Question in Cuba: An Analysis of Material Constraints on its Solution', *Signs*, 9(2), 1983.

A Critical Discussion of the Law on Rape in Namibia

Dianne Hubbard

*R*ape is a serious problem in Namibia. There were 352 reported rapes in 1988, 384 in 1989 and 419 in 1990. And this is only one small part of the problem – experts believe that only about *one-twentieth* of all rapes that occur are reported to the police.[1] This means that it is likely that one woman in Namibia is raped almost every hour, every day of the year.

A recent study of rapists in South Africa talks about the 'culture of rape'. Many of the rapists interviewed in this study actually did not believe that their actions were a violation of another human being. Most of the rapists interviewed in South Africa did not even try to conceal their actions, and court cases examined in Namibia for 1988–90 indicate that the same pattern of behaviour holds true there. The underlying presumption can only be the rapist's belief that other men will support his actions. Sadly, in a society where women are regarded as objects, this presumption may be all too accurate.[2]

Sociologists and anthropologists divide the world into societies which are relatively rape-prone and societies which are relatively rape-free, a distinction which can depend on cultural attitudes about rape. For example, a society where custom, law and religion forbid rape and punish it severely will be more likely to be rape-free than a society where rape is implicitly or explicitly endorsed or condoned.[3] Other important variables which affect the incidence of rape include the general level of violence in the society, the position of women in the division of labour and the society's stereotypes about gender.[4] According to one expert:

> In a transformed society where personal development is not defined by class, race or sex, the possibilities for egalitarian relationships abound. No longer would women be treated as sexual objects, or as human beings in the service of men. And no longer would their lives be restricted by discriminatory economic, social and sexual practices. In a society devoid of sexist conceptualisations of women and men, rape would be a strange phenomenon.[5]

Our own society is permeated with myths about rape:

- Women fantasise about being raped.
- Women say 'no' when they really mean 'yes'.
- Women secretly enjoy rape.
- Women are really responsible for rapes because they dress and behave provocatively.
- Rape is not really an act of violence, it's just rough sex.
- Women often consent to sexual relations with a man and then later claim that it was rape.

These myths have crept into the laws on rape and affected the application of laws by the courts.

The Namibian constitution clearly states that women and men in Namibia are to be equal before the law.[6] Surely this must be interpreted to mean that the law will accord them equal dignity and respect. There is no place for a 'culture of rape' in a society based on a fundamental principle of sexual equality.

Legal reform alone cannot alter attitudes which are deeply embedded in our society, but it can send out signals that the prevailing myths will not be condoned by the law or by the courts. The law can reflect the fact that rape is a serious crime of violence which warrants serious punishment, and it can show its concern for the victims of rape by incorporating procedures which protect their dignity and their privacy.

The following discussion is a critical appraisal of the existing law on rape in Namibia, and the treatment of rape cases by the Namibian courts. It includes proposals for legal reform in the hope that they will be discussed by a broad cross-section of women and ultimately guide action by the government on the issue.

The problem of rape in Namibia

In the past, rape and sexual assault were elements of the war in Namibia. There were reports of members of the security forces raping women as old as 80 and girls as young as four.[7] In the years prior to independence, the Oshakati State Hospital in northern Namibia treated rape victims once a week on average, and it is difficult to determine how many cases went untreated and unreported. In some cases, women failed to report cases because of fear of retaliation, or because of feelings of shame at having been raped by the enemy. In other cases, rapes occurred in isolated areas where access to police or medical assistance was difficult. Rape was one way in which the security forces threatened the local population to try to get information about the whereabouts of PLAN guerrillas. It was also a way of exerting power.[8]

It is difficult to measure the incidence of rape. The number of reported rapes can give at least some indication of the magnitude of the problem, but it must again be noted that rape has been found to be the most under-reported of all major crimes.[9]

As noted above, in 1988, there were 352 reported rapes in Namibia. In 1989, this figure was 384, and in 1990, 419.[10] In Windhoek alone, there were 98 reported rapes in 1988, 100 in 1989, and 121 in 1990.[11]

To put these figures into context, it is necessary to compare them to the population of Namibia. This is more difficult than it would seem, as estimates of the population vary widely. For example, one government estimate based on an extrapolation from the 1981 population census estimates that the population in 1990 was 1,294 million.[12] However, the United Nations Institute for Namibia estimated that the 1985 population of Namibia was approximately 1,597 million, while the UN Department for Social and Economic Affairs estimated that the mid-1989 population of Namibia was 1,711 million.[13] It is extremely likely that the 1981 census represents an undercount of the population, as many of Namibia's inhabitants may have been afraid to give information to government representatives during the period of colonial rule. Therefore, for the purposes of this paper, the United Nations estimate of 1,7 million will be used.[14]

Approximately 51 per cent of the Namibian population is composed of women.[15] This means that there would be about 867 000 women out of a population of 1,7 million. If we take only the rapes which were reported to the police, this means that approximately one out of every 750 women in Namibia experienced a rape in the last three years alone.[16] If we factor in the estimate that only one out of every 20 rapes is reported to the police, this means that it is likely that one out of every 37 women in Namibia experienced a rape or an attempted rape in the last three years.[17] Looking at it another way, more than one woman a day has *reported* a rape or an attempted rape during the last three years, meaning that it is probable that more than 20 women a day have been raped – almost *one woman every hour*.

To try to appreciate the magnitude of the problem from yet another angle, during a single week in June 1990 there were nine reported cases of rape from regions throughout Namibia. These complaints included the rape of a woman in Rehoboth, the rape of a 20-year-old woman and a 14-year-old girl in Katutura, the rape of a 28-year-old woman in Khomasdal, two cases of rape in Mariental, the rape of a 26-year-old woman in Stampriet, the rape of a 24-year-old woman in Schlip, the rape of a 20-year-old woman in Oshakati, and the rape of a 21-year-old woman near Keetmanshoop.[18]

In Zimbabwe, which had a population of almost nine million in 1988,[19] police statistics show that 1 021 women were raped during the period January to June 1988 – this means that in Zimbabwe, a woman *reported* a rape every 4 hours and 20 minutes in 1988. The number of reported rapes rose in 1989 to the extent that police estimated that a woman reported a rape every three hours.[20] (If the differing population sizes are taken into account, this means that the extent of the problem appears to be about the same in Zimbabwe as it is in Namibia.)

In South Africa, which has a population of about 52 million,[21] it is estimated that some 300 000 women are raped each year (including both reported and unreported rapes) – this is equal to 400 women a day, or one woman every 2,7 minutes.[22] Police statistics show that there were 20 458 rape complaints in South Africa in 1988. (Here, if the differing population sizes are taken into account, either the actual incidence of rape, or perhaps the rate of reporting, is slightly higher in South Africa than in Namibia.)

And what happens when a rape is reported in Namibia? Police statistics for 1988 record the disposition of 77 per cent of the reports of rape and attempted rape which were received. Out of a total of 400 reported crimes, 265 cases (66 per cent) went to court. Only 39 cases (ten per cent) were withdrawn, and only five cases (one per cent) were deemed to be unfounded.[23]

The cases which do go to court can be tried in either the regional magistrate's court or the Windhoek High Court, which was called the Windhoek Supreme Court prior to independence. The most serious cases go to the Windhoek High Court, which can impose sentences of up to life imprisonment, and was empowered to impose the death sentence prior to independence. The regional magistrate's court can impose sentences of up to ten years or fines of up to R10 000 for a single charge.

The decision as to which court a rape case goes to is made by the prosecutor-general.

The Windhoek High Court sits only in Windhoek. The regional magistrate's court is based in Windhoek but sits at 12 different locations throughout the country, visiting each location at least once every two months.[24] There is one regional magistrate and one public prosecutor for the regional court at present.

An examination of the Supreme Court/High Court files on rape cases for the last three years provides some indication of the profile of rape at its worst in Namibia. Rape survivors[25] in these cases ranged from one to 85 years old, including women up to 36 weeks pregnant. Rapes occurred in a wide variety of situations – night and day – in the woman's home, in the veld, along the road, in playgrounds and schoolbuildings – and in every part of Namibia. There are a distressingly high number of cases involving the rape of small children, as well as cases involving multiple rapists and rapes combined with serious assaults. One son was accused of raping his mother (not guilty), and one father was accused of raping his daughter (guilty). The average age of the accused in these cases was 23–24 years old, while the average age of the rape survivors was 18–20.

The definition of rape

Rape is a common law crime in Namibia. It is defined as *intentional unlawful sexual intercourse with a woman without her consent*. The key elements of this definition are: (a) intent; (b) unlawfulness; (c) sexual intercourse with a woman; and (d) the absence of consent. Each of these elements will be critically examined below.

Intent

'Intent' means that the crime was knowingly committed. It must be present for each element of the crime. However, the question of intent generally arises in connection with the issue of consent. If the accused rapist genuinely believes that there was consent to the acts which took place, even if this belief is unreasonable, there is no intent to rape.[26]

This legal principle, which is generally applicable to most crimes, is not unreasonable in itself, but it becomes problematic when it is applied in a society that is suffused with discriminatory assumptions about interactions between men and women. For example, if the prevailing attitude about women is that 'they often say no when they really mean yes', this will certainly affect a court's interpretation of the state of mind of the accused rapist.

But what option does a woman have for expressing a lack of consent other than saying or indicating no? If the law gives weight to a woman's right to be taken seriously when she expresses an attitude about sexual willingness, this will help lead the community to a point where men and women are treated with equal dignity. If the element of consent is not removed from the definition of rape altogether, the law should at least require that a belief on the part of the accused rapist that there was consent must be a *reasonable* interpretation of the signals advanced by the woman. Also, surely physical injury to the woman should be taken as *prima facie* evidence that there was no consent on her part – and therefore no possibility that the accused rapist could have formed a reasonable belief that consent was present.[27] (*Prima facie* evidence is literally evidence *at first sight*; in other words, it is evidence which will be considered sufficient to prove the point in question unless it is refuted.)

Unlawfulness

The law defines 'unlawful sexual intercourse' as any sexual intercourse other than that which occurs between husband and wife. This means that, generally speaking, a husband cannot be found guilty of raping his wife.[28]

The most commonly-cited reason for this exemption of marital rape from the general crime of rape is that upon marriage, a woman gives her irrevocable consent to sexual intercourse with her husband for the duration of the marriage. However, as many commentators have pointed out, it seems patently absurd to interpret the marriage vows as a blanket consent to sexual intercourse at any time, under any circumstances, for years to come.

Even the law itself is inconsistent on this point. For example, if the husband uses violence to force sexual intercourse on the wife, she can charge him with assault, even though she cannot charge him with rape. It is also legally permissible for a wife to refuse to have sexual intercourse with her husband if he is suffering from a contagious venereal disease.[29]

The law is also inconsistent in the sense that its attitude about the marital relationship holds true only for what the law defines as 'normal' sex – that is, penetration of the vagina by the penis. For example, if a husband forces his wife to have oral sex, he would have no immunity against a charge of indecent assault.

Another theory that is sometimes advanced to defend the marital rape exemption is that to allow a wife to charge her husband with rape would wreck the marital relationship – as if allowing the husband to rape his wife with impunity will do the relationship no harm![30]

What the exemption of marital rape from the definition of rape really does is to reinforce the view that wives are the property of their husbands. The law does not acknowledge that women, married or single, have the right to make choices about their actions and about their bodies. The law as it stands turns marriage into a power relationship which gives the husband the right to force his wife to submit to him, at any time, regardless of her wishes.

The legal history of the offence of rape reinforces this analysis. Rape was initially regarded as a property crime – the theft of the woman's virginity. Only unmarried virgins could be raped, and the crime was not committed against the woman, but against her parent or guardian.[31]

In Roman-Dutch law, which is the primary source of common law in Namibia, married women were clearly considered to be subordinate to their husbands in all matters:

> Husbands have, in the first place, such authority over their wives as is given by the laws of nature, of God and of all nations, namely that wives must be subject to their husbands in all things which do not clearly conflict with honour and virtue. Since no power in the world can be effective without compulsion, the husband must also possess certain means of compulsion, in case the wife refuses to bow to his sway in reasonable matters.[32]

Thus the current law on marital rape has its roots in a long legal tradition of inequality.

The findings of several US studies on rape within marriage indicate that it is a serious and widespread problem:

> Marital rape may be more common than all other kinds of rape combined, and may afflict one of every eight wives or more. Marital rape is commonly found among battered wives, being identified in between 18 percent and 41 percent of samples of wife-beating victims. The motivating factors in marital rape, as in rape by strangers, are anger, the need to dominate, and occasionally sexual obsession. Marital rape causes as much or more psychological upset in the victim as non-conjugal rape and has long-term effects of equal severity.[33]

One 1982 study concluded that at least 14 per cent of *all* married women are raped by their husbands.[34]

The marital rape exemption was criticised in a 1985 Natal Provincial Division case by Nienaber, J, who stated that 'the rationale for the rule is, to say the least, suspect, its support in authority is thin, and it offends against contemporary conceptions of morality'.[35] Judge Nienaber went on to comment that

> as for policy, the ultimate criterion for determining the lawfulness of the husband's conduct, if his marital privilege is contrasted to his wife's

interest in her bodily integrity, contemporary notions of *boni mores* [public morals] will assuredly regard it as intolerably offensive that a husband should be permitted to force himself sexually on his wife.[36]

In response to a questionnaire sent out by the South African Law Commission, Mr Justice Milne called the marital rape exemption 'a barbaric piece of nonsense that should be discarded without further ado'.[37]

In South Africa, the South African Law Commission recommended that legislation be enacted making it possible for a husband to be prosecuted for the rape of his wife, so long as the consent of the attorney-general is obtained for the prosecution.[38] However, this recommendation was *not* adopted by the South African parliament, which opted for the much weaker approach of making what would otherwise constitute rape within a marriage operate as an 'aggravating circumstance' if a woman's husband is convicted of the less serious charge of assault.[39] This compromise was widely criticised.[40] For example, Mrs Helen Suzman stated that the marital rape exemption implies agreement with

> an archaic view of the wife's duty towards her husband. In other words she is his chattel and must be available to him. Whether he is drunk or disorderly or whatever, she must make herself available to him whenever he has the impulse for sexual intercourse.[41]

In contrast, the marital rape exemption has been completely abolished in a number of jurisdictions – Australia, Canada, Czechoslovakia, Denmark, Israel, Poland, Norway, Sweden, the USSR, and many states in the United States.[42] Speaking on the proposal to eliminate it in Canada in 1982, the Canadian minister of justice said:

> This spousal immunity from rape derives from the traditional belief that marriage meant irrevocable consent to sexual intercourse. If the new law is to protect the integrity of the person... marriage should no longer mean forced sexual submission.[43]

As another writer stated in an article criticising the continued existence of the marital rape exemption in England, if we 'believe that marriage is a valuable institution, we should aim towards making it a just, equal and rewarding partnership in all ways, rather than a means of subordinating one person's will to that of another'.[44]

In Namibia, the marital rape exemption may be unconstitutional in any event. Article 124 of the Namibian constitution states that men and women 'are entitled to equal rights as to marriage, during marriage, and at its dissolution'. Allowing the husband, who is frequently the physically stronger marriage partner, to force sexual intercourse on his wife with impunity thoroughly undermines the notion of equality in marriage. Furthermore, in a country which emphasises human rights and equality of persons, the institution of marriage should not require that either party sacrifice the right to full self-determination or the right to bodily integrity.

Sexual intercourse with a woman

According to the current legal definition, rape occurs only when there is penetration of a vagina by a penis. There must be penetration, although it is not necessary for there to be an emission of semen.[45] Sexual actions other than intercourse might be indecent assault, but they are not rape. Also, a sexual assault on a *man* cannot be rape.

The inadequacy of this narrow approach can be illustrated by the following examples of situations which would *not* constitute rape under the existing law:

- X, Y and Z take Jane to a lonely spot. They force her to perform oral sex on X. Y penetrates her anally. Then Z forces his fist into her vagina, ripping her internally. Jane has not been raped.
- X assaults John and penetrates him anally. John has not been raped.
- X, a woman, overpowers Hannah and forces her to perform a variety of sexual acts. Hannah has not been raped.[46]

As one writer has put it:

Who is to say that the sexual humiliation suffered through forced oral or rectal penetration is a lesser violation of the personal private inner space, a lesser injury to mind, spirit and sense of self?... All acts of sex forced on unwilling victims deserve to be treated in concept as equally grave offences in the eyes of the law, for the avenue of penetration is less significant than the intent to degrade.[47]

The law should provide a broader, gender-neutral definition for rape. In fact, the existing definition may be a violation of the provision in the Namibian constitution which provides that all persons shall be equal before the law, as it protects women against certain bodily intrusions, but provides no protection for men against analogous sexual assaults.[48]

Another problem with this element of the existing definition of rape is that it presents rape as a *sexual* experience when rape is actually a crime of *power*. For the rapist, it is domination over the body of another. For the rape survivor, it is an invasion of bodily integrity and an insult to personal dignity. It is therefore erroneous, and actually demeaning, to refer to this experience in terms of a sexual encounter; the legal definition should highlight *the coercive aspect* of rape.

Psychologists who studied the accounts of 133 convicted rapists and 92 rape survivors in the US state of Massachusetts found that the dominant motive in all of the rapes was *power* or *anger*; they did not discover a single case in which sexual satisfaction appeared to be the dominant factor. Where power is the dominant motive (as it was in 65 per cent of the cases studied), the rapist seeks to control and intimidate his victim. Where anger is the dominant motive, the rape is often an expression of generalised hatred toward women, or a desire for revenge against women. In a small number of cases, the rapists could be categorised as pathological sadists who derived pleasure, not from the sexual elements of the assault, but from the suffering of their victims.[49]

One of the central findings of a recent study of rapists in South Africa is that 'the primary motivation for rape is the offender's need for power'.[50] Another recent South African study which compared 60 white rapists and a control group of 60 white armed robbers found that only 5,9 per cent of the rapists gave a sexual reason for their crime and only 39,3 per cent of them reached orgasm during the rape. Although there were no differences between the two groups with regard to aggression in general, the rapists were found to have more unconscious aggression towards women than the control group of robbers.[51]

Rapes are often accompanied by other non-sexual forms of violence. Information gathered on arrested and convicted rapists in the United States shows that about a third of all rapes involve more than one offender and that rapes are often accompanied by beatings. Where the victim and the offender know each other, the beatings tend to be more brutal, and where the victim struggles against her attacker, she is likely to receive more serious injuries or to be killed.[52] Rapists often have a record of other violent offences, suggesting that rape may be part of a 'subculture of violence'.[53]

Paradoxically, the existing law does in some respects acknowledge that rape is a crime of power. Section 261 of the South African Criminal Procedure Act, 51 of 1977 (as it is currently in force in Namibia) provides that common assault, indecent assault and assault with intent to do grievous bodily harm are all competent verdicts on a charge of rape.[54]

The courts have also acknowledged that previous convictions for crimes characterised by the use of violence are relevant to cases of rape, even more so where such crimes of violence also indicate a tendency to sexual deviation.[55]

Rape should first and foremost be conceptualised as an *assault*; the sexual aspect of the offence should be viewed only as a way of *categorising* the assault as one which is particularly invasive of personal integrity.

Absence of consent

As the law stands, the absence of consent is often the key element of the crime of rape. Generally speaking, consent must be freely and consciously given by a woman with the mental ability to understand what she is consenting to, and it must be based on a true knowledge of the material facts relating to the intercourse.[56]

The law does not require that either consent or lack of consent be expressed; either may be demonstrated by the woman's conduct. Thus, this can be a tricky and subjective question of fact which is coloured by societal attitudes about sex, rape and women.

The courts have recognised that *submission* by a woman is not necessarily *consent*: 'if her will is overborne by fear or intimidation as a result of which she fails to offer any outward resistance, this appearance of submission is not to be equated with consent.'[57] 'All the circumstances must be taken into account to determine whether passivity is proof of implied consent or whether it is merely the abandonment of outward resistance which the woman, while persisting in her objection to intercourse, is afraid to display or realises is useless.'[58] However, it has also been stated that 'it is essential that the victim's resistance be overcome by fear, force or fraud. When it is overcome by the prompting of her own passions, to the stimulation of which she consented, there can be no question of rape'.[59]

The law recognises that consent to intercourse can be vitiated in certain circumstances. For example, consent which is induced by threats or by certain kinds of fraud cannot prevent a rape conviction.[60] Also, factors such as mental defects or intoxication may be taken into account in the question of whether a person was capable of giving meaningful consent to sexual intercourse.[61] A girl under the age of 12 years is considered legally incapable of consenting to sexual intercourse.[62]

Making the absence of consent an element of the crime of rape places a portion of the burden of proof on the rape survivor. However, the law does not impose this requirement on the victims of other crimes, such as burglary or assault. In the case of crimes other than rape, consent is at most a *defence* that can be raised by the *accused*.[63]

As a practical matter, it is always more difficult to prove the *absence* of a thing in court. It is the issue of consent that usually stimulates questions about the woman's sexual history, or allegations of promiscuity, or suggestions that the woman's clothing or behaviour were provocative; it is this approach to the crime which puts the victim 'on trial' as well as the accused.[64]

The question of consent is a particularly difficult one in Namibia, because women in some communities are socialised to resist voluntary sexual encounters initially and not to 'give in' too easily.[65] This custom makes it all the more difficult to ascertain where consent has actually and freely been given.

The central issue in the charge of rape should be not the *absence* of consent, but the *presence* of coercion. If the focus is on the behaviour of the rapist, then the question is whether force or threats of force were used, instead of whether the woman's behaviour can legitimately be considered consent.

This is particularly important because of the prevalence of myths about rape, specially because of the widespread assumption that women 'say no when they really mean yes'. It is truly amazing to consider some of the behaviour by women that has been interpreted as 'consent' by men. For example, in a 1985 South African case, the accused argued that 'when she uttered a scream and threatened him with [a charge of] rape and the police, he thought that she was joking and tried to prolong foreplay'.[66] In another case, a 39-year-old woman was pulled into a car, raped by six men in succession and then pushed out of the car while it was still in motion. Her clothes were torn, her spectacles were broken and her face and body were bruised. The accused rapists admitted using force to get her into the car, but argued that they were 'only preventing a generally willing woman from wasting time by buying cigarettes'.[67]

It is far more logical to focus on the behaviour of the accused rapist instead of pegging rape cases to the troublesome question of consent. Such a change of focus would help the courts escape some of the myths about rape.[68]

However, in looking at the behaviour of the accused rapist, the law and the courts must remember that physical force is only one kind of coercion. Coercion can also take the form of threats of physical force, the use of economic leverage, fraud (for example, men have been known to manoeuvre women into vulnerable situations by posing as psychologists or pretending to look for fashion models), or even taking advantage of a subtle set of circumstances (such as where a woman finds herself alone with a larger man in a strange neighbourhood, or where there is a past history of violence in a relationship which communicates an implicit threat of force).[69] If the law switches its focus to the words and actions of the accused rapist, the definition of coercion must be broad enough to encompass all situations which may overpower another person's freedom of choice.

If the element of consent is not completely removed from the definition of rape, then the law should at least make it clear that simply saying or indicating 'no' is sufficient to constitute non-consent. As one commentator states:

> Viewing women as autonomous human beings would mean treating them as persons who know what they want and mean what they say. A woman who wanted sex would say yes; a woman who did not would say no, and those verbal signals would be respected.[70]

Traditional customs

The existence of any traditional custom which might permit rape in certain circumstances is *not* in itself a defence against a charge of rape.[71] However, although such customs are not technically defences, they may affect the perception of the event by the rapist, the rape survivor and the community. For example, in some communities in Namibia, it is customary for a widow to be passed into the custody of her late husband's brother. Although the origin of this custom is to ensure material security for the widow, there have also been sexual implications in some instances.[72]

Similarly, in some Namibian communities, an uncle is perceived as having a clear right to sexual intercourse with his niece. This is not considered rape, because women in these communities are educated in this custom and therefore generally agree to such sexual relations.[73] Furthermore, there is also a custom which may still be practised in some Namibian communities, whereby an uncle is given permission to acquaint a niece who has just reached sexual maturity with the facts about sexual relationships by having intercourse with her.[74] In such cases, does the woman feel that she has a right to refuse? Does the man understand that there can be a coercive aspect in the force of tradition? Do sexual relations under such circumstances constitute a rape?

These are difficult questions to answer, and they help to demonstrate why legal reform alone will not be sufficient to make Namibia into a rape-free society. Community organisations can help to empower women by communicating the idea that women have the right to self-determination in all the spheres of their lives – the right to say 'no' as well as the right to say 'yes'. This problem also illustrates why reducing the incidence of rape in Namibia must go hand-in-hand with making the equality of the sexes an everyday reality.

Traditional customs may also reduce the likelihood that a rape will be reported to the police. For example, in some communities in Namibia, rape is considered a domestic matter which should not be discussed outside the confines of the immediate family. Women who have been raped are also considered in some communities to be 'bad women' who are no longer good candidates for marriage, thus providing further discouragement against making an official report.[75] Again, in order to combat such perceptions, legal reform must be combined with community education and the empowerment of women.

Age of victim

If a girl is under the age of 12 years, she cannot legally consent to sexual intercourse. However, if the accused believed that there was consent and did not realise that the girl could be under the age of 12, then the element of intent may be absent.[76]

Age of offender

There is an irrebuttable common-law presumption that boys under the age of 14 are incapable of sexual intercourse. This is obviously a legal fiction, as there are a number of reported cases in which boys under the age of 14 have in fact engaged in sexual intercourse.[77]

In South Africa, the South African Law Commission recommended that this presumption be abolished.[78] This suggestion was adopted by the South African parliament; section 1 of the Law of Evidence and the Criminal Procedure Act Amendment Act, 103 of 1987 abolished the common-law presumption and provided that evidence may be adduced to prove that a boy under the age of 14 years has in fact had sexual intercourse with a female. However, this Act was not made applicable to Namibia.

Related statutory offences

The common law on rape is supplemented by the Combatting of Immoral Practices Act, 21 of 1980.[79] This Act makes it an offence for a male to have or attempt to have intercourse with a girl under the age of 16, to commit or attempt to commit an immoral or indecent act with such a girl, or to solicit or entice such a girl to the commission of an immoral or indecent act. This offence is punishable by up to six years imprisonment, with or without a fine of up to R3 000.[80] The Act also defines certain defences which are available to the accused; he can escape conviction (1) if the girl is a prostitute, he was under 21 at the time the offence was committed, and it is his first such offence, or (2) if he is under 16 and the girl deceived him into believing that she was over 16 years of age.[81]

It is also an offence under the Act for a male to have sexual intercourse with 'any female idiot or imbecile' in circumstances which do not amount to rape, to commit an immoral or indecent act with such a woman, or to solicit or entice such a woman to the commission of an immoral or indecent act. (Presumably, where the circumstances of the offence do constitute rape, a charge of rape would be laid instead of a charge under the Act.) The punishment for this offence can be up to six years imprisonment, with or without a fine of up to R3 000.[82]

The Act also makes it an offence to administer, apply or cause a woman to take any drug, intoxicating liquor, matter or thing with the intent to stupefy or overpower her to enable unlawful sexual intercourse. This offence is punishable by imprisonment for up to five years.[83]

Possibilities for change

The law needs a new definition of rape.

> To a woman the definition of rape is fairly simple. A sexual invasion of the body by force, an incursion into the private, personal inner space without consent – in short, an internal assault from one of several avenues and by one of several methods – constitutes a deliberate violation of emotional, physical and rational integrity, and is a hostile, degrading act of violence that deserves the name of rape.[84]

However, to some women, the term 'rape', with all its associated myths, carries a social stigma that deflects attention from the violence of the crime. 'Rape' in many jurisdictions has become sexual assault, sexual battery, criminal sexual penetration, criminal sexual conduct or sexual abuse.[85] Many new statutes include a continuum of offences of graduated degrees of seriousness, depending on such factors as the degree of coercion used, the amount of injury inflicted, and the age of the victim. These offences generally include a broad spectrum of sexual contact, not only penetration of a vagina by a penis, and they give equal protection to both men and women who have suffered a sexual assault.

Perhaps most importantly, progressive definitions of rape have removed consent as an element of the crime, focusing instead on the coercion used by the rapist, to reflect the reality that rape is a crime of force and not one of passion.

Examples from other countries

One example of a progressive rape statute is the one adopted in the US state of Michigan.[86] This statute covers a graduated ladder of offences called 'criminal sexual conduct', which are classified as 'first, second, third or fourth degree', depending on their severity. 'Criminal sexual conduct' includes 'sexual penetration', which is defined as:

> sexual intercourse, cunnilingus, fellatio, anal intercourse, or any other intrusion, however slight, of any part of a person's body or of any object into the genital or anal openings of another person's body, but emission of semen is not required.

It also includes, as a lesser degree of the offence, 'sexual contact', which is defined as:

> the intentional touching of the victim's or actor's intimate parts or the intentional touching of the clothing covering the immediate area of the victim or actor's intimate parts, if that intentional touching can reasonably be construed as being for the purpose of sexual arousal or gratification.[87]

The Michigan statute criminalises any sexual penetration which is accomplished by means of 'force or coercion', which is defined to include physical force, threats of physical force, and threats of future retaliation against the victim or any other person, including threats of physical punishment, kidnapping or extortion.

Thus, the Michigan statute focuses entirely on the conduct of the *defendant*; the question of consent by the victim arises only if the defendant puts forward some evidence of consent as a defence in a case where there is little or no evidence of force.

One serious weakness in the approach adopted by Michigan is that the definition of criminal sexual contact focuses on 'sexual arousal or gratification', rather than acknowledging that the purpose of such contact is more likely power or control by the actor over the victim.

A second fundamental weakness is that the Michigan statute's definition of force or coercion is too narrow; the cited examples do not give enough emphasis to non-physical forms of coercion, such as threatening to dismiss someone from a job, or to ruin a person's reputation. Another weakness is that it allows a spouse to lay a charge of criminal sexual conduct against the other spouse only if they are living apart and one spouse has filed for separate maintenance or divorce. However, on the whole, the Michigan law is considered to represent one of the most progressive reforms to date, and it has produced a marked increase in arrests and convictions for rape-related offences.

Similarly, the crime of 'rape' no longer exists in Canada. Instead, there are three graduated offences of sexual assault which are distinguished purely in terms of the level of violence involved. No distinction is drawn between penetration and other forms of sexual contact. Assault is defined as an act committed without the victim's consent, meaning that the prosecution must still prove the absence of consent. However, the statute lists a number of circumstances in which consent will be *deemed* to be absent, including situations where there is force or a threat of force. As noted above, the marital rape exemption has been abolished completely in Canada.

The report from the Law Reform Commission of Canada which recommended these reforms stated as its central proposition that

> rape is actually a form of assault and should therefore perhaps be treated as such under the law... The concept of sexual assault more appropriately characterizes the actual nature of the offence of rape because the primary focus is on the assault or the violation of the integrity of the person rather than the sexual intercourse.[88]

As noted above, categorising rape as an assault emphasises its nature as an act of violence and puts the focus on the actions of the rapist rather than on the actions of the rape survivor. However, this approach has been criticised on the grounds that it may understate the particular psychological harm suffered by the rape victim. Some commentators feel that to change the label of the crime is to risk 'obscuring the unique meaning and understanding of the indignity and harm of "rape"', which is 'a different and much more serious affront than assault'.[89]

A compromise might be to view rape as sexual assault, an approach which would stress rape's essentially violent nature while also recognising the particularly complex kind of damage rape inflicts.[90]

Namibia needs to reform the definition of rape along these lines. The main elements of a new law on rape should be:

- A focus on rape as a sexual assault rather than an act of sexual intercourse.
- A focus on the actions of the accused rapist rather than the question of consent by the rape survivor.[91]
- A gender-neutral definition of sexual assault.
- A recognition that a wide range of sexual contact is just as violative of the integrity of the individual as penetration of a vagina by a penis.
- The complete elimination of the marital rape exemption.

Procedure

There are two rules of evidence which make it particularly difficult to secure convictions for rape – one is the 'hue and cry rule' and the other is the 'cautionary rule'. Both of these rules reflect the prevailing societal myth that women are inclined to fabricate charges of rape, and should be discarded.

The most frequently-quoted statement of this myth comes from a prominent seventeenth-century English jurist, Lord Hale, who wrote that 'Rape is an accusation easily to be made and hard to be proved, and harder to be defended by the party accused, tho' never so innocent'.[92] In 1975, Susan Brownmiller made the following comment on this legal proverb:

> Since four out of five rapes go unreported, it is fair to say categorically that women do not find rape 'an accusation easily to be made'. Those who do report their rape soon find, however, that it is indeed 'hard to be proved'. As for the party accused... by and large a successful legal defense is nothing short of a cinch.[93]

This critique of the myth is even more valid today, now that recent studies have estimated that as many of 19 out of 20 rapes go unreported.[94]

There is also an urgent need for procedural changes which will protect the dignity and privacy of the rape survivor. At the moment, most rape survivors must testify about their intensely painful and traumatic experiences in open court, where they are often cross-examined on their previous sexual experiences or accused of being provocative by counsel for the alleged rapist. The rape survivor's character often comes under brutal attack in the course of a legal process which she may find bewildering. Yet, while the accused rapist has a lawyer present to defend his interests, there is no one whose primary task is to protect the rape survivor and her reputation. These procedural problems are examined in more detail below.

The 'hue and cry rule'

Generally speaking, in all criminal proceedings, evidence of previous consistent statements are inadmissible. In other words, a witness cannot add weight to his or her testimony by having other people testify that the witness made similar statements to them at some previous time. The rationale behind this rule is that if such statements were admissible, a witness would be able to bolster his or her credibility by simply repeating the same story to a number of people before testifying in court.[95]

There are a few exceptions to this evidentiary rule; one of them concerns complaints in cases of rape and other sexual offences.[96] Evidence that a rape survivor made a complaint soon after the alleged offence, and the specific details of that complaint, are admissible in court to show the consistency of the complainant's evidence. The previous complaint is admissible only for the purposes of corroboration; it cannot be used as independent evidence of the offence.[97] The admissibility of a previous consistent statement made by a rape survivor is not in itself problematic, as it merely allows the introduction into evidence of information which can corroborate the complainant's story. However, the exception comes trailing with it a history that may actually *undermine* the rape survivor's credibility.

In mediaeval England, an accused rapist could raise as a defence the fact that the complainant had not 'raised the hue and cry' immediately after the alleged offence. By the eighteenth century, it was considered to be a strong indication that the woman's story was false if she had not made a complaint within a reasonable time after the offence.[98]

Aspects of this history survive in the modern-day application of the rule. To be admissible, a complaint must have been made at the first reasonable opportunity after the offence. The question of what constitutes a reasonable lapse of time is a matter for the discretion of the judge, who may take into account the age and understanding of the complainant, and what opportunities there were for speaking to a person in whom she could reasonably be expected to confide.[99]

However, aside from questions of admissibility, the older form of the 'hue and cry rule' still operates in the sense that the courts sometimes question the credibility of the complainant if she did *not* make a complaint immediately after the alleged rape. For example, in an Appellate Division case in South Africa, Botha, JA allowed an appeal from a conviction of rape for the following reasons:

> ... I do not doubt the correctness of the magistrate's observation that the complainant's distress in the witness stand was genuine, nor his inference that it was also genuine when she went to the police. But that her distress was genuine means only that it was not simulated. It would be extremely dangerous, in my opinion, to regard the complainant's genuine distress in this particular case as a sufficient safeguard in itself for accepting that she was telling the truth. Her distress might well have been induced by her private knowledge that her charge against the appellant was a false one. There are cases, of course, where evidence of a complainant's distress at the time of making a complaint may be a powerful factor in satisfying the cautionary rule [see the discussion below on this rule]... In my judgement, however, the present is not such a case. On the complainant's own evidence, there was *an unexplained time lapse of considerable duration from the commission of the act of intercourse until the making of the complaint.* On the appellant's evidence, something happened in between which could have induced the laying of a false charge, as well as the signs of distress on the part of the complainant.[100]

Of course, this particular decision may well have been a correct one in light of the evidence before the court, particularly since we do not know what information was produced as a motive for a false charge by the complainant. However, in all fairness, the court should have also taken note of the fact that there are many legitimate reasons why rape victims may not make a complaint promptly – transport problems for those who live in remote areas, the trauma of the crime, hesitancy to discuss intimate or embarrassing details with a stranger, the very real fear that they will be 'accused' of consenting to the act.

Another example of the 'hue and cry rule' in action is a rape case heard in April 1990 by the High Court in Windhoek, where a 28-year-old man was charged with raping an eight-year-old girl. According to a newspaper report on the trial, the accused admitted to having previously attempted to have sexual intercourse with the girl, but said that he had been too big for her. He testified that he had abandoned the attempt when his girlfriend called from the next room. The girl subsequently complained of pain in her abdomen, and a medical examination revealed that she had been raped. On the advice of the doctor, the girl's aunt, who is her guardian, did not ask her what had happened. However, several days later, the girl told her aunt that the accused had engaged in sexual intercourse with her without her consent.

In his judgement, the judge noted that the permissibility of the report made by the girl to her aunt depended on the amount of time which had elapsed since the alleged offence. In this case, the crime had been reported only two to three weeks after it had allegedly occurred. The girl testified that she had not told her aunt earlier because she was afraid that her aunt would shout at her. The judge concluded that the report of the incident made by the girl to her aunt was probably not admissible as evidence. The defendant was ultimately acquitted.[101]

The exclusion of the girl's statement to her aunt was only one of many factors in the case which led to the acquittal, but we may still ask whether cases like this one *might* be decided differently if the law formally recognised the many understandable reasons why the victim of a sexual assault may not 'raise the hue and cry' immediately after the commission of the crime.

It should also be noted that it does not conversely strengthen the complainant's case if she *does* raise an immediate 'hue and cry'; evidence that a complaint *was* made immediately after an alleged offence took place *cannot* be used to confirm the truth of the complainant's testimony.[102]

The following observations relate to the effect of a delay in reporting a rape in the English legal system:

Defence Counsel invariably refers to any delay in reporting in cross-examination and comments on it in the closing speech; not making an immediate formal complaint is sometimes referred to as 'an extraordinary thing to do going against what you'd expect a girl who has been raped to do'. Is there any systematic link between the time of reporting a rape and the verdict? The findings of this study suggest that there is. About 40 per cent of the victims reported the offence following some delay after the departure of their assailant ranging from one day to around three months. The conviction rate for those accused of the rape of late reporters was 38 per cent as compared to 73 per cent for those whose victims made an immediate complaint.[103]

The 'cautionary rule'

The courts have identified several kinds of evidence which need to be treated with particular caution in deciding whether guilt in a criminal case has been proved beyond a reasonable doubt. Among such categories of evidence are the uncorroborated evidence of a single witness; the evidence of an accomplice to the crime; the evidence of young children – and the uncorroborated evidence of the complainant in cases which involve so-called 'sexual offences' such as rape.[104]

One of the leading cases on this point includes the following explanation of the rationale for the 'cautionary rule' in sexual cases:

> In rape cases for instance, the established and proper practice is not to require that the complainant's evidence be corroborated before a conviction is competent. But what is required is that the trier of fact should have clearly in mind that these cases of sexual assault require special treatment, that charges of the kind are generally difficult to disprove, and that various considerations may lead to their being falsely laid.[105]

It is not even necessary that there be any evidence of a motive for a false charge; the 'cautionary rule' allows the court to speculate, as the following statement from another rape case illustrates:

> In the present case, a number of possible motives for the complainant to have acted as the appellant alleged she did, suggest themselves. She may have been overcome by shame, disgust or remorse (perhaps even alcoholic remorse) at the fact that she had consented to intercourse with the appellant; she may have been sexually frustrated because of the appellant's drunken state (he may not have realised that they both did not enjoy the act); she may have been filled with revulsion at the unusual sexual acts to which the appellant had wanted her to submit, whether or not she was a willing party to such acts (as distinct from the act of intercourse); or she may simply have become afraid, with the coming of

the morning, that her male friend would arrive at the flat. *It is true that these possibilities are speculative and that a court is not usually required to speculate on possibilities having no foundation in the evidence placed before it...* but if the appellant were telling the truth there was no way in which he could have offered any explanation in evidence for the complainant's conduct, and *possibilities of the kind I have mentioned are inherently present in the circumstances of a case such as the present.* It is precisely because of the difficulty of discerning hidden motives that cases of this nature require special treatment.[106]

As the previous passage suggests, the range of reasons which the courts have cited for false charges in sexual cases is stunningly imaginative. One recent case quotes Glanville Williams, who relies in turn on Wigmore:

> ... [T]hese cases are particularly subject to the danger of deliberately false charges, resulting from sexual neuroses, fantasy, jealousy or simply a girl's refusal to admit that she consented to an act of which she is now ashamed. Of these various possibilities, the most subtle are those connected with mental complexes. Wigmore, who recites a number of instances where women have brought false sexual charges against men, explains one of the motivations as follows: 'The unchaste (let us call it) mentality finds incidental but direct expression in the narration of imaginary sex-incidents of which the narrator is the heroine or the victim. On the surface the narration is straightforward and convincing. The real victim, however, too often in such cases is the innocent man; for the respect and sympathy naturally felt by any tribunal for a wronged female helps to give easy credit to such a plausible tale.'[107]

It is hard to think of any other area of law in which the courts would be so willing to indulge in amateur psychology, without any supporting evidence from expert witnesses. Other reasons for caution which have been cited by the courts include the following:

- 'Where pregnancy has supervened and in that way it has become necessary for the girl to explain her condition, she may be tempted to shield some young friend who is the actual wrongdoer and to implicate someone of relatively sound financial standing who may be better able than the actual father of the child about to be born to provide it with maintenance'.[108]
- 'As a mode of obtaining vengeance for any affront to a woman's pride or dignity, the bringing of a charge of this kind is probably without equal. The very fact that the charge is brought at all is calculated to damage the man even if he is eventually acquitted'.[109]
- The difficulty of refuting a charge of sexual immorality.[110]

- Hysteria that can cause a neurotic victim to imagine things which did not happen.[111]
- Wounded vanity and spite against the person who may have rejected one's advances.[112]

Where there is no corroboration of the complainant's testimony in a case of rape, the court may look for other indications of trustworthiness, such as the falsity of the evidence of the accused.[113]

Thus, in cases of rape where the testimony of the complainant is uncorroborated, in addition to the understandable cautionary approach which the court is expected to take in *any* criminal case where there is a single witness against the accused, the court is to consider *other* reasons for caution which apply *only* to cases involving 'sexual offences'. In other words, where the rape survivor is the only witness against the accused rapist (as is often the case), the court must apply a '*double cautionary rule*'.[114]

This approach can only perpetuate the myth that women have a tendency to falsely 'cry rape'. In fact, the taking of extra precautions in rape cases is particularly *unnecessary*, since a woman who alleges that she has been raped is often accused of provocation or promiscuity; at best, she must be prepared to discuss with strangers details that may be painful or embarrassing to recount.

A US study found that the incidence of false reports for rape is *exactly the same* as that for other felonies – about two per cent.[115] Furthermore, as noted above, studies of the incidence of rape indicate that as many as *19 out of every 20* rapes are *unreported*. In a world with so many disincentives for women to report rapes which actually took place, is there really a need for such exaggerated concern about false charges of rape?

The Canadian legal reforms discussed above now prohibit the judge in a sexual offence case from requiring corroboration simply because of the category of offence. The requirement of corroboration in cases of sexual offences has also been repealed in most states in the Unites States and in Israel.[116]

The cautionary rule for single witnesses which applies equally to all crimes in Namibia is surely sufficient to protect against the possibility of wrongful convictions in cases involving 'sexual offences' as well.

Evidence of the character of the victim

In a prosecution for rape, the accused may lead evidence on the complainant's lack of chastity in order to try to discredit her testimony. On the issue of consent, the complainant may be cross-examined on sexual acts with other men, or on other sexual acts with the accused.[117]

The South African Law Commission examined this practice in its report 'Women and Sexual Offences in South Africa' and noted that it has been criticised as a relic from 'the days when it was a generally accepted code of conduct that no decent woman had sexual intercourse outside marriage'. The report observed that the complainant's character is often unnecessarily and unfairly attacked in court, noting that the disclosure of previous sexual history may be a traumatic experience for the complainant.[118]

The report examined legislation on this point in other jurisdictions and noted two trends. One approach has been to prohibit all evidence and cross-examination on the complainant's prior sexual behaviour and character, with the exception of prior sexual acts with the accused. Another approach has been to leave decisions on whether or not to allow evidence and cross-examination on sexual acts with persons other than the accused to the discretion of the judicial officer. The commission recommended that evidence on the complainant's prior conduct with persons other than the accused be prohibited, unless special permission was received after an application made *in camera* (in private, such as in a closed court or in the judge's chambers).[119]

The recommendation of the South African Law Commission on this point was followed in South Africa. In 1989, section 227 of the Criminal Procedure Act, 1977, was amended in South Africa to provide that neither direct evidence nor cross-examination regarding previous sexual experiences of the rape survivor is permissible, except with the express leave of the court. Such leave shall be granted only if the court is satisfied that the evidence is relevant, and the judge or magistrate must clear the court of all unnecessary persons before an application for such leave is heard. Subject to this limitation, evidence of the general character of the complainant continues to be admissible.[120]

This amendment was not made applicable to Namibia, where section 227 of the Criminal Procedure Act still reads as follows: 'Evidence as to the character of an accused or as to the character of any woman upon or with regard to whom any offence of an indecent nature has been committed, shall be admissible...'[121]

Thus, there is no limitation in Namibia on the admissibility of evidence about the rape survivor's sexual history. In contrast, evidence regarding previous convictions of the accused rapist is generally admissible only *after* conviction, as a factor which is relevant to the imposition of sentence.[122]

In Michigan, the statute which is discussed above also strictly regulates the scope of evidence about the sexual history of the complainant which is admissible – such evidence is allowed *only* where it involves past sexual conduct with the defendant, or where it relates to the origin of semen, pregnancy or disease.[123]

Police procedure

In Namibia, the police training material currently in use requires that rape cases must be dealt with by experienced investigators – someone with the rank of senior sergeant or above. The investigator is directed to be 'sympathetic' towards the complainant during interrogation. Where a minor is involved, police are instructed that her parents or guardian should be present during questioning, or, where this is not possible, another woman such as a policewoman. Police in Windhoek say that their policy is to try to have all rape cases dealt with by a policewoman, but the small number of women in the police force means that the investigating officer will in fact usually be male.[124]

The common myths about rape were discussed in a seminar conducted by a rape-counselling organisation, Women's Solidarity, for 18 plainclothes detectives in Windhoek in October 1990.[125] Because of police experience with actual rape cases, they do not suffer from many of the misconceptions about the crime that affect the rest of society. However, there were two myths about rape which did operate strongly within police ranks.

The first of these is the myth that rape is an uncontrollable act of sexual gratification perpetrated by abnormal perverts. It was difficult for men in a male-dominated society to come to terms with the concept of rape as a violent crime with sex as a weapon rather than a crime with sex as a motive.

The second myth that gave difficulty was the belief that women are prone to lay false rape reports. The police quoted several cases in which it appeared that a woman laid a charge of rape against a man who did not pay for sex as agreed upon before the act; in other words, rape as a cover for prostitution. There is no denying that prostitution is a complex social problem in Namibia, but a study of rape cases heard by the courts also reveals that in a number of cases where the accused was *convicted* of rape, he tried to defend himself by *alleging* that the woman consented to the act and requested money; obviously, confusion between rape and prostitution can be either a reality behind a false rape charge *or* an excuse to hide a genuine rape.

The police cited other cases in which a woman withdrew a rape complaint after the rapist or his family had offered her compensation in the form of money. This does indeed happen, but it would be a misunderstanding to interpret such cases as false charges of rape. It is traditional in some Namibian communities, particularly in the north, for a person who has suffered damage of any sort from another person, be it physical, emotional or material, to be entitled to payment in concrete form (such as money or cattle) from the offender. This serves as both punishment for the perpetrator and compensation for the victim (the latter of which is usually not provided by western legal systems without a separate legal action), and it is a procedure which takes place in crimes of many varieties.[126] Thus, when a case is withdrawn after such payment is made, it should not be seen as an indication that the rape report was false, but merely that it has been dealt with in an alternative manner.

The myth that women often lay false charges of rape affects the way that the police respond to rape charges. Where a police officer doubts the truth of the charge, he 'validates the victimisation' of the rape survivor, and there is little chance of a serious investigation of the case.[127] And yet, as has been noted above, there is no evidence that false charges of rape are laid any more often than false charges of any other crime.

The investigating police officer is often one of the first people to whom the rape survivor relates the incident in detail, so the way in which this officer responds can be extremely significant. Rape survivors would be better served by the police if all rape cases were investigated by officers, women where possible, who have had special training in the facts about sexual offences and in rape-counselling techniques. (Namibia might follow the example of Zimbabwe, where police reportedly receive extensive training in how to handle rape survivors.)[128]

There is another aspect of police procedure which should be considered – the identification parade. If the rape survivor does not know the rapist by name, she may be asked to pick him out from a line-up of several men. The procedure generally followed in such identification parades requires that the complainant or the witness identify the suspect by touching him on the shoulder. The purpose of this procedure is to eliminate any possibility of misunderstanding the identification. This is *not* a rule of law, but merely a standard police practice. Legal commentators on this procedure have stated that 'there may be circumstances where the identifying witness may be scared to approach and touch the suspect. In these circumstances, any other form of identification should suffice, for example merely pointing out the suspect'.[129]

The potential for trauma to the rape survivor in the standard procedure is obvious. It is perhaps made worse by the fact that the rape survivor most often has no lawyer or friend present to provide support. Ideally, the rape survivor should be allowed to view the identification line-up through one-way glass and indicate the rapist verbally. At the very least, no rape survivor should be requested by the police to make physical contact with the alleged rapist.

Medical procedure

Rape survivors who arrive at a hospital for treatment should be examined in private, by a female physician if possible, and they should be told how to contact a counselling service. They should also be advised to have tests for pregnancy and AIDS performed at the appropriate time. Doctors who examine rape survivors should be knowledgeable about the kinds of medical evidence which can help to secure a conviction against the rapist so that they will know what to look for.

Some rape crisis services have worked in co-operation with other institutions to set up innovative approaches for assisting rape survivors with the medical aspects of the ordeal. For example, in New Zealand, there is a Sexual Assault Centre which combines medical treatment and counselling. It is staffed by a roster of doctors who have received special training regarding the treatment of sexual abuse, as well as education on collecting forensic evidence and on presenting medical evidence effectively in court. Police sometimes take statements at the Sexual Assault Centre while a counsellor is present.[130]

Legal practitioners in Namibia have emphasised the importance of teaching medical personnel to collect good medical evidence, which can be crucial to the prosecution of a rape case. In smaller towns in Namibia, the standard medical form used in rape cases is sometimes completed by a less-experienced nurse rather than a doctor because of the unavailability of doctors. Even where a doctor fills in the form, an examination of case files shows that the information is often incomplete. A discussion of the importance of medical evidence in legal proceedings could be incorporated into workshops on violence against women for the medical profession.

Other procedural issues

South Africa

In South Africa, several procedural improvements have been made in the legal process:

- Publication of the name of a complainant in a rape case is now forbidden, unless authorised by a magistrate on an application made in chambers, giving due regard to the complainant's wishes.[131]

- Evidence by the complainant in any trial involving a sexual offence *must* now be heard in closed court unless the complainant requests otherwise.[132] The current position in Namibia – which was the position in South Africa prior to the 1987 amendment – is that such evidence will be heard in private only if the court grants a request from the complainant to this effect.[133]

- In 1989, the South African parliament went one small step further towards redressing the exemption of marital rape from the definition of the crimes of rape by providing that: 'Whenever a man has been convicted of assault in any form on his lawful wife and could, but for the existence of the marriage relationship between them at the time of the commission of the crime, have been convicted of rape, the fact that he could have been convicted of rape had he not been married to his wife, shall be regarded by the court as an aggravating circumstance at the passing of sentence.'[134] Thus, the law in South Africa continues to move gradually in the direction of abolishing the illogical marital rape exemption, but without going far enough.

None of these amendments is applicable to Namibia.

Swaziland

In Swaziland, where the definition of rape is the same as that in Namibia, the law was amended in 1986 to make provision for holding rape trials in closed court. The same amendment made it an offence to publish any information as to the identity of the rape victim, the place of the offence or the name of any witness.[135]

Denmark

In Denmark, rape victims have their own legal representation in court and are usually awarded financial compensation by the court where the defendant is convicted.[136]

Summary of proposals for procedural change in Namibia

The primary components of procedural change should be as follows:

- The law should formally recognise that there may be many valid reasons why a rape survivor may not report a rape immediately after it occurs.
- The 'cautionary rule' for cases involving sexual offences should be discarded.
- Evidence about the rape survivor's prior sexual conduct, with the exception of prior sexual acts with the accused, should be inadmissible.
- Police officers who deal with rape cases should receive special training in the facts about sexual offences and in rape counselling techniques.
- Rape survivors should not be required to make physical contact with the alleged rapist in identification parades.

- Medical personnel should be trained in the importance of collecting medical evidence in rape cases.
- Publication of the name of the complainant in rape cases should be prohibited.
- The evidence of the complainant should be heard in closed court unless the complainant requests otherwise.

Punishment
Relevant factors

The following factors are considered by the courts to be relevant to the degree of punishment imposed for rape:

- Previous convictions for rape.
- The degree of violence used.
- Whether physical or psychological injuries were inflicted, and their severity.
- The age and the health of the victim (for example, the crime may be considered more serious if the victim is very young or very old).
- The victim's character.
- Premeditation.[137]

In a 1958 Appellate Division case in South Africa, Schreiner, JA stated the following:

> The character of the complainant has always, and rightly, been regarded as of significance in deciding upon the penalty to be imposed upon the raptor. Rape upon a prostitute, for example, though it is the crime of rape would not ordinarily call for a penalty of equal severity to that imposed for rape upon a woman of refinement and good character.[138]

In another case, 'the consideration that the appellant's victim is *a lady of refinement*' was held to be a proper factor to take into account in sentencing.[139] Judicial consideration of the character of the rape survivor as a factor in imposing punishment implies that her character and degree of sexual experience are determinative in part of the seriousness of the crime. This merely reinforces the myth that some women really want to be raped, or at least do not mind too much. Is this the message that we want the law to send out?[140]

In a recent case in the High Court of Zimbabwe, Muchechetere, J, criticised a lower court for considering the complainant's 'questionable morals' a mitigating factor in the sentencing of her rapist:

There is, in my view, no reason why persons who rape prostitutes should be treated lightly when the prostitutes have neither made overtures to nor shown any interest in them. A prostitute in circumstances of this nature should be treated like any other complainant. A difference in treatment would be sending the wrong message to would-be rapists, which is that if they rape prostitutes they should receive lighter sentences in courts.[141]

Like the existing definition of rape, the consideration of the rape survivor's character puts the focus of the law on the rape survivor rather than on the rapist. Instead of examining the character of the rape survivor, the law should focus unswervingly on the actions of the accused rapist and the degree of force or coercion which was used. This is what the law must seek to punish and to prevent.

Severity of punishment

Rapists have a tendency to rape more than once.[142] Although longer prison sentences alone will not necessarily reduce the rate of recidivism among rapists, sentences must be imposed with the need to protect the community in mind. Furthermore, it appears that a real fear of arrest and conviction might act as an inhibiting factor in some cases, but a large number of rapists are aware that serious punishment for their actions will be unlikely.[143]

Namibia

In Namibia, an accused rapist will initially appear in a magistrate's court, where a decision will be made on bail and a plea entered. Rape cases are then referred to the prosecutor-general, who decides whether or not there is enough evidence to proceed with the case, and what court the case should go to. Depending on the severity of the case, it can be tried in either the regional magistrate's court, which has jurisdiction to impose sentences of up to ten years, or in the high court, which may impose sentences of up to life imprisonment.[144] Most rape cases end up in the regional magistrate's court.

Prior to independence, it was possible for the Supreme Court of South West Africa to impose the death sentence for rape, although this was usually done only where there were aggravating circumstances. The death penalty is no longer allowed, pursuant to Article 6 of the Namibian constitution, which reads: 'No law may prescribe death as a competent sentence. No Court or Tribunal shall have the power to impose a sentence of death upon any person.'

In the Windhoek Supreme Court, 94 persons from locations throughout Namibia were tried on charges of rape in 1988. Guilty verdicts were handed down for 78 charges of rape, or 80 per cent of the

charges which went to trial, while there were 11 verdicts of not guilty
(11 per cent). In 1989, 55 persons were tried for rape in the Supreme
Court; 50 guilty verdicts were handed down (83 per cent) and nine verdicts of not guilty (15 per cent). In 1990, based on the case files
available up to mid-November, 30 accused were tried for rape; 18 guilty
verdicts were handed down (60 per cent), and seven verdicts of not
guilty (23 per cent).[145]

During the years 1988–90, the sentences imposed by the Supreme
Court/High Court for a single count of rape ranged from nil (sentence
postponed, fine in lieu of imprisonment, warnings, etc) to 15 years. The
average actual sentence (the entire sentence imposed regardless of any
suspended sentences) was about six years, while the average effective
sentence (the sentence to be served taking into account suspended sentences and portions of sentences) was between four and five years.

The case record for the regional magistrate's court for 1988 was also
examined. It listed 146 cases involving 208 accused. The outcome of
many of the cases was not apparent from this record, but guilty verdicts
were handed down for at least 94 charges (44 per cent), while there were
at least 38 verdicts of not guilty (18 per cent). Sentences ranged from nil
to ten years. The average actual sentence was approximately four years,
while the average effective sentence was approximately three years.[146]
According to the public prosecutor for the regional court, the most
common sentences in rape cases are three–four years for a first offence,
six–seven years where there are previous convictions, and cuts for
juveniles.[147]

South Africa

In South Africa, it is estimated that only 50–55 per cent of rape prosecutions lead to conviction.[148] According to another source, only about one
in 11 rapists is convicted in South Africa.[149]

A study of the 118 rape convictions returned by the Durban and
Coast Local Division of the South Africa Supreme Court from 1970–79
showed that the average length of imprisonment was just over seven
years, while the median sentence was five years. Two persons received
the death sentence.

The victims in these cases ranged from two to 85 years old, with
over 25 per cent of the victims being under ten years of age, and 39 per
cent being under 16 years of age.[150]

The South African study found the following factors to have some
correlation with the severity of sentence imposed:

- The age of the rapist; younger rapists received heavier sentences.

- The education level of the rapist; the higher the education level, the more lenient the sentence.

- Rapists who lived alone were found to be treated more leniently than those who lived with others.

- Rapists without a psychiatric history were treated more leniently than those who did have such a history.

- The race of the victim; sentences were heavier where the victim was white.

- The age of the victim; sentences were heavier where the victims were older women and less likely to be heavy where the victims were very young children.

- The marital status of the victim; rapists were more likely to receive heavy sentences for raping married women. (The old patriarchal notion of rape as a property crime against the father or the husband instead of a crime against the person of the woman herself may well be insinuating itself into modern-day attitudes about rape.) Where the victims were women with children, there was also an increased likelihood of a heavy sentence.

- The occupation of the victim; a heavy sentence was more likely where the victim was a skilled person or a housewife than where she was unskilled or unemployed.

- The extent of injury suffered by the victim increased the sentence.

- What the study terms 'contributing conduct' by the victim was a mitigating factor for the rapist.[151]

- A rapist acting together with others was more likely to get a heavy sentence than someone acting alone.

- When the rape was accompanied by other crimes, the sentence was heavier.

- The sentence was heavier if the rape occurred in the victim's house, often where it followed a break-in.

- The use of a weapon increased the chance of a heavy sentence.

- Premeditated crimes received heavier sentences.

- Persons charged with more than one count of rape received substantially heavier sentences.

- Persons with previous convictions for other common-law crimes tended to receive heavier sentences.

- Rapists who were known to their victims received lighter sentences than rapists who were strangers to their victims.

- Interestingly, Afrikaans-speaking judges were found to impose heavy sentences more frequently than English-speaking judges. While there could be a number of explanations for this pattern, it can be read as

reinforcement for the argument that cultural attitudes about rape play
an important role in the way that the legal system deals with rape.

This study can be criticised on a number of methodological grounds.
However, it does indicate that a number of factors which have nothing to
do with the offence on any logical grounds actually operate to affect the
severity of the sentence imposed. Of particular concern is the fact that
variables such as the race, marital status and occupation of the rape survivor affect the punishment received by the rapist. The law should
clearly eliminate such considerations from the sentencing process.

Swaziland

A study of all sexual offence cases in Swaziland in 1984 and 1985,
which included a total of 168 charges of rape or attempted rape against
172 accused, revealed a conviction rate of only 59,8 per cent. Of the 172
accused in the cases studied 68 were found guilty of rape; eight were
found guilty of attempted rape; 16 were found guilty of statutory rape;
nine were found guilty of assault; two were found guilty of abduction;
57 were found not guilty; and 12 had the cases against them withdrawn
by the prosecution.[152]

The sentences imposed for rape ranged from a minimum of suspended sentences or strokes with a cane to a maximum of ten years'
imprisonment. The bulk of the sentences given in rape cases ranged from
three to seven years, and the average sentence imposed for rape was five
and one-third years.[153]

The study noted that in the past several years the Swazi government
has 'consistently expressed concern over the crime of rape and attempted
to deter rapists by increasing sentences'. Since 1980, all rape cases in
Swaziland have been tried in the high court to make it possible for
heavier sentences to be imposed than would be possible in a magistrate's
court. Also, in 1986, Swaziland's Criminal Procedure and Evidence Act
was amended to provide for a minimum sentence of nine years in any
rape case where aggravating circumstances are present. However, the
study concluded that there is still a need for a clear sentencing policy
which will provide for sentences that are 'heavy enough to underline the
seriousness of the crime and deter future rapes'.[154]

Recommendations in regard to sentencing in Namibia

While a discussion of sentencing warrants a study on its own, it is a
matter for concern that there are a number of cases in Namibia where a
convicted rapist has repeated the crime after coming out of prison, sometimes having been released early on parole.

Generally speaking, sentences for rape should be stiff enough to send out a message to society about the seriousness of the crime, and to reduce the chance of repeated crimes.

Conclusion

The current legal treatment of this cluster of issues relating to rape symbolises a lack of commitment to the right of all women to sexual self-determination. It is necessary to take a serious look at the laws and procedures in this area in order to send out a strong message about sexual offences.

It should be noted, however, that there is no such thing as a perfect statute. While the law can and does make a difference, it is always interpreted in the light of society's prevailing values. No legal approach to rape will be effective as long as the people who apply and interpret the laws still believe the myths about rape. Legal reform must be combined with education about the realities of the crime.

Furthermore, research indicates that there is a direct relationship between sexual inequality and rape; rape occurs more frequently in societies where women have not yet achieved total equality with men in the economic. political and legal spheres.[155] So, in order to combat rape effectively, Namibians must continue to work for complete sexual equality.

[A longer version of this paper has been published by the Namibia Institute for Social and Economic Research at the University of Namibia, Private Bag 13301, Windhoek, Namibia.]

Notes

1. The National Institute for the Prevention of Crime and the Rehabilitation of Offenders (NICRO) in South Africa estimates that only one in 20 rape victims reports the crime to the police. L Vogelman, *The Sexual Face of Violence*, Johannesburg: Ravan, 1990, p31. This figure is also quoted from another source in South African Law Commission, *Women and Sexual Offences in South Africa*, Project 45, 1985, p5, para 1.6. Namibian Police Commissioner, Siggi Eimbeck, has cited this same figure with regard to Namibia. (*The Namibian*, 13.11.1990, p2.)
    There is evidence that the true figure may be even higher; a study carried out by the Australian Bureau of Census and Statistics and the Australian Institute of Criminology in 1975 found that only 28 per cent of the rape survivors included in the study reported the rape to the police. ('General Social Survey of Crime Victims', Australian Bureau of Statistics, Canberra,

May, 1975, quoted in ED Mnangagwa, MP, 'Victims of Sexual Attacks and
Domestic Violence in the Context of Human Rights and Criminal Justice',
paper delivered at the seminar on Human Rights in the Administration of
Justice in Southern Africa, Gaborone, Botswana, October 1990, p4.) The
problem of under-reporting of rapes also holds true for Zimbabwe,
according to the Zimbabwe Republic Police and the Musasa Project, a
non-governmental organisation set up to address the issues of sexual assault
and domestic violence. (Mnangagwa, 'Victims of Sexual Attacks', p4.)

2. Vogelman, *The Sexual Face of Violence*, particularly pp29, 76, 168, 172 and
    197–8. Mr Vogelmen is the director of the Project for the Study of Violence
    at the University of the Witwatersrand in Johannesburg, South Africa. (See
    also interview with Mr Vogelman in the *Sunday Star* Review, 11.2.1990.)
    The 'culture of rape' is examined in detail in S Brownmiller, *Against Our
    Will: Men, Women and Rape*, (Britain: Penguin, 1975) which is considered
    to be one of the classic feminist analyses of rape. The concept was
    graphically portrayed in a recent film called *The Accused*, starring Jodie
    Foster. In this film, a young woman was gang-raped on a pinball machine
    in a crowded bar while other men watched and cheered. The film was based
    on an actual incident which occurred in the United States. See Vogelman,
    The Sexual Face of Violence, p160. The relationship between the position of
    women in society and the incidence of rape is highlighted in another study
    of rapists, which concluded that most rapists are unable to conceive of
    women as people. J Fremont, 'Rapists Speak for Themselves', quoted in
    Vogelman, *The Sexual Face of Violence*, p12. There was a vivid example of
    the way that myths about rape condition society's response to it in the news
    recently; in response to reports that Philippine women in Kuwait were being
    raped by invading Iraqi troops, the Philippine foreign secretary remarked at
    a congressional hearing: 'If rape is inevitable, relax and enjoy it.' (*The
    Namibian*, 5.9.1990.)

3. See, for example, PR Sanday, 'Rape and the Silencing of the Feminine', in
    S Tomaselli and R Porter (eds), *Rape: An Historical and Social Enquiry*,
    Britain: Basil Blackwell, 1986.

4. R Porter, 'Does Rape Have a Historical Meaning?', in Tomaselli and Porter
    (eds), *Rape*, p230. According to another expert on rape: 'Rape must be
    examined within the context of patriarchy and the social control of women.
    This is because it is oppressive structures and social relations which relegate
    women to a relative position of powerlessness that contributes substantially
    to their susceptibility to rape.' (Vogelman, *The Sexual Face of Violence*,
    p23.)

5. Vogelman, *The Sexual Face of Violence*, p198.

6. Article 10 of the Namibian Constitution reads as follows: '(1) All persons
    shall be equal before the law; (2) No person may be discriminated against
    on the grounds of *sex*, race, colour, ethnic origin, religion, creed, or social or
    economic status' (emphasis added).

7. Information from the Legal Assistance Centre, Windhoek, Namibia.

8. See, for example, M Hinz and NG Leuven-Lachinski, *Koevoet Versus the
    People of Namibia*, Utrecht: Working Group Kairos, 1989, pp13–14.

9.　S Estrich, 'Rape', *Yale Law Journal*, 95, 1986, p1087 at p1163 (quoting a US study), and pp1164–9.

10.　Statistics supplied by General Thomasse, Namibian Police Head Office. It is interesting to note that while newspapers across the political spectrum have reported that the incidence of rape has increased dramatically since independence, the police figures for reported rapes do not bear this out. (See, for example, 'Murders, rapes up but Police believe situation stabilising', *The Namibian*, 13.11.1990.) In fact, there is a *greater* increase in the number of reported rapes between 1988 and 1989 than between 1989 and 1990.

11.　This includes Khomasdal and Katutura, the areas of Windhoek which are still, respectively, predominately 'coloured' and black. As a point of comparison, in 1988, there were 21 reported rapes in 'white' Windhoek as compared to 77 in Khomasdal and Katutura combined; in 1989, 28 as compared with 72; and in 1990, 38 as compared with 83. This difference is probably due to the much higher population of Khomasdal and Katutura.

12.　This figure is calculated from the 1981 census by assuming a growth rate of 1,5 per cent for whites and a growth rate of 3 per cent for blacks. The figure of 1,284 million excludes returnees, who number 40 000–50 000.

13.　International Labour Conference, 77th Session, Special Report of the Director-General on Apartheid, Geneva, 1990. The annual growth rate has been estimated to be as high as 4,5 per cent.

14.　Approximately 18 per cent of the population lives in urban areas (towns of 5 000 or more). *Namibia: Development and Investment*, revised edition, First National Development Corporation, October 1989, p15. However, if the police statistics from districts where there are concentrations of 10 000 people or more are looked at by themselves (Grootfontein, Katima Mulilo, Katutura, Keetmanshoop, Mariental, Otjiwarongo, Rehoboth, Swakopmund, Tsumeb and Windhoek), it can be seen that *more than one-half* of all reported rapes occur in and around these larger urban areas (approximately 51 per cent in 1988, 52 per cent in 1989 and 52 per cent in 1990).

15.　1981 Population Census.

16.　The total number of reported rapes for 1988–90 is 1 155. If this figure is compared to the estimate of a population of 867 000 women, the result is that these reported crimes have affected approximately one out of every 750 women, assuming that the same women did not suffer more than one sexual assault during this period.

17.　Multiplying the figure of 1 155 for 1988–90 by 20 produces the estimate of 23 100 women who were raped during this three-year period.

18.　*Windhoek Observer*, 9.6.1990, p9.

19.　C Stoneman and L Cliff, *Zimbabwe: Politics, Economics and Society*, London: Pinter, 1989, p8.

20.　Mnangagwa, 'Victims of Sexual Attacks', p3.

21.　Figure supplied by the Office of South African Interests, Windhoek, October 1990. This estimate includes the population of all of the so-called 'homelands'.

22.　Quoted in South African Law Commission, *Women and Sexual Offences*, pp4–5, para 1.6. The current estimate of Rape Crisis in Cape Town is that

200 000 women per year are raped in South Africa. See D Hansson in this volume, p180.

23. Statistics provided by General Thomasse, Namibian Police Head Office. As a point of comparison, there were 20 458 rape complaints in South Africa in 1988, and 10 424 prosecutions for rape from July 1987 to June 1988.
C Murray and C O'Regan, 'Women's Rights', *South African Human Rights and Labour Law Yearbook 1990*, Cape Town: Oxford University Press, 1990, p270.

24. The regional magistrate's court sits at Gobabis, Grootfontein, Katima Mulilo, Keetmanshoop, Lüderitz, Mariental, Oshakati, Otjiwarongo, Rundu, Swakopmund, Tsumeb, and Windhoek.

25. The term 'rape survivor' is favoured over the term 'victim' by many Rape Crisis groups, as it emphasises the woman's strength and ability to cope with the situation; it is perceived to be a more empowering term than the passive concept of 'victim'. However, the term 'victim' also appears in this paper in places, particularly in quotes, as it is still frequently employed in legal contexts.

26. This principle was established in a controversial English case decided by the House of Lords – *DPP v Morgan* [1975] Appeal Cases 182. The case was publicly debated at the time, and the finding was ultimately entrenched in England by the Sexual Offences (Amendment) Act 1976. The decision has more recently been criticised by legal scholars. For a discussion of this case, see J Temkin, 'Women, Rape and Law Reform' in Tomaselli and Porter (eds), *Rape*, pp36–7. In the United States, a mistaken belief in consent is a defence only where it is based on reasonable grounds. See Temkin, note 133.

27. One writer on the subject has stated that the law should 'impose a duty on men to open their eyes and use their heads before engaging in sex – not to read a woman's mind, but to give her credit for knowing her own mind when she speaks it… [B]eing treated like an object whose words or actions are not even worthy of consideration adds insult to injury.' Estrich, 'Rape', pp1104–5.

28. There are a few exceptions to this general rule. Where a husband and wife are separated pursuant to a decree of judicial separation, it is possible for a husband to be convicted of raping his wife. This may also hold true in the case of an extrajudicial separation agreement. However, the fact that divorce proceedings have already been instituted by the wife does *not* suffice to make a charge of rape against the husband possible. PMA Hunt and JRL Milton, *South African Criminal Law and Procedure, Volume II – Common Law Crime*, Cape Town: Juta, 2nd edition, 1982, pp438–9.

29. South African Law Commission, *Women and Sexual Offences*, p29, para 2.29.

30. Other rationales which have been used to defend the exemption are the risk of false accusations (which have been shown to be no higher than for other crimes); evidentiary problems (which are present in any number of crimes which tend to be committed in private); and the existence of alternative remedies (which are not adequate for the particular emotional and psychological damage which is caused by a sexual assault). See F Kaganas

and C Murray, 'Rape in Marriage: Conjugal Right or Criminal Wrong?', *Acta Juridica*, 1983, p125.

31. See, for example, Porter, 'Does Rape Have a Historical Meaning?', p217; Vogelman, *The Sexual Face of Violence*, pp25–6; and Brownmiller, *Against Our Will*, pp16–30.

32. Huber, *Heedendaegse Rechtsgeleertheyt*, (trans. by Percival Gane, 1939), quoted in Felicity Kaganas, 'Rape in Marriage: Developments in South African Law', *International and Comparative Law Quarterly*, 35, April 1986, p456 at p457.

33. LH Bowker, 'Marital Rape: A Distinct Syndrome?', *Social Casework: The Journal of Contemporary Social Work*, 64(6), June 1983, pp347–8.

34. 'To Have and to Hold: The Marital Rape Exemption and the Fourteenth Amendment', *Harvard Law Review*, 99, 1986, p1255 at p1258 (referring to D Russell, *Rape in Marriage*, 1982).

35. *S v H* 1985 (2) SA 750 (N), p752 (obiter dictum).

36. *S v H*, p756.

37. South African Law Commission, *Women and Sexual Offences*, p25, para 2.22.

38. South African Law Commission, *Women and Sexual Offences*, p36, para 2.43.

39. See 'Report of the Joint Committee on the Criminal Law and the Criminal Procedure Amendment Act Amendment Bill', *Hansard*, South African Parliament, 7th session, 8th Parliament, 10 February 1989.

40. See, for example, 'The Report of the Joint Committee on the Criminal Law and the Criminal Procedure Act Amendment Bill' (a critique of the report of the Joint Committee signed by a number of South African academics); 'Memorandum on the Criminal Law and Criminal Procedure Act Amendment Bill' (an uncredited refutation of the reasons put forward by the Joint Committee for rejecting the recommendations of the South African Law Commission); and JRL Milton, 'Law Reform: Marital Rape', *South African Journal of Criminal Justice*, 2, 1989, p79.

41. Debates of Parliament, *Hansard*, 7th session, 8th Parliament, 13 March 1989, p2682.

42. Brownmiller, *Against Our Will*, p382; South African Law Commission, *Women and Sexual Offences*, p24, para 2.22; D Hanson and W Van der Vent, 'Rape: The Husband Factor', *South*, 17–23 August 1989. A draft penal code currently under consideration in Zimbabwe has also recommended abolition of the marital rape exemption. G Feltoe, 'Reforming the Penal Law and the Criminal Justice System in Zimbabwe', paper presented at a seminar on Human Rights in the Administration of Justice in Southern Africa, Gaborone, Botswana, October 1990, p4.

43. Quoted in Temkin, 'Women, Rape and Law Reform', pp33–4. Temkin discusses the Canadian law reforms in detail at pp29–35.

44. C Murray, 'Some Comments on Rape in Marriage and the English Criminal Law Revision Committee's Report on Sexual Offences', *South African Law Journal*, 102, 1985, p157 at p162.

45. *S v W* 1988 (3) SA 450 (A), p463.

46. Examples adapted from C Hall, 'Rape: The Politics of Definition', *South African Law Journal*, 105, 1988, p67 at p68.

47. Brownmiller, *Against Our Will*, p378.

48. See Article 10 of the Namibian Constitution.

49. Coleman, Butcher and Carson, *Abnormal Psychology and Modern Life*, Scott, Foreman & Co, 7th edition, 1984, p475. According to Vogelman, 'an essential ingredient of rape is a man's need to gain power and build up his depleted self- concept...' (Vogelman, *The Sexual Face of Violence*, p109) Further: 'Although multiple causation is a feature of every rape, recent studies and most feminist writers stress that a cardinal feature of rape is the rapist's desire to express his power and superiority over his victim.' (Vogelman, *The Sexual Face of Violence*, p132)

50. Vogelman, *The Sexual Face of Violence*, p165. See also p197.

51. ET Verwey and DA Louw, 'Die verkragter – 'n empiriese ondersoek', *South African Journal of Criminal Justice*, 2, 1990, p150.

52. Coleman, Butcher and Carson, *Abnormal Psychology*, p474.

53. Vogelman, *The Sexual Face of Violence*, p128.

54. See Hall, 'Rape', p70.

55. See, for example, *S v J* 1989 (1) SA 669 (A), p675 (gang-rape of a 19-year-old woman who died from injuries received in connection with the rape).

56. CR Snyman, *Criminal Law*, Durban: Butterworths, 2nd edition, 1989, p447.

57. *R v K* 1958 (3) SA 420 (A), p421.

58. *R v Swiggelaar* 1950 (1) PH H61 (A), p110–11.

59. *R v M* 1953 (4) SA 393 (A), p398.

60. There are only two kinds of fraud which can vitiate consent. One is where the rapist impersonates another person, such as the victim's husband or fiancé. Another is where the victim is induced to believe that what she is consenting to was not actually sexual intercourse, but an act of a different nature (such as medical treatment). Hunt and Milton, *South African Criminal Law*, p443–4.

61. On the subject of intoxication, Schreiner, JA, has stated: 'At the one end of the scale, if the woman is insensible from any cause she clearly cannot be a consenting party, nor is it easy to see how the impression could arise that she was consenting. At the other end of the scale is the case where the woman is only slightly affected by liquor. It may be that her judgment, moral as well as intellectual, is impaired, but it would be going too far to say in such cases that, although by words or conduct she could convey the impression of consent, such impression was really false, and consent must be taken to have been absent. It is no doubt reprehensible for a man to have connection with a woman if he has reason to think that her consent to intercourse is in any degree the result of her having taken intoxicants, and it certainly more reprehensible if he has induced her to take the intoxicants with the object of making her more pliant, but the law does not make such conduct the offence of rape.' *R v K* 1958 (3) SA 420 (A), p421–2.

62. Hunt and Milton, *South African Criminal Law*, p443.

63. In other crimes, such as assault, theft, kidnapping and abduction, unlawfulness is an element of the crime; consent would be one of several

defences which could arise under the element of unlawfulness. In contrast, in rape *both* unlawfulness and the absence of consent are elements of the crime. To illustrate the point more clearly, consider the crime of assault, which is defined as an unlawful, intentional application of force to the person of another. In certain situations where there was consent to the physical contact (such as in sport or medical treatment), the element of unlawfulness will be lacking. Hunt and Milton, *South African Criminal Law*, p467–8. The defence of consent is available only where public policy warrants legal recognition of the fact of consent. See *S v Collett* 1978 (3) SA 206 (A), p211 (where the court held that the unequal power relationship between the assailant and the victim – master and servant – meant that there could have been no legally meaningful consent by the victim). Where the charge is assault with intent to cause grievous bodily harm, the defence of consent is not available at all. See *S v Sikunyana and Others* 1961 (3) SA 549 (ECD).

64. Vogelman (*The Sexual Face of Violence*, p187) gives an example of the accusatory kind of questioning which can take place on the issue of consent.
65. Information based on personal interviews by members of Women's Solidarity, June 1990.
66. *S v H* 1985 (2) SA 750 (N), p751. (The court did not accept this evidence.)
67. *Rex v D and Others* 1951 (4) SA 450 (A), p454–5. (The jury convicted the accused rapists in this case.)
68. Interestingly, 'the present day circumscription of the crime, with its shift in emphasis from sexual intercourse *with force* to sexual intercourse *without consent*, is a conception of English and not Roman-Dutch origin'. *Rex v D and Others*, p752 (emphasis added). See also South African Law Commission, *Women and Sexual Offences*, p19–20, para 2.11.
69. See Estrich, 'Rape', generally.
70. Estrich, 'Rape', p1127.
71. Hunt and Milton, *South African Criminal Law*, p440.
72. Information based on personal interviews by members of Women's Solidarity, June 1990.
73. Based on interviews by Women's Solidarity.
74. Based on interviews by Women's Solidarity.
75. Based on interviews by Women's Solidarity.
76. *R v Z* 1960 (1) SA 739 (A). See also Hunt and Milton, *South African Criminal Law*, p443.
77. See Hunt and Milton, *South African Criminal Law*, p439, note 115.
78. South African Law Commission, *Women and Sexual Offences*, p37–40, paras 2.44–2.32.
79. This law applies only to Namibia, but is similar to the South African Sexual Offences Act, No 23 of 1957 (previously known as the Immorality Act). In addition to sexual offences which are related to rape, the Act also covers a number of offences which are related to prostitution.
80. The Combatting of Immoral Practices Act, 21 of 1980, section 14(1).
81. The Combatting of Immoral Practices Act, 21 of 1980, section 14(2).
82. The Combatting of Immoral Practices Act, 21 of 1980, section 15.
83. The Combatting of Immoral Practices Act, 21 of 1980, section 16.

84. Brownmiller, *Against Our Will*, p376.
85. P Searles and RJ Berger, 'The Current Status of Rape Reform Legislation: An Examination of State Statutes', *Women's Rights Law Reporter*, 10, 1987, p25, at note 5.
86. Michigan Penal Code, MICH. COMP. LAWS ANN., 39, section 750.520 (Supp. 1982). It is not known whether this statute has been amended since 1982. For a detailed discussion of this statute and the grassroots pressure for its adoption, see Temkin, 'Women, Rape and Law Reform', p26–9. A critique of the Michigan statute appears in Estrich, 'Rape', p1147–57.
87. 'Intimate parts' are defined to include the 'primary genital area, groin, inner thigh, buttock or breast'.
88. Law Reform Commission of Canada, *Sexual Offences*, Working Paper No 22, 1978, quoted in Temkin, 'Women, Rape and Law Reform', p31. Temkin includes a detailed discussion of the Canadian reforms at pp29–35.
89. Estrich, 'Rape', p1148.
90. Cape Town Rape Crisis in South Africa has proposed centering the law around the offence of 'an unlawful sexual act', defined as 'any act of a sexual nature committed by one or more persons without the latter's consent', with the following graduated ladder of offences: (a) *sexual injuria*: offences involving the infringement of the sexual dignity of the complainant, such as indecent exposure and crimen injuria; (b) *sexual assault*: offences involving the infringement of the person of the complainant including (i) *sexual assault (common)*: relatively minor offences of a sexual nature, involving physical contact with the complainant, such as touching a woman's breast without her consent; (ii) *grievous sexual assault*: serious offences of a sexual nature, involving gross infringement of the person of the complainant, including rape as presently defined and oral/anal/object penetration; and (iii) *sexual assault with aggravating circumstances*: sexual offences involving the use of severe force, causing serious physical and psychological injury, including rape as presently defined and oral/anal/object penetration. (M Van Zyl, D Rudolph and S Stewart, Rape Crisis (Cape Town), 1985.) A more recent proposal from Rape Crisis (Cape Town) recommends two new statutory offences: sexual assault and sexual assault with intent to do grievous bodily harm. (Hansson, 'Working Against Violence', p7.)
91. Consent should become a *defence* which can be raised by the accused, eliminating *absence of consent* as an element of the crime to be proved by the state.
92. Quoted in Brownmiller, *Against Our Will*, p369.
93. Brownmiller, *Against Our Will*, p369.
94. As noted above, Police Commissioner Eimbeck in Namibia and NICRO in South Africa both estimate that only one in twenty rape victims report the crime to the police. Vogelman, *The Sexual Face of Violence*, p31.
95. LH Hoffmann and DT Zeffertt, *The South African Law of Evidence*, Durban: Butterworths, 4th edition, 1988, p117–18.
96. The other common law exceptions are: previous statements which may disprove a suggestion that a witness's story is a recent fabrication, evidence of a prior act of identification, and statements made by an accused when

confronted on a previous occasion with incriminating facts. Hoffmann and Zeffertt, *The South African Law of Evidence*, p121–3.

97. See *S v M* 1980 (1) SA 586 (B). Hiemstra, CJ, is of the opinion that the fact of a prior complaint is admissible only to prove absence of consent, and that the contents of the prior complaint can be used only to test the credibility of the complainant's allegation that there was in fact a complaint. Steenkamp, J, is of the opinion that 'consistency' is the only ground for admissibility.

98. Hoffmann and Zeffertt, *The South African Law of Evidence*, p118–19.

99. Hoffmann and Zeffertt, *The South African Law of Evidence*, p118–21.

100. *S v Balhuber* 1987 (1) PH H22 (A), p44–5.

101. *Windhoek Observer*, 12.5.1990; *S v Aimongwa*, Windhoek High Court, Case No 17/1990 (O'Linn, J, unreported judgement). After examining the other relevant factors in the case, the court concluded that the guilt of the accused had not been proved beyond a reasonable doubt. The judge noted that the girl had made a good impression as a witness, and that, despite her age, she seemed able to make the distinction between truth and lies. The court was not prepared to reject any of the girl's evidence as being false. However, the judge then applied the cautionary rule, correctly stating that the court was obliged to treat the complainant's evidence with particular caution in the absence of any supporting evidence. This rule is required in all cases where evidence is being given by young children, as well as in all cases of sexual offences. (See the discussion of the cautionary rule below.)

102. Hoffmann and Zeffertt, *The South African Law of Evidence*, p580.

103. Z Adler, *Rape on Trial*, London: Routledge and Kegan Paul, 1987, p119, quoted in Mnangagwa, 'Victims of Sexual Attacks', p6.

104. Hoffmann and Zeffertt, *The South African Law of Evidence*, pp572–84.

105. *Rex v W* 1949 (3) SA 772 (A), p780. The court went on to state: 'Had the charge against the appellant been, for instance, one of theft, requiring no more than the ordinary high but not exceptional standard of careful scrutiny… the verdict of guilty must have stood. But because the magistrate appears to have treated the case as if it were an ordinary one, save for the fact that the complainant was a child, it becomes possible and in the circumstances necessary for this court to interfere. Although the magistrate was convinced that the complainant had told the truth and that the appellant had lied and was guilty, he reached this conclusion without realising the special risks involved in the case and the consequent necessity of taking precautions above the ordinary. In these circumstances the fact that he found strongly in favour of the truthfulness of the complainant and against that of the appellant cannot relieve this court of its duty to find that the case against the appellant was not proved beyond reasonable doubt.' *Rex v W*, p783.

106. *S v Balhuber* 1987 (1) PH H22 (A), p45 (Botha, JA) (emphasis added). See also *S v F* 1989 (3) SA 847 (A).

107. *S v Balhuber*, quoting Glanville Williams, *The Proof of Guilt*, p158–78, as cited in *S v Flanagan* 1989 (2) PH H75 (A), p209.

108. *Rex v W* 1949 (3) SA 772 (A), p780.

109. *R v M* 1947 (4) SA 489 (N), p493–4.

110. *R v M* 1947, p493–4.

111. *R v Rautenbach* 1949 (1) SA 135 (A), p143.

112. Hoffmann and Zeffertt, *The South African Law of Evidence*, p580. (The editors cite *Potiphar v Joseph* for this point.)

113. Hoffman and Zeffertt, *The South African Law of Evidence*, p580.

114. See *S v S* 1990 (1) SASV 5 (A), p8 ("n dubbele versigtigheidsreël').

115. Brownmiller, *Against Our Will*, p366. According to another source, 'the ordeal to which rape victims are subjected after reporting a rape makes it unlikely that false accusations would be numerous. Furthermore, there are no indications that false accusations about rape are made more frequently than those about any other kind of crime'. Vogelman, *The Sexual Face of Violence*, p48.

116. Temkin, 'Women, Rape and Law Reform', p35 and at note 146; M Benson, 'Rape Law: A Feminist Legal Analysis,' *Medicine and the Law*, 8, 1989, p303–9.

117. Hoffmann and Zeffertt, *The South African Law of Evidence*, p47.

118. South African Law Commission, *Women and Sexual Offences*, p43, para 3.9, and at p48–9, paras 3.26 and 3.28.

119. South African Law Commission, *Women and Sexual Offences*, p45, para 3.13 and at p48–50, paras 3.24–3.31.

120. Criminal Law and Criminal Procedure Act Amendment Act, 39 of 1989.

121. The South African Criminal Procedure Act, 51 of 1977 is applicable to Namibia as it was in force in South Africa in 1979. The administration of most of the provisions of this Act were transferred from South Africa to 'South West Africa' by the Executive Powers (Justice) Transfer Proclamation, 1979 (AG 33/1979, as amended). The effect of this transfer was that subsequent amendments to the Act in South Africa were not automatically applicable to 'South West Africa' unless the amending Act (or some other law passed after the date of the Transfer Proclamation) expressly stated that the amendment was also applicable to 'South West Africa'. (See section 3(5) of the Executive Powers Transfer (General Provisions) Proclamation, 1977 (AG 7/1977), as amended by AG 10/1978 and AG 20/1978.) The Criminal Procedure Act as it applies in Namibia has been amended or affected by: the Criminal Procedure Amendment Act, 1981 (Act 15/1981) (affects sections 114 and 116); the Police Amendment Act, 1983 (AG 21/1983) (affects section 20); the Appeals Amendment Act, 1985 (Act 29/1985) (affects sections 315–19 and section 323); and the Criminal Procedure Matters Amendment Act, 1985 (affects sections 24, 37, 42, 55, 56, 57, 60, 68A, 112, 119, 121, 145, 146, 169, 170, 188, 262, 296, 297, 300, 302, 307, Schedule 2 (Part II)).

122. Criminal Procedure Act, No 51 of 1977, sections 211 and 271.

123. Temkin, 'Women, Rape and Law Reform', p28.

124. M Venter, 'Police and Rape', unpublished paper available from Women's Solidarity, Windhoek, October 1990.

125. Martsie Venter, 'Police and Rape'.

126. Zimbabwe has recognised the compensatory approach of customary law and is currently exploring ways to incorporate compensation and restitution to the victim into its civil court system. Feltoe, 'Reforming the Penal Law', p16.

127. Brownmiller, *Against Our Will*, p364ff.

128. Mnangagwa, 'Victims of Sexual Attacks', p5.

129. E du Toit, FJ de Jager, A Paizes, A St Q Skeen and S van der Merwe, *Commentary on the Criminal Procedure Act*, Cape Town: Juta, 1987, pp3–6, 3–11, 3–12.

130. F Goodyear, 'Sexual Assault Centre, Auckland, New Zealand,' *Medicine and the Law*, 8, 1989, p297–302.

131. Amendment of section 154 of the Criminal Procedure Act, 51 of 1977, and addition of new section 335A by the Law of Evidence and the Criminal Procedure Amendment Act, 103 of 1987.

132. Amendment of section 153 of the Criminal Procedure Act, No 51 of 1977 by the Law of Evidence and the Criminal Procedure Amendment Act, No 103 of 1987.

133. In both South Africa and Namibia, the court may also direct that the entire trial be closed to the public if this is requested by the complainant, or if the court thinks that it would be in the interest of public morals to close the proceedings. Criminal Procedure Act, 51 of 1977, section 153(3).

134. Section 1 of the Criminal Law and Criminal Procedure Act Amendment Act, 39 of 1989.

135. Criminal Procedure and Evidence Act 6/1986. See A Armstrong, 'Women as Victims: A Study of Rape in Swaziland', in A Armstrong (ed), *Women and Law in Southern Africa*, Harare: Zimbabwe Publishing House, 1987.

136. Temkin, 'Women, Rape and Law Reform', note 146.

137. Hunt and Milton, *South African Criminal Law*, p451.

138. *R v Sibande* 1958 (3) SA 1 (A), p6. Here the court found that had the fact that the complainant was living in 'incest' with her husband's brother been known, it might well have affected the sentence imposed on the rapist by the trial judge. To throw this point into an even starker light, consider the case of Turkey, where a law which is currently the subject of much protest provides for the automatic reduction of a sentence for rape by two-thirds if the victim is a prostitute. (*Die Republikein*, 6.2.1990.) The character of the victim can also be taken into account in deciding upon the amount of compensation to be awarded in civil claims for damages arising from a rape case. Consider the following statement in this regard: 'Mrs M was at home alone with the children. She was dragged out of her home by a relative of her husband and there is no evidence of any provocative or suggestive attitude on her part. She suffered a most terrifying, shocking and humiliating experience. Any *respectable* woman would have felt dirty and soiled, terms used by Mrs M to describe how she felt. Mrs M did not try to exaggerate her experience or its consequences. She and her husband are obviously *respectable* people... Mrs M is a young happily married woman of good character and the insult, indignity and terror to which she was subjected entitle her to substantial damages.' (*M v N* 1981 (1) SA 136 (T), p138–9 [emphasis added].)

139. *R v S* 1958 (3) SA 102 (A), p105 (emphasis added).

140. Although the age or physical condition of the victim may arise as a factor in the imposition of sentences for other forms of assault, it would be extremely rare for the *morals* of the victim to be considered relevant.

141. *State v Adam Bwanusi*, High Court of Zimbabwe, judgment HC-B-48-87, quoted in Mnangagwa, 'Victims of Sexual Attacks', p13.
142. Vogelman, *The Sexual Face of Violence*, p189. This fact also appears from examination of the court files in Namibia.
143. See Vogelman, *The Sexual Face of Violence*, p165.
144. See Hunt and Milton, *South African Criminal Law*, p447. Namibia has only one regional magistrate's court, which is based in Windhoek but travels on circuit throughout the country.
    Before 21 March 1990, rape cases in Namibia could be tried in either the regional magistrate's court or in the Supreme Court of South West Africa. (The High Court now occupies a place in the judicial system similar to that of the Supreme Court prior to independence. See Articles 80 and 138 of the Namibian Constitution.)
145. Some accused were tried for more than one charge of rape. Some accused did not show up for trial, and some cases were withdrawn by the state. As a point of comparison, there were 10 424 rape prosecutions in South Africa from July 1987 to June 1988, resulting in 5 243 convictions (50,3 per cent). Murray and O'Regan, 'Women's Rights', p270.
146. This is only an approximation; the 1988 index of cases is handwritten and difficult to decipher in places, and the figures have not been cross-checked with the actual court files.
147. Interview by Women's Solidarity with Mr Jooste, 15 November 1990.
148. Vogelman, *The Sexual Face of Violence*, p1. (This estimate is supported by the figures cited by Murray & O'Regan for 1987–88, 'Women's Rights', p270.)
149. Quoted in South African Law Commission, *Women and Sexual Offences*, pp4–5, para 1.6.
150. O Salmon, 'Sentences for Rape' in MCJ Olmesdahl and NC Steytler (eds), *Criminal Justice in South Africa*, Cape Town: Juta, 1983, p162–75.
151. The concept of 'contributing conduct' or 'victim participation' in criminology does not hold the victim responsible for the crime, but questions whether the crime might have been avoided if the victim had behaved in a different manner. It is disturbing to note what the Salmon study considered to be 'contributing conduct' by the rape victim: the fact that the victim was an acquaintance of the rapist, accepting a lift, or accepting an invitation to accompany the accused. As a point of comparison, consider the definition of 'contributing conduct' used by the National Commission on the Causes and Prevention of Violence in Washington, DC: 'Where the victim agreed to sexual relations but retracted before the actual act or when she clearly invited sexual relations through language, gestures, etc.' However, even the narrower definition still implies that it is the responsibility of *women* to change their behaviour if they want to avoid being raped. (This would support Brownmiller's thesis that rape is a conscious process of intimidation by which *all* men keep *all* women in a state of fear. Brownmiller, *Against Our Will*, p15.) Obviously, like the law, research about rape can be coloured and shaped by the myths about rape. See Brownmiller on the concept of 'victim participation', pp352–3.

152. Armstrong, 'Women as Victims', p255–75. These figures includes charges of contravening the Girls' and Women's Protection Act 39/1920, which makes it an offence to have carnal knowledge of a girl under the age of 16, or with a female idiot or imbecile, even with her consent. The study noted that government figures for the years 1980–83 indicated a conviction rate of 90 per cent on average, but the reason for this discrepancy in conviction rates was unclear.
153. Armstrong, 'Women as Victims', p255–75.
154. Armstrong, 'Women as Victims', pp272–3.
155. See, for example, L Baron and MA Strauss, 'Rape and its Relation to Social Disorganisation, Pornography and Inequality in the USA', *Medicine and the Law*, 8, 1989, p208–32.

Working Against Violence Against Women

Recommendations from Rape Crisis (Cape Town)

Desirée Hansson

*I*n principle, Rape Crisis (Cape Town) is committed to the liberation of all people and to the elimination of all forms of oppression. As feminists, our priority in practice is the liberation of women and the eradication of gender oppression. Our chosen focus is violence against women, for we believe that this is one of the central mechanisms of women's oppression.

During the past year, women's oppression has been made an issue within liberation politics in South Africa. Probably the best written example of this is paragraph 4 of the preamble to the African National Congress's constitutional guidelines which states that:

> [w]e also have to acknowledge that oppression of women in South Africa is not only a consequence of conquest and white domination, and make commitment to abolish all vestiges of patriarchy in our institutions and practices, not just those that followed conquest.[1]

'Indeed, it is no longer fruitful to debate whether or not gender should be on the agenda. It is there already, having been put there by the women's movement in a way that cannot be ignored.'[2] If we are to move women's liberation from the level of political rhetoric to reality, however, we must campaign now for specific and concrete changes. The aim of this paper then, is to propose a number of practical ways in which we can start to reduce one aspect of women's oppression, namely, that which results from male violence. The changes proposed here are not merely theoretical abstractions, they are recommendations which have been derived from suggestions made by abused women themselves and from our practical experience in working with these women.

The magnitude of the problem

In our society, problems defined as 'women's issues' are usually cast aside by those in power as insignificant. Violence against women is an issue which has long been treated in this manner. A few statistics dispel this myth of insignificance and demonstrate the magnitude of the social problem of violence against women in South Africa.

It is estimated that approximately 200 000 women will be raped this year.[3] At least four women will be raped every ten minutes.[4] One in every six adult women is assaulted regularly by her male partner,[5] and in at least 46 per cent of these cases, the men involved also abuse children who live with the women concerned.[6] Every week an average of four women are forced to flee from their homes, because their lives are being endangered by their male partners.[7] It is estimated that over half of those who admit to a killing are men who have killed their female partners.[8] Such violence can hardly be considered insignificant: instead, '[v]iolence against women is a [profound] social problem and reducing it is one of the major challenges facing a new South Africa.'[9]

The problem of family rights

As a feminist organisation, Rape Crisis (Cape Town) is deeply concerned about the clause in the ANC's constitutional guidelines, which reads, '[t]he family... shall be protected'.[10] We understand that the intention of this clause is to guard against oppressive practices, such as influx control and migrant labour, which have divided African families. We acknowledge that to those who have been denied family unity, the family must appear to be a desirable institution, for we live in a society which regards the family 'as a place of safety in which members can escape the stresses of the world'.[11] Yet, it is this romantic view of the family institution which has been used to 'hide the extent of the violence and [to] protect the abusers. It has discouraged the legal profession from intervening, with the result that battered women are often isolated from sources of assistance'.[12]

One need only work with battered women to shatter the illusion of the family as a 'haven in a heartless world', for in reality, it is 'one of the least safe places for women and children'.[13] Furthermore, it has been shown consistently that existing family structures, whether they be nuclear or extended in nature, are founded on and serve to perpetuate the subordinate position of women which is reproduced in political, economic and social relations outside of the family.[14] Thus, to protect the family is to entrench women's subordination, for existing family structures serve the interests of men at the expense of women. At the Malibongwe Conference Frene Ginwala stated that:

> The constitution should protect women from cultural practices that discriminate against them and promote inequality... We can no more accept even at a social level, a cultural practice that relegates the status of women, than we would accept a claim by Afrikaners that respect for their culture requires the separation or segregation of races. Just as commitment to racial equality is absolute, so too we should consider the commitment to the equality of women and men. The latter cannot be diminished on the grounds of sensitivity to cultural practices, or respect for the privacy of family relations...[15]

We would submit that because existing family structures are cultural practices that discriminate against women, they *cannot* be protected in a new constitution, for nowhere in the world has the family been strengthened without patriarchy being bolstered.

Practical recommendations for addressing violence against women

Before proposing concrete changes in the specific spheres of rape and battery, we must consider the broader reforms on which such recommendations are predicated.

The history of women's liberation in other countries has shown that if the interests of women are to be served in the long term, structures having this specific objective must be set up at the highest levels of government. To be effective such structures must receive budgetary allocations and must be headed and run by, at very least, a majority of women. Hence, we would propose that a structure, similar to the Australian Office of the Status of Women in the Department of the Prime Minister and Cabinet,[16] be developed to meet the specific needs of the South African context and that it be established as part of the new government of South Africa.

It is also proposed that addressing the problem of violence against women be one of the first priorities of such an office. Again, the Australian initiative could be used to inform the development of programmes for South Africa. Australia has established a Family Violence Prevention Committee (FVPC), consisting of various government departments and agencies, as well as community organisations, the aim of which is to ensure that legislative reforms and policy changes are implemented at the grassroots level. To this end, the committee co-ordinates three task forces, namely,

[t]he Housing Task Force – to address housing needs and questions of equity and access. This task force is chaired by the Ministry of Housing and Construction. The Professional Education Task Force – to address the training and education needs of professionals at both the tertiary and in-service training levels. This task force is chaired by the Education Department. The Community Education Task Force – to address the issues of changing community attitudes, improving services offered to victim/survivors, and providing information to victim/survivors. This task force is chaired by the Health Department...[17]

Indeed, this Australian programme seems particularly suited to the South African situation, for Rape Crisis (Cape Town) has found that the three spheres of housing, training of service providers and popular education, must be addressed if survivors are to be assisted effectively and if violence against women is to be reduced significantly.

The South African system of health and welfare is particularly inadequate, especially for African people, the working classes, and those living in rural areas. Historically, not only in South Africa but in most other countries, when the state shirks the responsibility of providing adequate health and welfare services, it is women who are tied to the domestic sphere to carry the burden of such tasks. 'Women are the ones who look after the young, the aged, the ill, the disabled, the abused, [as well as] the unemployed.'[18] Thus, a state-funded national health system and a much improved system of social welfare are two of the fundamental preconditions for women's liberation in South Africa. Furthermore, it is important that both systems be designed to meet the particular needs of women, especially women who are abused. Examples of the ways in which this may be achieved are highlighted in the next two sections which deal with concrete recommendations for change in the spheres of sexual assault and domestic violence.

Sexual Assault

Under existing South African common law 'rape consists in a male
having unlawful and intentional sexual intercourse with a female without
her consent... Sexual intercourse consists in the penetration of the
female's sexual organ by that of the male.'[19] This definition and the legal
procedures for dealing with rape survivors have been criticised extensively.[20] The requirement that it be proven that a survivor did not consent
to sexual relations has been central to most critiques. In theory a woman

> need not expressly indicate her objection to intercourse; if her will is
> overborne by fear or intimidation as a result of which she fails to offer
> any outward resistance, the crime [of rape] is committed, since mere
> submission is not equated with consent.[21]

In practice, sexist assumptions, such as 'women cannot be trusted to tell
the truth' and 'women say no to sex when they mean yes', inform the
courts and legal practitioners and ensure that in most cases rape survivors are assumed to have consented, unless they can provide strong
evidence to the contrary, such as severe physical injury. Even the legally
less serious offence of indecent assault hinges on the issue of consent.
Furthermore, the common law conception of rape excludes acts which
do not involve the penetration of a vagina by a penis, acts committed by
males against males, females against males, and it indemnifies men who
rape their wives, since this is considered to be lawful intercourse.[22]

We would argue that the core issue in the legal conception of rape
should be *coercion* and not consent,[23] and that when a women claims to
have been raped by a man, the legal presumption should be that coercion
has been used, because

> truly consensual sexual activity requires independent, equal parties and a
> context in which neither can coerce the other. Given the economic
> dependence of many women on men, (or at least their relative economic
> weakness), and men's stronger social, organizational and physical power
> the sexes can rarely meet on a footing of complete equality.[24]

Hence, to overcome the abovementioned shortcomings it is proposed
that the offences of rape and indecent assault be abrogated and that two
new statutory offences be introduced, namely, sexual assault and sexual
assault with intent to do grievous bodily harm. These new offences
would comprise the elements of the existing offences of assault and assault with intent. At present assault in South Africa is defined as:

unlawfully and intentionally (a) applying force, directly or indirectly, to the person of another, or (b) threatening another with immediate personal violence in circumstances which lead the threatened person to believe that the other intends and has the power to carry out the threat.[25]

Assault with intent requires the additional element of an intention to inflict grievous bodily harm.[26] For the offence of sexual assault then, an element stipulating that the purpose of the force or threatened force is to commit an act which is sexual in nature would have to be added to the elements of assault and assault with intent.

It is noteworthy that sexual assault centres on coercion or the threat of force, rather than on consent. The legal presumption here is that it is not possible to consent to being assaulted. Furthermore, this definition does *not* require that there be any physical impact on a person's body, because the mere threat of force constitutes an assault. Like assault with intent, the offence of sexual assault with intent to do grievous bodily harm would not require that grievous bodily harm actually be inflicted, but that there be an intention to do such harm. In cases in which no physical force or threat of physical force is present, but in which women are coerced into sexual acts or acts with sexual connotations, certain existing laws, like extortion, could be used. To illustrate, the offence of extortion is 'committed when a person unlawfully and intentionally obtains some advantage which is not due to [her] him from another by subjecting the latter to pressure which induces [her] him to hand over the advantage'.[27]

As for the offence of assault, sexual assault can be committed by a person of either sex against a person of either sex and the relationship between the people involved is of no legal relevance. Sexual assault is not limited to acts involving the penetration of a vagina by a penis, so includes penetration of any of the body orifices by animate or inanimate objects, including for example a penis, a finger, a bottle or stick. It also includes acts which do not necessarily involve penetration, like fondling a person's genitals or breasts. This new legislation would also prevent the secondary victimisation which many rape survivors experience when they are cross-examined in court regarding their sexual histories, since neither consent nor the relationship between the complainant and the accused is to be of legal relevance.

The secondary victimisation of rape survivors in court has been exacerbated by the double cautionary rule, which requires that courts exercise additional caution when assessing the credibility of the testimony of rape survivors whose evidence is not corroborated.[28] This rule is frequently brought into operation, because rape victims are commonly the sole eye-witnesses to rape. The rationale for this rule is overtly sexist for it is assumed that rape victims/survivors are more likely to fabricate testimony than are other victims of violence. For as leading authors explain: 'The bringing of the charge [of rape] may [be] motivated by spite, sexual frustration or other unpredictable emotional causes.'[29]

This is blatant and unfounded prejudice against women, for in practice it has been found that women are ashamed and afraid of bringing charges of sexual abuse. In fact in the case of rape, under-reporting is the norm. It is thus proposed that the double cautionary rule be abolished.

Sexual assault laws have already replaced rape laws in many other countries including Canada, New Zealand, Australia and many American states. A related proposal is that the common law prohibitions on 'sodomy' and 'unnatural sexual offences' be abrogated insofar as they criminalise sexual relations between consenting adults, and that the Sexual Offences Act[30] be altered in such a way that lesbian and gay sexual relations between consenting adults are decriminalised; that the age of consent to sexual relations becomes 16 years; and that all sections of the Act apply equally to males and females, as well as to heterosexual, lesbian and gay sexual relations.

Abortion

A serious problem facing rape survivors is the real possibility of pregnancy resulting from sexual assault. Rape Crisis (Cape Town) has estimated that at least ten per cent of rape survivors become pregnant as a result of rape. Yet, in South Africa it is very difficult to obtain a legal abortion, even following rape. To illustrate, although approximately 16 000 rapes were reported to the police in 1984, which meant that at least 1 600 women were likely to have become pregnant as a result of these rapes, only 40 legal abortions were granted to rape survivors.[31]

Under existing South African law[32] a legal abortion must be procured by a medical practitioner in a state hospital with two other medical practitioners certifying in writing that the abortion is necessary. Legal abortions may only be granted where a state psychiatrist deems it necessary to protect the mental health of the woman concerned; where the medical profession considers that the child is likely to be born with a severe mental and/or physical handicap; or where a district surgeon is convinced that the foetus was conceived as a consequence of rape or incest. In the lattermentioned instance, the survivor is required to report the rape or incest in order to obtain a legal abortion.

Since the majority of survivors do not report rape or incest, they are not eligible for legal abortions. Although it is difficult to acquire accurate figures regarding illegal abortions in South Africa, it has been estimated that approximately 200 000 teenagers undergo illegal abortions annually.[33] In 1985, 32 500 women, of whom 13 600 were aged between 15 and 19 years, underwent surgery for the removal of the residues of pregnancy. Doctors believe that most of these operations were conducted to deal with the complications of illegal abortions.[34]

Denying women control over their own fertility is one of the many mechanisms for the social control of women, the aim of which is to keep women dependent on men.[35] Although the matter of abortion should not be considered in isolation from the broader issue of whether women have access to effective and safe contraception, neither of which is the case in South Africa, the limitations of this paper prevent due consideration of this complex matter. Nevertheless, we would propose that the existing law on abortion be replaced with new legislation allowing women abortion on demand during the first three months of pregnancy. The final decision to have an abortion must be that of the woman concerned and not of the legal or medical professions. After three months of pregnancy, women should be informed of the risks of abortion and the decision should then become that of the woman concerned and her doctor. Furthermore, so-called abortificants which produce 'spontaneous abortion' should be made available and accessible to all women free of charge, and they should be encouraged to use abortificants should they miss a period and not wish to be pregnant.

Resources

Rape survivors consistently report a severe lack of resources and facilities and a range of practices which constitute secondary victimisation. For instance, they have been routinely required by the police to identify assailants by touching them on the shoulder and have had to give statements to unsympathetic male police officers in crowded charge offices. To avoid such additional trauma and to effectively assist those who suffer sexual assault we would propose the establishment of state-funded but community-managed Assistance Centres for Abused Women, similar to the Sexual Assault Centres in New Zealand.[36] These centres would be the *first* point of referral for survivors of sexual assault, rather than the police. Instead of district surgeons, specially trained female doctors attached to the centres would conduct the necessary forensic examinations, provide prophylactic treatment for venereal disease and pregnancy, administer necessary medical treatment and collect, prepare and present evidence for court cases. The centres would also provide temporary safe accommodation if necessary and the services of trained counsellors; women's advocates to provide information about legal matters, prepare complainants for and support them through legal proceedings; and social workers to assist survivors in matters of material assistance such as obtaining victim compensation and other forms of social welfare.

Domestic violence

In South Africa, battered women express little confidence in police assistance. The common experience is that the police either fail to respond to calls for help, or merely warn male abusers. By contrast the police complain that

> the biggest problem facing them is that the majority of battering charges laid by women are later withdrawn... Often there are no witnesses and it is the man's word against the woman's... Invariably they [battered women] go back to their husbands or boyfriends.[37]

At Rape Crisis (Cape Town) we have found that it is fear of retaliation by abusers which drives many battered women to refuse to lay charges or to later withdraw their complaints. The legal devices, interdicts and peace orders, available for protecting women from continued male abuse, have usually proved to be inadequate in practice. Interdicts have generally been the more effective of the two devices, in so far as the police tend to respond more consistently and effectively to violations of interdicts. However, interdicts are not granted timeously, they are expensive and are often inflexible and not well-suited to the requirements of particular domestic violence situations. Peace orders, although more economical and easier to acquire, are frequently ineffective in practice, because the police do not treat violations of such orders as matters which deserve serious attention.

It is true that there are few willing witnesses in cases of domestic violence, because it occurs in the home and outsiders are often reticent to become involved. It is also typical for abused women to leave and return to their abusers many times before making a final break.

> Economic dependence on their partner, coupled with the high unemployment rate and poor educational standards leave many women with little choice but to stay. [Additionally] [w]hen a relationship breaks down, economic and emotional dependency mitigates against women leaving, while the social stigma attached to divorce and the emotional effects on children encourage women to tolerate the violence, often to their disadvantage.[38]

We would propose the following changes to overcome some of the problems which face battered women in South Africa. A Women's Protection Unit, akin to the Child Protection Unit, should be established by the police and staffed by specially trained personnel. Every woman who reports abuse should be referred to an Assistance Centre for Abused Women (discussed above) and should be offered assistance by a team from this unit comprising a specially trained female doctor, counsellor, advocate and social worker, as well as a member of the Women's Protection Unit.

Since available interdicts and peace orders are ineffective, legislation should be introduced enabling specially designed Domestic Violence Intervention Orders (DVOs) such as those used in Australia.[39] These DVOs are more flexible legal instruments which can be shaped to meet the requirements of specific situations. They are not limited to preventing only physical violence, but also sexual, financial, social, verbal, psychological and emotional abuse. Furthermore, such DVOs may be used by *de facto* partners, parents, children and all of those comprising a household.

Legislation should be passed making it the legal duty of the police to respond to every call for assistance from abused women and it should be mandatory that the police arrest and hold male abusers in custody for at least 12 hours. On release, women should be offered the protection of a DVO automatically and free of charge. The police should be given the authority to issue emergency DVOs, which could be formalised subsequently by magistrates' courts. In addition, the prison services should keep the police and survivors informed of the release of male abusers from prison.

Increasing numbers of those who assist abused women agree that legislation should be introduced to make it the duty of the police, and not just of women, to lay charges of domestic violence against male abusers and to take such complaints to trial, despite the withdrawal of charges by survivors. This approach has been adopted in Ontario, Canada, and research on the efficacy of this legal strategy has shown that prosecuting male abusers prevents domestic violence for an average of 18 months following arrest.[40] This proposal remains controversial, for some feminists argue that it disempowers women by denying them the right to choose. I would argue, however, that in reality women's oppression has placed them in a position where they do not have real choice. How can one argue that a woman who withdraws a domestic violence charge because she is threatened by her abuser, or that a woman who returns to her abuser because she has no accommodation or financial means of supporting herself and her children, has any real choice? I would add that strategies like mandatory charging and prosecution should be viewed as temporary methods of assistance to be discontinued when women have real options.

As was mentioned above, cases of domestic violence and rape often fail in court due to a lack of evidence, especially evidence which the court deems to be 'independent' in nature. Typically, both domestic violence and sexual assault are patterned offences, that is, they are repeated over time. We would thus propose that it be made possible for male abusers, sexual and otherwise, to be tried for a *pattern* of abuse, rather than only for a single offence.[41] Although it is beyond the scope of this discussion, this proposal should also be considered for the offences of child sexual abuse and sexual harassment. To this end, a register should be kept by the office of the attorney-general of the names of alleged and convicted male abusers and of the characteristics of their alleged or actual offences.

> However, to guard against the abuse of such a record, we suggest that it consist of sworn statements made to the police... [which] should then be lodged at the office of the Attorney-General, and be kept in abeyance until a reasonable trial can be held.[42]

At present there are no state-funded refuges for battered women in South Africa and only three non-state run shelters, two in Cape Town and one in Johannesburg. It is proposed therefore, that the Department of Health and Welfare bear the responsibility for providing sufficient, free and safe accommodation for those abused women and their children who wish to leave their abusers.

To ease the financial burden of abused women, a state-funded compensation scheme should be established for the victims of male abuse. Where feasible, abusers' sentences should include some kind of direct financial compensation for their victims such as payment for medical, legal and therapeutic assistance. Furthermore, abused women should receive free services and special welfare grants for the maintenance of themselves and their children, as in Canada.

At this point let me address an issue which has been neglected thus far, namely, the 'treatment' of the perpetrators of domestic violence and of sexual abuse. For, as has been pointed out, '[m]en are responsible for their own violence. There is nothing women can do to make a man violent if he chooses not to be'.[43] Regrettably, however, the majority of programmes designed to deter male abusers have met with little success. This does not mean that we cannot learn from the experiences of others, especially from those few programmes which are now beginning to succeed, such as the programme of the Domestic Violence Service in South Australia.[44] Accumulated experience has shown that programmes are more effective when conducted with volunteers, when participation does *not* serve to reduce sentences and when groups also include men who have not abused women. We would thus suggest that efforts be made to develop programmes appropriate for South Africa. As a start, we would propose that a small number of pilot programmes be initiated through existing organisations like the National Institute for the Prevention of Crime and the Rehabilitation of Offenders (NICRO), and that they be monitored and evaluated carefully, before being introduced on a wide scale.

Conclusion

To conclude, some may feel that too great an emphasis has been placed on legal reform in this paper. In response, I would urge that the power of law not be underestimated, for

> not only does the law serve to reproduce social order (not that it always does this) but it actually constitutes and defines that order. The law is a 'cultural underpinning'. The legal form is one of the main forms of social practise through which actual relationships embodying sexual stratification have been expressed.[45]

Historically, the law has served effectively to mould public opinion, to express public disapproval of certain conduct whilst supporting other types of conduct. Thus far, the law has worked largely to the disadvantage of women and now is the time for us to turn it to our advantage.

At another level, some may feel that the recommendations made here accord the state too great a degree of control over women. It should be noted, however, that these proposals should be implemented using political methods of negotiating change through consultation and involvement at the grassroots level, particularly with those organisations which are already active in the field. Accordingly, we would require that women be actively involved in any changes affecting them and that future services for abused women be state-funded, but community managed, and then mainly by women.

Another point of criticism may be that the suggested changes are not feasible, because they require substantial financial support on the part of a state which is facing the enormous expense involved in trying to compensate the victims of 40 years of apartheid. In this respect I would emphasise that 'the responsibility for ensuring equality, racial as well as sexual *should* be placed upon the state',[46] for women are as much victims of gender oppression as black people are of racial oppression.

In this paper, I have attempted to outline some of the specific changes which Rape Crisis (Cape Town) believes will not only assist women who are abused by men, but will also contribute toward the transformation of the deeper roots of gender oppression in South Africa.

It is our firm hope that these concrete suggestions for change will constitute part of the process of 'giving reality to notional equality', for

> [t]he emancipation of women requires more than a declaratory commitment to equality and legislation prohibiting discrimination. A declaration that there shall be no discrimination on the basis of gender is necessary and serves as a statement of intent and has a normative value. However, such a declaration, whether or not it is entrenched in a constitution, can amount to no more than a token gesture, if the material, ideological, educational and cultural underpinnings of gender oppression are not simultaneously addressed, so as to provide a basis for giving reality to notional equality.[47]

[This paper was written for Rape Crisis (Cape Town). The author wishes to acknowledge and to thank all those members of Rape Crisis (Cape Town) and the women with whom we work who contributed their ideas to this paper, particularly Pat Anderson and Mikki van Zyl.]

Notes

1. The ANC Constitutional Guidelines for a Democratic South Africa, *Weekly Mail*, 7–13.10.1988, p3.
2. A Sachs, *Protecting Human Rights in a New South Africa*, Cape Town: Oxford University Press, 1990, p57.
3. Rape Crisis (Cape Town), *Violence in South Africa*, Training Manual, Cape Town, 1989, p5.
4. Rape Crisis (Cape Town), *Violence in South Africa*.
5. Co-ordinated Action for Battered Women (CABW), *Battering is a Crime: An Information Booklet for Battered Women*, Cape Town, 1990, p1.
6. T Angless, *Battered Women*, Cape Town: University of Cape Town, 1985, p7.
7. National Institute for the Prevention of Crime and the Rehabilitation of Offenders (NICRO), quoted in S Sorour, 'Women on the Receiving End', *The Weekend Argus*, 1989.
8. Unpublished Research, Institute of Criminology, University of Cape Town, 1986.
9. CABW quoted in Sorour, 'Women on the Receiving End'.
10. ANC Constitutional Guidelines, px.
11. Sorour, 'Women on the Receiving End'.
12. N Hill, quoted in Sorour, 'Women on the Receiving End'.
13. P Anderson, quoted in Sorour, 'Women on the Receiving End'.
14. F Ginwala, 'Formulating National Policy Regarding the Emancipation of Women and the Promotion of Women's Development in Our Country', proceedings of the Malibongwe conference, Amsterdam, 1990.
15. Ginwala, 'Formulating National Policy', p6.

16. J Mugford, 'Domestic Violence', *Violence Today*, 2, 1989, pp1–8.
17. G Marcus, 'Family Violence: Whose Responsibility? A Community Development Strategy for Dealing with the Problem of Family Violence', Occasional Papers on Family Violence, Melbourne: Community Education Task Force on Family Violence, 1989, p66.
18. Western Cape Region, 'What do we Mean by the Emancipation of South African Women?', proceedings of the Malibongwe conference, Amsterdam, 1990, p10.
19. CR Snyman, *Criminal Law*, Durban: Butterworths, 2nd edition, 1989, p400.
20. C Hall, 'Rape: The Politics of Definition', Master of Laws Dissertation, University of Cape Town, 1987.
21. Snyman, *Criminal Law*, p401.
22. Snyman, *Criminal Law*, p401.
23. Hall, 'Rape'.
24. Hall, 'Rape', p24.
25. Snyman, *Criminal Law*, p438.
26. Snyman, *Criminal Law*, p438.
27. Snyman, *Criminal Law*, p438.
28. LH Hoffmann and DT Zeffertt, *The South African Law of Evidence*, Durban: Butterworths, 1981, 4th edition, 1988.
29. Hoffmann and Zeffertt, *The South African Law of Evidence*, p455.
30. The Sexual Offences Act, 23 of 1957, as amended.
31. Commissioner of the South African Police, Annual Report, 1985, p18.
32. The Abortion and Sterilization Act, 2 of 1975.
33. The Natal Organisation of Women, 'The Nature of Women's Oppression', proceedings of the Malibongwe conference, Amsterdam, 1990, p15.
34. B Oswell, 'Abortion: A Woman's Right to Control her own Fertility', unpublished seminar paper, University of Cape Town, 1990.
35. G Greer, *Sex and Destiny: The Politics of Human Fertility*, London: Picador, 1984.
36. F Goodyear, 'Sexual Assault Centre, Auckland, New Zealand', *Medical Law*, 8, 1989, pp297–302.
37. S Crewe, quoted in Sorour, 'Women on the Receiving End'.
38. Hill, quoted in Sorour, 'Women on the Receiving End'.
39. Australian Crimes Family Violence Act of 1987.
40. Canadian Broadcasting Corporation, 'Punching Judy', video, 1989.
41. Rape Crisis (Cape Town), 'Report to the Commission of Inquiry into the Inclusion of Psychopathy as a Certifiable Mental Illness and the Handling of Psychopathic and other Violent Offenders', Cape Town, 1990.
42. Rape Crises (Cape Town), 'Report to the Commission of Inquiry', p5.
43. R Brand, 'Why Should we be Surprised when Wife Bashers Change?', *Criminology Australia*, April/May 1990, pp16–18.
44. Brand, 'Why Should we be Surprised', pp16–18.
45. MDA Freeman, 'Violence Against Women: Does the Legal System Provide Solutions or Itself Constitute the Problem?', *British Journal of Law and Society*, 7, 1980, p226.
46. Ginwala, 'Formulating National Policy', p5.
47. Ginwala, 'Formulating National Policy', p2.

Paying for Stolen Kisses?

The law and sexual harassment in South Africa

Carla Sutherland

> Sexual harassment, depending on the form it takes, violates that right to integrity of the body and personality which belongs to every person and which is protected in our legal system both criminally and civilly. An employer has a duty to ensure that its employees are not subjected to this form of sexual harassment.[1]

J v M Ltd, the first reported case of sexual harassment in South Africa, was heard in the industrial court in February 1989.[2] The case is worth examining in some detail as it provides a useful framework within which to discuss sexual harassment in South Africa. It highlights many of the problems associated with sexual harassment and illustrates the limited legal protection currently offered to employees. In looking at this legal protection, the focus of the paper is limited, primarily, to the provisions contained within the Labour Relations Act. No serious examination of the options offered by civil and criminal law is entered into.

> The applicant sexually harassed another complainant, a much older woman, by caressing and/or slapping her buttocks and fondling her breasts. She found his behaviour offensive and told him not to come near her. Eventually she told him to remain on the other side of the desk whenever he entered the office.[3]

The case in question concerned a senior executive of an unnamed company. He was charged with sexual harassment at an internal company hearing, following numerous complaints about his behaviour. Specifically he was accused of having 'sexually molested and harassed' a female employee 'against her will'.[4]

He was alleged to have 'fondled her breasts'. This was one of many complaints of similar acts that had been received 'from the time the applicant first joined the (company)'. The company claimed that the general manager had on 'several occasions discussed (the) applicant's behaviour with him', and that he had been issued with a 'final warning'. This was disputed by the applicant, but accepted by the court. At the disciplinary hearing, chaired by the general manager of the company, he was found guilty of sexual harassment and given the opportunity to resign. This he did, but subsequently withdrew his resignation and was dismissed.[5]

The senior executive then brought an application for reinstatement to the industrial court. The application was brought in terms of section 43 of the Labour Relations Act, 28 of 1956, which gives the industrial court the authority to reinstate employees if the court is satisfied that an 'alleged unfair labour practice' has taken place. The applicant contended that the company had not followed company procedure and that the sanction imposed had been 'too harsh'.[6]

In his defence the applicant argued that his behaviour was 'no more than mildly flirtatious... [or] mediterranean type behaviour'. In support of this contention, the applicant submitted two petitions. The first was signed by '*all* the ladies in the office controlled by [the applicant]... pleading for compassion and stating that they did not feel offended or sexually harassed' by his past behaviour (own emphasis). The second was signed by 'some 500 employees of the company, requesting the management to "reconsider his dismissal"'.[7]

The application was dismissed. The court found the senior executive guilty of sexual harassment. Sexual harassment was viewed as a 'serious matter which require[d] attention from employers'. The sanction imposed by the company, namely dismissal, was upheld, as the seriousness of the matter warranted this action.

Neither of the submitted petitions were given serious consideration by the court. In response to the first, De Kock argued that he could 'not accept that all of them [the signees], consented to the applicant fondling their buttocks and breasts and took pleasure in doing so. The evidence that many have objected to and resigned because of his fondling habits is clear'. The second petition was dismissed on the grounds that the employees who signed it '[did] not know the facts' and 'natural[ly]... would have sympathy with the applicant'.[8]

It seems unlikely that the people who signed the second petition would have done so without any knowledge of what the applicant was accused of. For instance, it is implausible to suppose that he would have received the support he did if he had been accused of rape, murder or theft. The implication therefore is that sexual harassment in the workplace, even of the nature that the applicant was found guilty of, is regarded as acceptable, or at the very least as a somewhat trivial disciplinary offence. The widespread nature of the support may have been instrumental in persuading some of the women under the applicant's authority that what they had experienced was not serious or offensive, hence encouraging them to sign the first petition. While this remains at the level of speculation, these issues do, however, support the more general contention that sexual harassment in South Africa is both widespread and not treated seriously.

In addition, it appears that the court was also persuaded by a concern that 'it should be careful not simply to substitute its (the court's) own assessment for that of the employer'. It is argued that 'the standard of conduct which an employer expects from its employees... is a clear management prerogative'. The company's 'most senior executives' had decided that the applicant's conduct had 'fallen short of what is regarded as acceptable behaviour'. He had been warned of this several times and finally dismissed. The court found that there was 'no basis' on which to find the 'judgement' of the company 'clearly unfair or unreasonable'.[9]

Definition of sexual harassment

'At least until 1976, no one had a name for this collective experience.'[10] The definition of sexual harassment used in *J v M Ltd* was 'unwanted sexual attention in the employment environment'. Different *forms* of sexual harassment were also identified:

> [I]n its narrowest form sexual harassment occurs when a woman (or a man) is expected to engage in sexual activity in order to obtain or keep employment or obtain promotion or other favourable working conditions. In its wider view it is, however, any unwanted sexual behaviour or comment which has a negative effect on the recipient.[11]

While De Kock, the presiding member of the court, relied largely on the article by Mowatt[12] for his definition, in recognising different forms of sexual harassment it is very similar in scope and nature to the US Equal Employment Opportunity Committee's (EEOC) 'Guidelines on Sexual Harassment'. These guidelines were adopted in 1980, and set out the 'legal definition' of sexual harassment which has been 'analysed extensively by the courts'.[13] The guidelines define sexual harassment as:

Unwelcome sexual advances, requests for sexual favors, and other verbal or physical conduct of a sexual nature... when (1) submission to such conduct is made either explicitly or implicitly a term or condition of an individual's employment, (2) submission to or rejection of such conduct by an individual is used as the basis for employment decisions affecting such individual, or (3) such conduct has the purpose or effect of unreasonably interfering with an individual's work performance or creating an intimidating, hostile, or offensive working environment.[14]

The first two sections of this definition deal with what has become known as *quid pro quo* harassment. This occurs when specific employment opportunities or benefits are withheld as a means of coercing sexual favours. In other words, an individual in a position of power, either explicitly or implicitly, uses his/her authority to hire, fire, promote or allocate work to 'persuade' an employee to engage in sexual activities. These activities can include complying with requests for dates or sex, being touched or fondled, or responding positively to sexual comments and flirtations.[15]

The latter section of the definition deals less explicitly with direct power relationships in employment. It focuses instead on the work environment. If this is made unpleasant or uncomfortable for anyone on the basis of their sex or sexual preference, then it constitutes sexual harassment. This type of harassment, therefore, can include sexist or homophobic jokes or comments, unwelcome verbal and/or physical advances of a sexual nature, offensive sexual flirtations, graphic comments about an individual's body, sexually degrading words used to describe an individual, and the public display of sexually suggestive objects or pictures. In a 'working conditions sexual harassment' case, an employee must demonstrate that a superior has either 'create[d] or condone[d]' such an atmosphere.[16]

Importantly, in *J v M Ltd*, De Kock recognised both the wide spectrum of activities that constituted sexual harassment, and the fact that these actions could be of a physical or verbal nature. Moreover, unlike many definitions, he argues that these acts do not have to be repeated to be harassment:

Conduct which can constitute sexual harassment ranges from innuendo, inappropriate gestures, suggestions or hints or fondling without consent or by force to its worst form, namely rape. It is in my opinion also not necessary that the conduct must be repeated. A single act can constitute sexual harassment.[17]

Within both of the definitions three points are emphasised. Firstly, that the acts are of a *sexual nature*. Secondly, that sexual harassment covers a wide range of activities that may be *either physical or verbal*. Finally, these acts are *unwanted* by the recipient of them. There remains, however, a fundamental distinction.

In the United States sexual harassment is recognised as a form of unlawful sexual discrimination. Under Title VII of the Civil Rights Act[18] it is an unlawful practice 'for an employer to discriminate against applicants or employees on the basis of sex', and, as 'by definition, sexual harassment occurs because of the harassed employee's sex' it is unlawful. The EEOC has the 'responsibility of administering Title VII' and their guidelines provide a legal definition of sexual harassment.[19] Moreover, under Title VII, if sexual harassment can be proved, an employer can be held liable for such acts. Under this legislation employees can apply for 'interdicts preventing certain conduct' as well as be awarded 'back pay [and/or] damages for injured feelings'.[20]

The law in South Africa

> There is reason to suggest that a remedy (for sexual harassment) may now exist in South African law with the introduction of the concept of unfair labour practice.[21]

No legal definition of sexual harassment exists in South Africa. According to Mowatt[22] it is a 'wrong which can presently be redressed by the appropriate criminal sanction or civil action'. He argues that the 'concept of sexual harassment' is covered under the criminal law by a such crimes as 'rape, through indecent assault, extortion to crimen injuria'. Civilly, a victim of sexual harassment 'may also be entitled to recover damages under the delictual head of injuria'.[23]

In *J v M Ltd*, this view appears to be endorsed as it is argued that sexual harassment 'violate[s] that right to integrity of body and personality which belongs to every person and which is protected in our legal system both criminally and civilly'. This is different, although not contradictory, from the view that sexual harassment is a form of sexual discrimination. Mowatt recognises the limitations of this approach in relation to the workplace:

> [Criminal or civil] redress is obviously punishment of the offender, or damages for past wrongs, but it essentially fails to compensate the victim for the harm suffered in terms of her work environment. Although justice is done, the woman may have lost her employment, or promotion opportunity, or some other tangible asset.[24]

He contends that what might address this issue is the use of the 'concept "unfair labour practice" contained within the Labour Relations Act'.[25]

The 1979 amendments, responsible for the deracialisation of the original Act, also made provision for the establishment of the industrial court. The industrial court was given the responsibility of defining an 'unfair labour practice' as the 1979 definition was 'embarrassingly wide... simply "any labour practice which in the opinion of the court is an unfair labour practice"'. A year later, and subsequently in 1988, the Act was amended to include a more specific definition of this concept.[26]

Mowatt, writing prior to the 1988 amendments, argues that subparas (a)(1) and (a)(iv), of the 1980 version of the Act are of 'particular significance in the case of sexual harassment': where subsection (a)(1) defines as 'unfair' any practice which has the 'affect' of prejudicing or unfairly jeopardising 'any employee's or class of employee's' employment opportunities, work security or physical, economic, moral or social welfare'; and subsection (a)(iv) states that any practice which has the effect of 'detrimentally' affecting (or doing so in the future) 'the relationship between employer and employee' is an unfair labour practice. Mowatt suggests that both of these are applicable to sexual harassment, and as such are subject to the jurisdiction and protection of the industrial court.[27] His argument remains relevant, however, as these particular aspects of the definition appear in the current, amended Act.[28]

The definition of an 'unfair labour practice' expressly includes 'the unfair discrimination by any employer against any employee solely on the grounds of... sex...',[29] a definition that was maintained within the current Act.[30] Mowatt, while recognising that it could be used in relation to sexual harassment, implicitly warns against it: 'But a delicate and exotic plant, such as anti-discriminatory legislation, would whither and die in an environment in which discrimination is an "institutionalised form of government".'[31]

Certainly there is little evidence to suggest that until recently sexual discrimination would be treated seriously. To the contrary, in the Wiehahn Report,[32] dealing with 'Women in Employment', it was reported that '[m]any instances of discrimination against women in employment were recorded', but that 'in the limited time available' it was not able to 'sponsor any research' into it.[33] In the current political context, however, there may be greater scope for its use, as, for example, in the ANC constitutional guidelines and the bill of rights, specific attention is paid to this question.

This remains at the level of speculation as there have been no reported cases that have tested these suggestions. While *J v M Ltd* did deal with sexual harassment it was both unusual and ironic that it did so, not in the context of a victim of sexual harassment seeking reinstatement, protection, or compensation, but of a perpetrator seeking relief from sanction.

The court did, however, find the applicant 'guilty' of sexual harassment and refuse to reinstate him. Given that there is no legal definition of sexual harassment, it is worth examining the grounds on which the applicant was found guilty. The court was satisfied that the applicant had repeatedly and 'without consent' touched 'in a sexual way' female employees 'under his control'. These actions included caressing/slapping buttocks and fondling breasts. That the actions were 'unwanted', a critical aspect of sexual harassment, was supported by the fact that there were complaints and resignations in response to the applicant's behaviour from the time he joined the company. Secondly, he was warned several times by more senior executives that his behaviour was unacceptable. Finally the court argues that: 'His conduct was also such that if he had been charged criminally, for indecent assault he would have found it difficult to defend himself.'[34]

In the absence of a legal definition of sexual harassment this latter point may be of the most significance. It certainly raises the question of how willing the court would have been to find the applicant guilty of sexual harassment if he had engaged in 'less serious' forms of it, particularly those that did not involve any physical contact. There are, however, two more fundamental criticisms of the approach argued for by Mowatt. The first is that the industrial court only offers protection and relief to those people already in employment.[35] The unfair labour practice concept does not include people *applying* for employment. The EEOC guidelines in the US specifically recognise that this category of person may be especially vulnerable to sexual harassment and explicitly prohibit employers from engaging in it. Bird suggests that sexual harassment, including 'jobs in exchange for sex', is common:

> The position of women workers is too heavy with many things: say you are a woman and you are looking for a job. When you reach a factory, you find the induna there and you ask him. If you like the job the induna will tell that you must sleep with him before you get the job. And you've got no choice. You want to work and your children are starving in Soweto. So, some women sleep with those men.[36]

The industrial court offers no protection or redress to persons in this situation. Moreover, the Labour Relations Act does not cover all categories of workers. Domestic workers, for example, are exempt from even the limited protection offered by this Act.[37] It is inadequate to offer, as a legal option for the prohibition of sexual harassment in the workplace, legislation that does not cover all categories of workers.

Finally, in his article Mowatt concedes that '[o]ne problem in regarding sexual harassment as an "unfair labour practice" is the relief which the victim may obtain'. Prior to the 1988 amendments of the Labour Relations Act, the industrial court could only instruct an employer to 'cease an unfair labour practice', or to 'restore the position to that which prevailed before the introduction of the unfair labour practice'. In addition, the industrial court could not 'award... damages for... humiliation suffered or for lost promotion opportunities'. This led Mowatt to conclude that while the industrial court could provide a 'remedy' for sexual harassment, 'the relief is relatively ineffective'.[38]

With the 1988 amendments this situation has been addressed. Expressly included in Section 46(9) is the provision that the industrial court may order 'compensation'; that is 'to order the payment of "the value, estimated in money, of something lost"'.[39] Under this provision claims for lost promotion opportunities, as well as humiliation or mental anguish, could be submitted.

The judgement offered by *J v M Ltd*, however, remains significant. Within the limitations already explored, the industrial court sounded a firm warning to employers that sexual harassment would not be tolerated. Moreover, it was argued that it was an *employer's responsibility* to see that it did not occur: 'An employer undoubtedly has a duty to ensure that its employees are not subjected to this form of violation (sexual harassment) within the work-place.'[40]

Particular significance is attached to this in a case note on *J v M Ltd*. Employers are 'advised' to 'take immediate appropriate action' if an allegation of sexual harassment is brought to their attention, as failure to do so 'could lead to an allegation of the employer committing an ULP (unfair labour practice). In addition, the failure to act could possibly be regarded as constituting breach of contract or form the basis for other common law liabilities'.[41]

Caveat Emptor

'[T]he standard of conduct which an employer expects from its employees... is a clear management prerogative.'[42] *J v M Ltd*, as the only reported judgement on sexual harassment has many positive points that need to be welcomed. It identifies sexual harassment in the workplace as a serious problem that needs to be dealt with. And perhaps most importantly, it stresses that it is an employer's responsibility to ensure that it does not occur.[43]

While these points are made explicitly in the judgement given, there are other factors within the case that need to be stressed. De Kock appears to recognise and appreciate many of the problems associated with sexual harassment. He dismisses the petitions offered in defence of the applicant. While he does so on technical grounds, ruling that they are inadmissible, it is to be welcomed that he is not swayed by the common misperceptions and myths about sexual violence that form the basis of both petitions. Moreover in dismissing as mitigating evidence the fact that the complainant withdrew her accusations he asserts that:

> The first complainant subsequently sought to withdraw her complaint on the basis that the applicant did not intend to harass her sexually. She at no time withdrew the facts. The facts establish sexual harassment. The fact that she subsequently felt sorry for the applicant proves no more than she is a nice person.[44]

There are, however, some aspects to the judgement that give cause to concern. The first is the stress placed on conduct within the workplace being 'a clear management prerogative'. It is clear in South Africa, as elsewhere, that management structures are dominated by men. Konrad and Gutek, in their study, demonstrated that men are less willing than women to both identify sexual behaviour in the workplace as sexual harassment and to see it as a serious issue.[45] In this context it does not seem adequate to place the responsibility of dealing with sexual harassment with this group of people. The applicant himself was a senior member of the firm, responsible presumably for determining the code of conduct within the area that he controlled. It took four years for management to effectively deal with what the court labelled as 'a serious matter'.[46] This approach, at the very least, begs the question of what would happen if employees labelled particular behaviour as sexual harassment, while management did not. De Kock's judgement suggests that the industrial court might, in such an instance, find in favour of management and not offer relief to the victims.

This concern is heightened in the context of De Kock's argument against a previous judgement of the industrial court. In the case referred to, a female employee and a senior partner in the firm had a consential affair. Both parties were married. The affair was terminated when the wife of the partner found out about it. Subsequently, the female employee was asked to resign on the grounds that the manager found it stressful to work with her, and because of his wife's concern that the affair might begin again. The employee refused to do this, and instituted a means of continuing with her work while limiting work-related contact with the manager concerned. He was not happy with this situation and the employee was subsequently fired on the basis of a number of 'unsubstantiated allegations against her'. These included that she showed a 'perceptible reluctance to take instructions from other partners or even consider their wishes' and that she displayed 'an air of superiority which was not warranted'.[47] She filed an unfair labour practice suit, and was subsequently reinstated by the industrial court.[48]

In this situation, a particular code of conduct is being endorsed by the management of the firm concerned. It is considered as 'acceptable' that members of management engage in sexual relations with employees and when those sexual relations are terminated, that the employment relationship is also ended. De Kock implicitly endorses this practice, as he concludes that the industrial court should not have reinstated the employee. Instead he argues that the stress caused by the presence of the employee in the workplace would have a negative effect not only on the business but also on the marriages of both the manager and the employee. In such an instance he argues that 'the other directors (of the firm) are surely in a far better position to judge what is in everyone's interest, bearing in mind the natural tension evoked by the situation'. As such the industrial court should not have 'substitute[d] its own opinion in a matter of [this] nature'.[49]

He fails to recognise that the directors would be likely to act, not in 'everyone's interest', but in their own interests, without regard to the position of employees. It is this point that is made within the original judgement of *G v K*:

> For this court to approve of the applicant's dismissal would be tantamount to rendering every female employee vulnerable and expendable once she has slept or cavorted with her employer. It would also imply that in any amatory situation it is the employee who is to be regarded as the party who bears the guilt and, therefore, the one who must come out the worst for it. Such discriminatory treatment would be completely at variance with the standards of fairness and equity laid down by this court in its numerous standards.[50]

It is on these grounds that the employee was reinstated. In addition, the court is highly critical of the code of conduct endorsed by the management, and subsequently by De Kock:

> There is no basis, whether in law or in equity, for the proposition that when an employer has had an affair with his employee he may dismiss her once the affair is over on the ground that the employee's presence is a source of embarrassment for him. *In casu* the senior director should, at the outset, have been acutely aware of the possible consequences which the affair held in store, not only for himself but also for his wife and his company... The words of Catullus, the Latin poet, spring here to mind:
>
> The kiss I stole... how dear for it I paid![51]

Secondly, throughout his judgement, De Kock is at pains to stress that
the social code of conduct he is referring to is part of western culture:

> This case concerns relations between people who belong to the Western
> culture. In Western culture one expects gentlemanly conduct. Sexual
> harassment is unacceptable at any level in Western society. No warning
> or counselling is required and certainly not at senior management level.[52]

There are obvious problems with his stereotyped understanding of
acceptable roles for men and women, and the fact that 'gentlemanly conduct' can in his view include firing ex-mistresses. The cause for
particular concern, however, is that in a multi-cultural society like South
Africa the implication is that in some cultures sexual harassment is
acceptable. All employees, whatever their cultural background, deserve
protection in the workplace from harassers, whatever their cultural background. For the industrial court to suggest otherwise is to render women
in particular, but all employees in general not from a 'western culture',
vulnerable to sexual harassment, and denies them the full protection they
are entitled to by the court. What makes this particular argument offered
by De Kock the more surprising is that prior to this he states: 'Sexual
harassment... violates that right to integrity of the body and personality
which belongs to every person and which is protected in our legal system both criminally and civilly.' [53] 'Integrity of body and personality' is
a *right* that belongs to everybody. To suggest, as De Kock does, that a
court of law, such as the industrial court, cannot intrude into the cultural
integrity of 'groups' which are not part of 'western culture' in order to
offer protection from violation of 'body and personality' is unacceptable.

All of these suggest that what is needed within the 'unfair labour
practice' code is an explicit definition of what constitutes sexual harassment. In other words, while it should remain an employers' responsibility
to see that sexual harassment does not occur in the workplace, it should
not be their prerogative to define it. Such a process would afford much
greater protection to employees and encourage the reporting of such acts.

Prevention is better than cure

> Employers have already recognized the necessity of introducing rules in
> regard to racial tension. Perhaps they should also consider introducing
> rules expressly prohibiting sexual harassment.[54]

Mowatt concludes that at best the law offers limited protection and redress to victims of sexual harassment. Moreover, it is the powerless that
have the least access to redress in the courts, as the process is often
time-consuming, expensive and alienating. For example, in a South

African context, it is difficult to imagine a black female domestic worker taking her white male employer to court for sexual harassment.

Mowatt draws a useful parallel between racial and sexual harassment and points to the advantages that have been gained through establishing rules of appropriate conduct around racial tensions in the workplace. He suggests that a similar approach should be adopted with regard to sexual harassment.[55] Explicit guidelines around sexual harassment, by making it clear what behaviour constitutes sexual harassment and that such behaviour is unacceptable, could encourage the labelling and reporting of inappropriate sexual conduct in the workplace. Rules localised in the workplace, and supported by legislations expressly outlawing such behaviour, could act as a deterrent to perpetrators, as well as an encouragement to victims to report such actions.

In assessing the effect of the EEOC guidelines and specific rules in workplaces in the US, it has been concluded that these need to be supplemented with training and education. It has already been argued that sexual harassment is often regarded as normal and acceptable behaviour. It is this attitude that needs to be addressed if sexual harassment is to be effectively dealt with. Changing accepted ways of co-workers and managers and workers relating to one another cannot only be done with rules. A more successful approach is through education and training:

> Training... is a proven mechanism for promoting an organization's policies and procedures, while increasing the awareness of managers and supervisors of their roles and obligations under these policies... [H]aving a training program may well be the best defense for an institution in a sexual harassment case, both as a preventative measure and as a remedy... By providing appropriate training, the institution can apprise both managers and employees, as well as other potential victims, of methods for handling situations involving harassing behavior. Training can stop such behavior, provide coping mechanisms, and offer individuals a means of differentiating true sexually harassing activity from behavior that is not so intended. Training can help to eliminate an environment that encourages situations of sexual harassment.[56]

The role of trade unions

> Over the years there have been many complaints about sexual harassment and exploitation of women members by management and particularly middle management such as foremen... What became clear to us was that it is all very well discussing the issue as it manifests itself with management, but sexual exploitation was taking place within our own union structures.[57]

Wilson argues that it was a 'struggle' to get trade unions in the United Kingdom to address sexual harassment. Women within union structures had to be organised in order to 'insist' that the issue be taken up. 'But it is even harder for women in non-unionized workplaces to get sexual harassment dealt with.'[58]

At the 1989 Cosatu congress a motion on sexual exploitation was put forward by the Transport and General Workers Union (TGWU). It identified 'sexually exploitative' behaviour and sexual harassment, as a problem *within* the ranks of the union:

> [M]ale comrades in our organisation often get involved in relationships with newly recruited women members of our affiliates... [T]hese relationships are often characterised by an imbalance of power because of the greater political experience and organisational seniority of the male comrade... [W]hen these unequal relationships collapse, the women often drop out of the organisation. In other cases, divisions start to develop in the organisation because of the broken relationship... [M]any incidents of sexual harassment of women comrades by male comrades have occurred.[59]

No resolution was passed, as 'delegations from most unions disagree[d] about the issue'. Perhaps of greatest importance, however, was not so much the motion itself as the debate that it generated on the congress floor:

> Women say that it is a fact that men in the unions take advantage of their leadership positions as organisers or shopstewards. They make sexual advances towards women... But most men saw the resolution differently. Unionists say that the whole tone of the congress changed when the sexual conduct resolution was discussed. Before delegates were tired and serious, but suddenly there was excitement, laughter and lots of joking.[60]

This response points to the significant problems that will be encountered in addressing sexual harassment. Some of the points raised in the debate demonstrate the nature of these problems. These are in keeping with problems associated generally with sexual violence, namely that it is often regarded as 'normal', or that the victim is blamed:[61]

> Some delegates argued that there was no such thing as sexual exploitation – that women asked for it and that women can say no. Others argued that it was a problem of discipline but that it did not warrant debate at national congress.[62]

Jane Barrett, the TGWU general secretary, in assessing the response to the motion argued that '[i]t was no surprise that there was not overwhelming support for the resolutions'. However, she recognised the value of the issue being raised and concluded that this was the start to a process that in 'the next few years' would result in a 'shift in consciousness'.[63]

Conclusion

The judgement offered by *J v M Ltd*, and the encouraging signs of organised labour finally addressing this problem, suggest that in South Africa this pervasive and until now almost invisible problem may at last be getting the attention it deserves.

Notes

1. *J v M Ltd, Industrial Law Journal (ILJ)*, 10, 1989, pp755–62.
2. *J v M Ltd*, pp755–62.
3. *J v M Ltd*, pp755–62.
4. *J v M Ltd*, pp755–62.
5. *J v M Ltd*, pp755–62.
6. *J v M Ltd*, pp755–62.
7. *J v M Ltd*, p761.
8. *J v M Ltd*, p761.
9. *J v M Ltd*, pp755–62.
10. E Stanko, *Intimate Intrusions: Women's Experience of Male Violence*, London: Routledge and Kegan Paul, 1985, p61.
11. *J v M Ltd*, p757.
12. JG Mowatt, 'Sexual Harassment: New Remedy for Old Wrong', *ILJ*, 7, 1986, p652.
13. Lanora Welzenback (ed), *Sexual Harassment: Issues and Answers. A Guide for Education, Business and Industry*, Washington: College and University Personnel Association, 1986, p4.
14. See Welzenbach, *Sexual Harassment*, p23.
15. Welzenbach, *Sexual Harassment*, p4.
16. Welzenbach, *Sexual Harassment*, p4.
17. *J v M Ltd*, p757.
18. The Civil Rights Act of 1964.
19. Welzenbach, *Sexual Harassment*, p9.
20. Mowatt, 'Sexual Harassment', p645.
21. Mowatt, 'Sexual Harassment', p638.
22. Mowatt, 'Sexual Harassment', p638.
23. Mowatt, 'Sexual Harassment', p645.
24. Mowatt, 'Sexual Harassment', p645.
25. Labour Relations Act of 1953 as amended in 1979, 1980, and 1988. Referred to in Mowatt, 'Sexual Harassment', p646.
26. E Cameron, H Cheadle and C Thompson, *The New Labour Relations Act*, South Africa: Juta and Co, 1989, see p22 and pp161–5.

27. Mowatt, 'Sexual Harassment', pp646–7.
28. See subparas (o)(i) and (iv) of the Labour Relations Act, and Cameron et al, *The New Labour Relations Act*, p165.
29. Labour Relations Act, section 1(k).
30. Labour Relations Act, section 1(i).
31. Mowatt, 'Sexual Harassment', p646.
32. The Wiehahn Report, chapter 6 of part V, cited in Mowatt, 'Sexual Harassment', p646.
33. Cited in Mowatt, 'Sexual Harassment', p646.
34. *J v M Ltd*, p760.
35. Cameron, et al, *The New Labour Relations Act*, p139.
36. A Bird, cited in J Cock, 'Trapped Workers: Constraints and Contradictions Experienced by Black Women in Contemporary South Africa', *Women's Studies International Forum*, 10(2), 1987.
37. Cock, 'Trapped Workers', p134.
38. Mowatt, 'Sexual Harassment', p652.
39. Cameron, et al, *The New Labour Relations Act*, p251.
40. *J v M Ltd*, p758.
41. Bulbulia, 'Sexual Harassment as Grounds for Dismissal', *Labour Law Briefs*, 15 April 1989, p70.
42. *J v M Ltd*, p757.
43. *J v M Ltd*, p755.
44. *J v M Ltd*, p760.
45. A Konrad and B Gutek, 'Impact of Work Experiences on Attitudes Toward Sexual Harassment', *Administrative Science Quarterly*, 31, 1986.
46. *J v M Ltd*, p755.
47. *G v K*, p316.
48. *G v K*, p314.
49. *J v M Ltd*, p762.
50. *G v K*, p317.
51. *G v K*, p316.
52. *J v M Ltd*, p761.
53. *J v M Ltd*, p760.
54. Mowatt, 'Sexual Harassment', p652.
55. Mowatt, 'Sexual Harassment', p652.
56. Welzenbach, *Sexual Harassment*, p19.
57. I Obery, 'Challenging Sexual Exploitation', *Work In Progress*, 61, June 1989, p30. Interview with Jane Barrett, General Secretary of Transport and General Workers Union (TGWU).
58. E Wilson, *What is to Be Done About Violence Against Women?*, Great Britain: Penguin, 1983, pp181–2.
59. B Klugman, 'The Personal is Political', *South African Labour Bulletin*, 14(4), October 1989, p33, quoting the TGWU resolution from the Cosatu congress.
60. Klugman, 'The Personal is Political', p33.
61. L Vogelman, *The Sexual Face of Violence*, Johannesburg: Ravan, 1990.
62. Obery, 'Challenging Sexual Exploitation', p32, quoting Barrett.
63. Obery, 'Challenging Sexual Exploitation', p31.

Women and Reproductive Rights

Helen Rees

Reproductive rights could be defined as the right of women to decide when and how to have their children. It includes issues of contraception and abortion, infertility and childbirth. It also covers the rights of minority groups, such as lesbian women, to have children. This paper outlines the present situation in South Africa, and will look at policy development and areas requiring future legislation and policy decisions. One of the problems faced when putting together a paper on the subject is the lack of accurate information in some areas, which could be constructively used to inform us about future policy. At this point in South Africa's history, we must move beyond the kind of rhetoric used in discussion of issues like abortion and depo provera (a contraceptive injection), and develop policy based on sound appropriate research.

Contraception

Numerous surveys have been done in South Africa on contraceptive patterns and attitudes towards contraception. In one study of black women in the urban and rural areas of Cape Town and Ciskei, the fertility pattern of the 'average' woman was described. The age of the woman at the time of her first pregnancy was 19,8 years. She had 3,5 pregnancies, 2,9 living children and wished for 3,9 children. A sizable minority of the women experienced the death of at least one living child. Fifty-seven per cent of women were using contraception when interviewed but all but 20,7 per cent of these were receiving an injectable progestogen. In urban areas a significant minority used sterilisation or oral contraception.[1] The low utilisation of contraception was shown again in a study of coloured women attending antenatal clinics and family planning clinics. Forty-two per cent had never used contraception or had done so only after their third child was born. Sixty-nine per cent said their pregnancies were unplanned. Sixty-seven per cent indicated lack of knowledge or fear of contraception.[2]

This lack of knowledge about contraception is exaggerated in teenage girls. A study done in Transkei on pregnant rural schoolgirls showed that in nearly all cases the pregnancy was unplanned. Most of the girls were misinformed about sexual development, conception, sexual relationships and appropriate use of contraceptives. Teenage sex has become the norm rather than the exception. An extensive study from a teenage clinic in Cape Town showed that 81 per cent of girls attending for their first visit were already sexually active.[3] An AIDS survey done in Cape high schools revealed that three-quarters of the students had had sexual intercourse, and 25 per cent of boys and five per cent of girls had had more than one sexual partner in the previous year.[4]

While the lack of family planning facilities and the lack of education could be seen as an omission by the state, the abuse of Internal Uterus Contraceptive Devices (IUCDs), high-dose oestrogen pills and injectable progestogens must be seen in a different light. In urban areas, where the incidence of pelvic inflammatory disease is high, we are seeing a significant number of nulliparous women (women who have never been pregnant), including teenagers, fitted with IUCDs. IUCDs in this group cause a significantly higher incidence of pelvic infection, sometimes with resulting infertility. IUCDs are in fact prohibited from being fitted to members of this group in all standard medical text books.

A second inappropriate use of contraceptives is the widespread prescribing of high-dose oestrogen pills. In so-called developed countries, these pills have a restricted usage, but in South Africa state health services and general practitioners are continuing to prescribe these drugs to non-questioning, compliant women.

On an equally large scale we are seeing the abuse of injectable progestogens. A joke that comes out of many of our black hospitals is that 'depo is the fourth stage of labour'. Many women do not give informed consent for the injection, and women who try to refuse are often given a hard time.

In 1988, factories in Natal and the Western Cape were using injections to curb pregnancies among women workers to ensure maximum production. Women interviewed from one such factory in Natal related how, when looking for jobs, they were told that they would be injected every three months to stop them from 'breeding a lot'. They were told that childbirth should not interfere with production. The women said they felt defenseless and had to agree to the injections because they needed jobs.[5]

In these three examples of improper contraceptive use, we must ask why a woman agrees to any of these methods. I would suggest that in most cases we are not dealing with informed consent from the woman, but rather a paternalistic decision taken by the health worker on behalf of the woman. If women using the injectable progestogen were asked whether they knew about the side effects of bleeding or amenorrhoea (no periods) that the injection can cause, I am sure most women would have no idea. If we go back to the original statement that it is a woman's right to choose about contraception or not, then clearly there can be no real choice if the woman does not have the necessary knowledge about that contraceptive.

The assumption made here then is that the health worker believes that the choice of contraceptive method is better made by the 'informed' health worker rather than the 'ignorant' consumer. On a global scale it would seem that governments and drug companies have taken similar decisions. In the late 1970s there was an outcry by feminist lobby groups against the dumping of depo provera on poor women in developing countries. This resulted in countries like Zimbabwe banning depo after independence, because the drug had the reputation of being a tool of colonialist oppression. However, there is another side to this problem. Many South African women may now choose to use an injectable progestogen, partly because they are used to it and it suits them, but also because it is a method of prevention that can be concealed from controlling male partners. Progressive health workers working in family planning clinics are also finding that depo is the safest method of contraception in teenage girls who forget pills, and who should not be fitted with the loop.

This is a good example of the conflict involved in policy making. Should we follow the example of Zimbabwe and ban injectables, or should we first canvass South African women's opinion and make a decision about injectable usage based on this? If we do consult women and find a significant number are happy with injectables, do we end up overriding their views on the subject because of the bad reputation that depo has rightly earned for itself as a tool of women's oppression?

In contrast to enforced contraception, we have an example of the opposite problem in Gazankulu. Here, women's groups and care groups had a lot of input and discussion around contraception. Many women recognised the advantages of child spacing. However, when attending the local family planning clinics, they were told they must bring either a letter of consent from their husband or their husband's reference book before being given contraception. This was a directive from the Gazankulu government.

The powerful role of men in this example is in stark contrast to the way men are omitted as a target group when discussing contraception. This omission, and the complex cultural and political reasons that have led to it, is one that urgently needs to be addressed. It is a particular concern when you remember that condoms are being promoted as the major tool in the prevention of the spread of the AIDS epidemic. The experience in Zimbabwe on targeting men for condom usage is not an optimistic one. The Zimbabwe Women's Group says that when wives insist on condoms being used 'they are told that they are married and have children, or get accused of sleeping around or, alternatively, get a slap for accusing the man of having slept around'.

We have been talking about the rights of women to take decisions. However, the example of the depo ban in Zimbabwe is an example of the state asserting its rights. In South Africa today we have two conflicting problems. Firstly, we are told that we are facing a population explosion, but in contrast to that we are told that the AIDS epidemic may stop population expansion. In either scenario, what right does the state have to control the behaviour of the people? Could there be a scenario of a future state intervening to limit family size, or perhaps to compel HIV positive women to have terminations? Should these scenarios be avoided by writing into the new constitution that decisions about reproduction lie with women? Perhaps the only duty that the state should assume is one of education and the provision of services.

In summary, the problems we have with present contraceptive policy are poor education and knowledge of contraceptives by women and men, the poor utilisation and availability of contraception, and the abuse of contraceptives by health workers and by the state. The challenge for future policy makers is how to take scientific knowledge and political views on contraception, and turn them into a policy that is acceptable to our people and is based on the principle that it is the woman's right to control her fertility. What is clear from the review of contraceptive practice in South Africa is that the majority of women are, for one reason or another, falling through the net of effective contraception. There are four main reasons for this: no contraceptive is 100 per cent effective; no contraceptive is universally available; no contraceptive is universally acceptable; and knowledge of contraception is lacking for most women.

Abortion

When we add the lack of economic security experienced by women, and a migrant labour system that forces women into single parenthood to the above, it is hardly surprising that many women resort to abortion. Under present legislation, abortions are almost impossible to obtain legally in South Africa. Only 1 000 abortions a year are done legally inside South Africa. Seventy-seven per cent of these are on psychiatric grounds, near-ly all on white women. On the other side, it is estimated that 300 000 abortions a year are done illegally in South Africa.[6] These figures are difficult to establish accurately, but it is recognised that septic abortion rates reflect the illegal abortion rate. Figures from King Edward Hospital in Durban for 1983, 1987 and 1988 showed a 26 per cent, 16 per cent and 17 per cent septic abortion rate out of all abortion admissions, re-spectively. A two per cent mortality rate and a four per cent hysterectomy rate resulted from these septic abortions.[7]

No amount of legislation will stop desperate women from resorting to 'back street' abortions, with their attendant morbidity and mortality. In 1939 the Birkett Committee in the UK estimated that about 111 000–150 000 illegal abortions were performed there annually. After abortion was legalised in 1968, the number of legal abortions steadily rose to a plateau of about 140 000 by 1985. What seemed to have happened was that women who were earlier condemned to illegal abortions now came forward in similar numbers to have abortions legally and safely.

To legalise abortion is to give women real control of the decision when and if to have children, a choice which directly challenges the patriarchal society of South Africa. At its recent congress, Cosatu passed a motion in favour of free abortion on demand. A similar recommen-dation was passed by delegates at a joint ANC and Health Worker Organisation conference held in April 1990 in Maputo.

The question is, what do we mean by this? Do we mean that women can have 'over the counter abortions' with no questions asked? Or do we believe that the interests of women would be better served by a liberal policy that requires them to have the signature of two health workers? If we believe that, who should those health workers be? Nurses come from a notoriously conservative profession, and doctors are not available in the rural areas. If we set up joint contraceptive and abortion counselling clinics, will this service be equally available in rural areas, or will poor women be missed out despite their greater need? Clearly there is much work that still needs to be done on this issue. Any change in the abortion laws can only be made with an understanding of South African women's living conditions and of its health services. If we are committed to allowing women who need abortions the right to have them, we may be looking at an 'over the counter service' as the only way that would allow this to happen.

Childbirth

It is clear that the majority of pregnant women continue with their pregnancies, whether wanted or not. This takes us into the area of childbirth, which by its nature targets women. It is generally agreed that the perinatal mortality rate of a society reflects the health and health services of that society. The perinatal mortality rate is the number of deaths of babies taking place between 28 weeks of pregnancy and the first week of life. Some examples of perinatal mortality rates are as follows:[8]

- White Johannesburgers   16:1 000
- Soweto   38:1 000
- Transkei   49:1 000
- In some rural areas as high as: 130:1 000

The figures for both black urban and rural deaths are probably underestimates.

There are many reasons for the differences in rates and perhaps the first is the poor nutritional status of working-class black women. In Cape Town a study looking at factors influencing perinatal mortality showed that being unbooked (a woman who has no antenatal care prior to delivery), uneducated, and smoking increased perinatal mortality.[9] Unbooked patients show a higher percentage of complications.[10] A study in Alexandra township showed 20 per cent unbooked deliveries and 70 per cent deliveries when booked after 28 weeks.[11] Reasons given by a mother for non-booking vary with her situation, but a study done in KwaZulu brought out some factors common to many attenders: the clinic is too far away, no money, and lack of transport.

Even when women do book, antenatal care is haphazard with suboptimal care being offered. General practitioners who do much of the antenatal care in South Africa frequently do no blood tests because of cost. Less forgivably, they often omit basic monitoring such as blood pressure readings. Clinics are variable in quality, but records are often poorly kept, with one clinic in the Orange Free State keeping no records at all.[12]

Teenage pregnancies with their increased risks are common. Ross found that 18 per cent of parturient women were under the age of 18 years. Maternal deaths during labour are very rare in 'first world' countries but in South Africa they do occur. When emergencies happen, the primary referral centres are usually not equipped to handle them.

Emergency transport is a problem in both urban and rural areas. This makes it even more imperative that women attend antenatal care so that problems can be picked up early.

The focus of attention for childbirth in South Africa has been largely physical until recently. Although international figures show that one-third of women suffer from post-partum depression in the first year after delivery, very little attention has been paid to this. An understanding of the traditional concepts of pregnancy, delivery and child care have also been ignored until recently.

Support for women during labour is traditional in many South African cultures, with older women giving emotional support as well as being midwives. In a study at Coronation Hospital in Johannesburg, layworkers were trained to give emotional support during labour. The effect of this on the labour and its outcome was followed up. Supported mothers had their labour time cut by half, breastfed for longer, had a better self-image and a more positive perception of their children.[13] Despite this, most South African women labour alone and without support whether it be in clinics or hospitals. A new policy on childbirth requires not only practical changes in both facilities and education, but a fundamental change in our society's view of the dignity and needs of the pregnant woman. This is not something that can be legislated for.

A right to pregnancy

The final question that must be raised is a woman's right to be pregnant. Firstly, what can infertile women claim as a right under a future government? It is simple to talk about the rights of infertile women to be pregnant. But present health services simply couldn't provide the facilities for this to happen. Secondly, what are the rights of minority groups to have children. Here we could include lesbian women, and disabled women. These questions need much more research and discussion

Conclusion

As a last thought on the subject of reproductive rights, I would like to consider the example of Kerala State in India. Kerala was one of the poorest states in India when in 1953 a communist government was elected. That government introduced two significant pieces of legislation. Firstly, land reform and secondly, an uplifting in the status of women. Following that, Kerala had one of the highest uptakes of contraception found in India and a decline in the birth rate. I am sure that the situation in South Africa will be the same. Improvements in health policy on women's reproductive rights will have no impact without an upliftment of women that is written into the constitution, that is legislated upon, and that is reflected in their socio-economic position in society.

Notes

1.   M Roberts and M Rip, 'Black Fertility Patterns in Cape Town and Ciskei', *South African Medical Journal (SAMJ)*, 66(13), 29 September 1984, pp481–4.
2.   A Roux, 'Family Planning Among a Group of Coloured Women', *SAMJ*, 65(13), 20 June 1987, pp898–901.
3.   HA van Coeverden de Groot and EE Greathead, 'The Cape Town Teenage Clinic', *SAMJ*, 71(7), 4 April 1987, pp434–6.
4.   'AIDS Education in Schools', *Urbanization and Health Newsletter*, 4, February 1990, Centre for Epidemiological Research of the South African Medical Research Council (CERCA).
5.   *True Love*, April 1989.
6.   Abortion Reform Action Group (ARAG), *Star*, 30.11.1988.
7.   A Richards, E Lachman, SB Pitsoe, and J Moodley, 'The Incidence of Major Abdominal Surgery after Septic Abortion: An Indicator of Complications due to Illegal Abortion', *SAMJ*, 68(11), 23 November 1985, pp799–800.
8.   A Herman, 'Perinatal Mortality in Soweto', Proceedings of the First Conference on Priorities in Perinatal Care in South Africa, 1982; CW van der Elst and C Vader, 'Mortality Studies in Cape Town', Proceedings of the First Conference on Priorities in Perinatal Care in South Africa, 1982; M Zwarenstein and D Bradshaw, 'An Overview of Health Status and Health Care Provision in Southern Africa' in CP Owen (ed), *The Case for a National Health Service*, Department of Adult Education and Extra-mural Studies, University of Cape Town, 1989.
9.   HA van Coeverden de Groot, S Isaacs and CG Lawley, 'The Effects of Antenatal Care, Education Standard and Smoking on the Perinatal Mortality Rate in Cape Town', Proceedings of the Second Conference on Priorities in Perinatal Care in South Africa, 1983, pp79–83.
10. FR Prinsloo, 'The Effects of Booking Status on Pregnancy Outcome', Proceedings of the Second Conference on Priorities in Perinantal Care in South Africa, 1983.
11. Unpublished research done retrospectively on maternity cards, Alexandra Health Centre.
12. Anecdotal information from doctor working in the area.
13. GJ Hofmeyr, 'Ways of Making Birth Difficult', *SA Family Practice*, 11, 1990, p164–9.

Women and Law in Post-independence Zimbabwe

Experiences and lessons

Mary Maboreke

Zimbabwe shares with South Africa – and, indeed, all the other African countries in the region – the history of a colonial past as well as the legacy of the multiple oppressions of class, race and gender. This common historical legacy has bequeathed to us comparable concerns. Consequently, despite the occasional diversity and difference in our various countries, we still have a lot of similarities. We possess a great potential for learning from each other's experiences.

Zimbabwe attained independence on 18 April 1980. At the helm of the ship of state was a black nationalist government which described itself as Marxist-Leninist and therefore inherently opposed to discrimination in any form.[1] The government set itself the task of demolishing all the support systems of discrimination and creating a more just and equitable society. In addition to setting the parameters for what can legitimately be done, law also expresses the values of any given community or society. Pre-independence Zimbabwean society (or should I say Zimbabwe-Rhodesian society?) was based upon divisions of class,

race and sexism. Its laws reflected these divisions. Presumably such laws
would be on the new government's agenda for change.

The government's programme for change took the form of a series of
legislative enactments addressing the various areas in which discrimination had been identified. Some areas identified were the application and
content of customary law, family law, the legal status of women and
labour law. This paper discusses the changes made, what the old position
was, what change was effected, how and why the change was introduced
and received and the way this was done.

The constitutional position

The constitutional position of women has not changed. The constitution
forbids discrimination on all other grounds except sex. And one must
assume that what is not expressly forbidden is implicitly permitted. So in
Zimbabwe it is quite constitutional to discriminate against women for no
other reason than that they are women. This is a permissive, as opposed
to a mandatory, power. It is within the absolute discretion of the legislature whether to enhance or detract from women's status.

There are both advantages and disadvantages. A constitutional guarantee of sex equality would mean women's status would not be
dependent upon the whims or benevolence of successive governments.
Such a guarantee would give women a right to equality enforceable in a
court of law. The guarantee would also make it possible to remove all
sexually discriminatory laws as unconstitutional. Then there would be no
legal ambiguity about the status of laws which are sex-specific either in
their formulation or in their effect.

However, such a provision is no magic wand with which to wipe out
sexual discrimination in practice. In fact, such an approach might make
the problem legally invisible by driving it underground.

Men and women have different life paths and lived experiences. It
follows that rules of law will not always or necessarily affect them in the
same manner. A good example of this is the very restrictive law on abortion in Zimbabwe. The law is sex-neutral in its wording. But as only
women get pregnant they are the ones directly or more adversely
affected by this law – they have either to limit or otherwise control their
sexuality or else carry an unwanted pregnancy to full term.

If we want men and women to be affected in the same manner by a
particular law we may need to make provision for their different lived
realities, rather than attempting to abolish these differences. At the same
time, these differences should not be used to divide people. In most instances it is neither possible, nor advisable, to abolish difference. A
general or absolute constitutional guarantee of equality strikes out at any

sexual discrimination. Arguably, it does not allow for the flexibility necessary to cater for the different lived realities of men and women.

What is needed is a constitutional provision which is firm enough to uphold women's anti-discrimination claims but also flexible enough to allow 'discrimination' that is to women's advantage. This involves a recognition of 'difference' and a new understanding of old concepts such as discrimination and equality. 'Discrimination' should not be understood to mean just any distinction between two or more phenomena but refers also to distinctions which have the intention or effect of giving one group an advantage over and/or at the expense of the other. Such a constitutional position would go some way to creating substantive equality.

In Zimbabwe the constitutional status of sex discrimination has not been unduly restrictive as women still have a lot of room to manoeuvre. The greatest advantage has been the flexibility to respond to women's needs as they emerge.

The Customary Law and Primary Courts Act, 6 of 1981

Zimbabwe has a dual legal system. The customary law of the indigenous people operates side by side with the general law of the land. The Customary Law and Primary Courts (CLPC) Act, 6 of 1981, sets out which system of law, customary law or general law, applies. The CLPC Act was one of the first major pieces of legislation passed by the government of newly independent Zimbabwe. The aim was to bring the country's judicial and legal system in line with the state's professed socialist ideology.[2]

People have queried the retention of this dual legal system and court structure by a country whose avowed ideological leanings are inherently opposed to racial segregation. This is most relevant when dealing with questions of women's status. Customary law categorises women as perpetual minors, under the authority of one male or another.

The application of customary law is based in section 89 of the Zimbabwe Constitution Order.[3] This Constitution Order states that application of customary law is not racial discrimination within the meaning of the constitution.[4] However, it can be argued that the continued application of customary law to Africans and general law to non-Africans perpetuates legalised racism. Customary law entrenches the objectification, control and quasi-ownership of women by men, and it is clear that its continued application legitimates and perpetuates women's subservience to men.

While customary law denies the ideals of women's emancipation, it is doubtful whether an outright rejection of this form of law is the appropriate answer. Most African people have neither completely moved away from the customary way of life, nor have they remained squarely rooted within it. In most cases they have a foot in each world. Very often the modern executive moving sleekly along the streets of the capital city is 'transfigured' into an ancestor-worshipping traditionalist overnight when he/she goes 'home' to the rural area to appease some disgruntled ancestor or avenging spirit believed to be manifest through some misfortune.

Indeed, it is often said that most Africans wear at least two hats at all times – the customary traditional one and the modern progressive one – depending on their immediate context. The metamorphosis is far from complete and is the 'double bind' of the African:

> A village born, mission-taught, Oxford-anointed African has lived a synopsis of human history. He has outgrown pre-history so quickly that nothing has had time to die: the village gods, the Christian God and the modern absence of God (all) co-exist in him [sic].[5]

Given this transitional situation, it may not be advisable to argue for only one system of law. People whose lives are still steeped in custom may well be more comfortable with, and better served by, customary than general law. However, the retention of customary law in this context should not be seen as a move away from the principle of a non-racial society for which the liberation struggle was fought. Rather, it should be seen as a transitional need borne out of the great diversity of Zimbabwean society.

Prior to the passing of the Customary Law and Primary Courts Act there was not only a dual system of law but also a triadic system of courts. This hierarchical system was composed of headmen's and chief's courts, native commissioners and district commissioners courts, and the magistrates and high courts. Headmen's and commissioners courts applied customary law only, while magistrates courts applied only general law.[6] The high court could apply customary law, but it routinely sent such cases to district courts.[7]

As a general rule, customary law applied to Africans and general law governed non-Africans.[8] This remained, despite attempts through the African Law and Tribal Courts Act[9] to introduce some flexibility into the choice of law process. In fact, the Act was merely part of the colonial government's policy of appeasement to arrest the nationalist aspirations of up-and-coming middle class Africans spawned by the modernisation process. Rigid legal segregation along racial lines meant African women could not benefit from the more favourable provisions contained in general law. The CPLC Act of 1981 was passed to redress this racially based imbalance. The Act contained several aspects of importance to women: a) the introduction of new choice of law criteria; b) the creation of new courts; c) the introduction of new maintenance provisions.

The new choice of law criteria

Presently customary law applies where (i) there is no controlling statute; and (ii) the parties formally agree that customary law should apply; or (iii) looking at the surrounding circumstances, the parties have apparently agreed that customary law should apply; or (iv) having regard to the circumstances surrounding the case, it appears just that customary law should apply.[10]

Therefore, race is no longer the sole determinant, but only one of the factors in decisions about which system of law applies in any given case.

This process contains mixed blessings for women's rights. On the one hand it opens up to African women, who make up more than 96 per cent of the Zimbabwean female population,[11] enactments previously not applicable due to the strict legal segregation in pre-independence Zimbabwe. Some of these enactments give women more rights than they enjoy under customary law.

A good example is the Guardianship of Minors Act.[12] Under customary law, a father who has paid lobola is always entitled to the custody of his children. This Act provides that upon divorce, separation or judicial separation, the mother has custody of any minor children until a court makes a final ruling on the issue.

However, the new choice of law rules have not gone far enough. For instance, section 13 of the African Marriages Act[13] still provides that:

> The solemnization of a marriage between Africans in terms of the Marriage Act, Chapter 37, shall not affect the property of the spouses which shall be held, may be disposed of and unless disposed of by will shall devolve according to African law and custom.

Section 69 of the Administration of Estates Act[14] still states that:

- If any African who has contracted a marriage according to African law or custom or who, being unmarried, is the offspring of parents married according to African law or custom, dies intestate, his estate shall be administered and distributed according to the customs and usages of the tribe or people to which he belonged.
- If any controversies or questions arise among his relatives or reputed relatives regarding the distribution of the property left by him, such controversies or questions shall be determined in the speediest and least expensive manner consistent with real and substantial justice

> according to African usages and customs by the Provincial Magistrate or a Senior Magistrate of the province in which the deceased ordinarily resided at the time of his death, who shall call and summon the parties concerned before him and take and record evidence of such African usages and customs, which evidence he may supplement from his own knowledge.

In other words, even if general law is the applicable law using what I term 'mode of life' criteria, these enactments mandating the application of customary law will apply. In effect, then, customary law still applies. Once it is accepted that people's lived experiences should be the yardstick in deciding which law to apply, there seem no logical reason for limiting this to selected aspects of people's lives. It makes more sense to go the whole hog and make the social criteria absolute.

For women, the current position is good in so far as it protects them against being forced to agree to the application of customary law where such agreement might divest them of rights conferred by statute. But the converse is just as true: this rigidity also bars women from enjoying some of those 'better' rights contained in general law. The challenge lies in formulating choices of law criteria which allow women to enjoy better rights while protecting them against the possibility of being divested of certain rights.

The fact that women's access to such rights depends on their way of life means these rights are only available to certain classes of women. Thus the class distinctions which have always existed between women have now found legal expression and sanction. This is good in that there are now laws which correspond to people's way of life and to their expectations of the law.

However, the two legal systems sometimes make different provisions for the same issue. For woman, whatever her social class, the provisions of one system of law on a particular issue may be more favourable than those contained in the other system. A good illustration of this is the issue of seduction damages. Under customary law seduction is defined as having sexual intercourse with a woman with her consent but without the consent of her guardian. Therefore, the offense is committed against the woman's guardian and not the woman herself. Under customary law a woman has no right to sue for damages for her own seduction. General law, on the other hand, recognises seduction as an offense against the woman herself and she can sue on her own behalf. Whether a woman is closer to customary law or general law, she may still want to claim damages for her own seduction. The current choice of law rules would allow only the woman subject to general law to get seduction damages, while the one subject to customary law has no action at all.

Remedies in any particular system may depend not so much on their substantive content, but on the class of the woman concerned. A practical illustration of this is inheritance law. Under general law, a wife can inherit from her husband, but she has absolutely no other claims upon her husband's family. In terms of customary law, the wife does not inherit from her husband. Rather, she is herself part of his inheritable property. However, she can claim maintenance and other rights against her husband's estate and family. For a woman whose deceased husband leaves four oxen, three goats, eight chickens, a plough, a scotch cart and a field, customary law might actually offer the best solution. The widow can continue to occupy the matrimonial home, have continued access to the fields allocated to her husband, and continued use of the oxen, plough, goats, chickens, scotch cart and other matrimonial property. And in addition she has a 'husband' – or at least a person who is cast in that role – to go to should the need arise. This situation is surely better than selling the little property the husband leaves and dividing it between the wife, children and other dependents, customarily quite a large number. Alternatively, an economically independent woman capable of taking charge of her and her children's lives may find the customary law position quite untenable.

However, it cannot be denied that the reason customary law appears to offer some classes of women a better solution is because they are not economically independent enough to undertake the sole responsibility which goes with some of these general law rights. The answer to this does not lie in rejecting class distinctions and pulling all women back to the position they occupied prior to the enactment of the CLPC Act. It might be better to accept the new position as a step forward and work towards enabling all women to become economically independent and able to utilise these rights. It could also be argued that these 'better' rights should be available to all women coupled with an option exercisable at the individual woman's instance to opt for the lower level of rights.

The new courts

The CLPC Act creates new courts. Primary courts composed of village and community courts are grassroots courts spread extensively all over the country. Their procedure has been relaxed and simplified to the maximum level consistent with a legal forum. The fees charged are very low, making them affordable to the poor, the majority of whom are women. Any of the three major languages in Zimbabwe – English, Shona or Ndebele – can be used in these courts. Village courts are courts of first instance only, while community courts are courts of first instance, of record and of appeal from decisions of village courts. The village court has no criminal jurisdiction and a civil jurisdiction of Z$500 limited to cases where customary law applies.

The community court has no jurisdiction to dissolve a marriage contracted in terms of the Marriages Act,[15] although it can tie up loose ends when such a marriage is dissolved by a competent court: for example, issues of maintenance and division of matrimonial property on divorce. Apart from this, the community court has an unlimited civil jurisdiction. Its criminal jurisdiction is limited to specified crimes and a financial ceiling of Z$200.

Lawyers may not appear in a village court but they can appear in a community court. The presiding officers of the community courts are not as qualified as the lawyers who appear before them. They are, therefore, usually reluctant to find against a lawyer whom they regard as better qualified than themselves. But legal representation is not necessary when appearing in community courts.

Women are also not only the least educated but also the least able to afford lawyers, as well as being most likely to be intimidated by the impersonal, formal and imposing court process. All the new changes have made justice, or rather the legal system, both closer and more accessible to the poor and/or illiterate, many of whom are women. The majority of rural dwellers are women and they have used these courts so much that they have been dubbed 'women's courts'.

Despite these gains, however, the fact remains that these courts are staffed by people who have attitudes which can either facilitate or obstruct the accessibility of justice. Zimbabwe's experience shows that the attitudes of primary court staff have not made these courts work for women as well as they might.

To aggravate matters, most presiding officers tend to be more responsive to the needs of their immediate community than to strict legal doctrine. This is good to the extent that court responsiveness makes them alive to new customs which may have emerged and which may be more favourable to women. This is increasingly the case with inheritance cases where families allow the widow to retain possession of the matrimonial property, a practice which the higher courts are striking down as uncustomary. The court's responsiveness to the immediate community is bad, however, if community attitudes lag behind legal developments. A good example is the way primary courts responded to the Legal Age of Majority Act (LAMA). It has been denigrated as uncustomary and alien. Some court officials who tried to uphold this Act have had to flee from axe-wielding fathers who find it difficult to accept that under the LAMA fathers are no longer entitled to seduction damages for their major daughters if the daughters waited until they were 18 years old before getting themselves seduced!

Most of the gains discussed above have come under increasing threat from the Customary Law and Local Courts Act[16] which has been passed but not yet come into force. This Act abolishes the current primary courts and replaces them with local courts composed of primary courts and community courts. The primary court with a headman presiding is the lowest court with a civil jurisdiction of Z$500 only in cases in which customary law is the applicable system of law. Immediately above the primary court is the community court which acts as a court of first instance as well as a court of appeal from decisions of primary courts. This court has a civil jurisdiction of Z$1 000 and is presided over by a chief. Appeals against community court decisions go to a provincial magistrate and from there to the supreme court. These community courts have no criminal jurisdiction at all, and this is limited to cases where customary law applies. Issues such as custody and guardianship of minors, maintenance and other support obligations, dissolution of any marriage, determination of validity of wills, as well as the determination of rights in land and other immovable property, are outside the jurisdiction of local courts even if customary law is the applicable system of law. All these matters now have to be heard in the magistrates courts.

The current primary courts have been widely used by women because they are fairly extensively spread all over the country and their procedure is relatively simple and cheap. The new system removes the issues for which women most often use primary courts from the jurisdiction of primary courts to that of magistrates courts. This effectively reduces women's access to the judicial process.

The new maintenance provisions

In terms of customary law a man has no obligation to maintain either his illegitimate child or his former spouse. The CLPC Act reversed both positions and made him primarily responsible for the maintenance of both dependents. This goes beyond putting African women and children on a par with their non-African counterparts and actually places them in a better position. No doubt these provisions represent a major victory for women who normally have to take responsibility for the care of children. However, the provisions have only been directed towards the substantive content of the law rather than its structure and administration. This means their effect has been limited as cultural attitudes continued to impact negatively on the administration of the law. Strategies to improve women's status should be formulated in such a way that they address all aspects of an issue as women actually experience it in life.

The Legal Age of Majority Act, 15 of 1982

The next major piece of legislation to be passed was the Legal Age of Majority Act[17] (LAMA). The size and brevity of this Act belies the resounding impact it has had within the legal sphere. Section 3(1) is pertinent: 'On and after the fixed date a person shall attain the legal age of majority on attaining eighteen years of age.'

The importance and novelty of LAMA lies in its radical departure from the previously existing position which was as follows: (i) those people capable of attaining majority status did so on attaining 18 years of age; (ii) all non-Africans were capable of attaining majority status; (iii) African males could attain majority status; (iv) African women could never attain majority status whatever their age. This meant that African women could not exercise those rights attendant upon majority status. African women had no *locus standi in judicio*, no proprietary capacity, no contractual capacity and they could never be guardians of their own children whether legitimate or illegitimate. The harshness of this rule prompted even the colonial courts to make inroads into it by allowing exceptions. This was done, inter alia, by treating a divorced woman who did not return to the *patria potestas* of her father or his representative as a major and allowed a woman trader to be treated as a major for purposes of business. Consequently, by 10 December 1982 when LAMA came into effect, customary law rule consigning women to perpetual minority had already been substantially eroded.

With the enactment of LAMA, the legislature had, with a stroke of the pen, axed a very fundamental rule of customary law upon which some of its oldest and most hallowed institutions such as lobola were premised. All hell broke loose when the supreme court began to chart out some of the implications of this change on some of the established customary law principles. The first historic decision was in the case of *Katekwe v Muchabaiwa*[18] where the court ruled that an African father is no longer entitled to seduction damages for a daughter who is a major (18 years) at the time of seduction.

The 'powers that be' hastened to distance themselves from, and disclaim responsibility for, the Katekwe decision. The then prime minister, and now president, Robert Gabriel Mugabe, when quizzed on this issue during parliamentary question time, had this to say: '[I]f there has been a flaw in the drafting of the regulation that flaw will be amended.'[19]

He also added, apparently in a jocular manner, that if his sister were to get married he would demand lobola and if the prospective husband pointed to the Katekwe decision he would say to him, 'OK. That is the judgement. Do you want to marry my sister or not?'[20], clearly implying that if the prospective husband sincerely wanted to marry the president's

sister he would just have to pay the lobola demanded. It was not just the
current president who disowned LAMA and Katekwe. The then minister
of Community and Co-operative Development and Women's Affairs, and
the perceived embodiment of the struggle for women's emancipation,
Teurai Ropa Nhongo alias Joyce Mujuru, had the same view. When
questioned during the 1984 pre-election campaign she promised that
LAMA would be amended to restore parents' control over their children.
She said: 'We want to retain our cultural values and we shall invite
parents, elders and traditional leaders to advise us on the necessary
amendments needed to retain those social values we cherish.'[21]

The government went so far as to set in motion the machinery for
effecting the necessary changes, but the proposed amendments never
saw the light of day. This was partly because the ruling party, ZANU
(PF), was returned to power in another landslide victory, and did not
need to amend LAMA to win more votes. It was also because the government had apparently not really made up its mind about its policy
regarding women. Despite Teurai Ropa's 7 November 1984 pledge to
have LAMA amended to something more acceptable to conservative elements, a week later, on 14 November 1984, in her opening speech to the
Colloquium on the Rights of Women in Zimbabwe organised by the
Ministry of Justice, Legal and Parliamentary Affairs, she said:

> It should be borne in mind also, that in the context of the national
> ideology and the principles on which the liberation struggle was fought, a
> perpetuation of (the) inferior status of women is a real embarrassment for
> it negates the very principles of socialism... Cultures and traditions are
> not static but change as circumstances and situations change. Customs
> are made by people and it is people who can change them. They are
> fashioned to suit the prevailing socio-economic order and it is on this
> basis that women feel certain aspects of customary law are simply
> obsolete and out of step with the situation in Zimbabwe today.[22]

For a while it appeared the controversy sparked off by the Katekwe
decision had died a natural death. But the debate has surfaced again and
LAMA is being blamed for almost all current social ills. The November
1989 ZANU (PF) National Women's League Conference resolved:

> That a thorough search on the efforts [presumably 'effects'] of the Legal
> Age of Majority Act be carried out. The League further resolves that [the]
> Act be amended to allow parents to give consent to their children before
> they enter into Marriage. There is a general feeling that the Act have [sic]
> possible contributions towards baby-dumping, prostitution, ngozi[23], and
> suicide.[24]

LAMA's critics have not demonstrated how LAMA supposedly causes all these social ills. Objectively speaking, LAMA has scored major gains for women. Now, as long as women are married, and over 18, they are legally on a par with their male counterparts. Women should be jubilant about LAMA, not lambaste it. But many women have been inaccurately informed about LAMA's negative aspects. This demonstrates that it is terribly important to inform people thoroughly and accurately about new laws and how these impact on their lives.

The misunderstandings and misconceptions about LAMA have made both the public and the legislature hypersensitive about enacting 'women-specific legislation'. Consequently, those interested in women's issues have had to work more and more through the judicial process rather than through parliament.

However, the legislature is not monolithic. It is possible to identify allies among those in power and give these people the back-up support necessary to make them stay in power and be heard. Clearly, this calls for a good networking system among people and organisations interested in women's issues.

In Zimbabwe, many successes in the area of women's rights are attributable to a good working relationship with the supreme court. The relationship is symbiotic. The supreme court has used the results of our academic research; which in turn has meant this work has been translated into action via the judicial process.

But these legislative gains have not always translated into practical gains for women. For instance, although the current legal position is that a father's right to lobola for his major daughter depends upon that daughter's discretion, in practice such fathers have continued to exercise an unfettered and independent right to lobola and all concerned have taken such 'entitlement' as a matter of course. This is largely because of the way women and men perceive women.

Africans in general and African women in particular identify themselves through a maze of relationships; namely, mother to so-and-so, daughter of so-and-so, wife of so-and-so, etc, in which 'so-and-so' is always a man. African women are never viewed as separate individuals but rather as appendages of a man. Almost all Africans see themselves as an integral part of a big and complex machine called 'the family'. The individual alone is seen as almost useless and certainly powerless. African women feel this powerlessness when removed from the family wheel, and so attach themselves to the family organism even more tightly. The obligation this family membership generates is the price women pay for membership of their family.

Societies such as ours are tightly structured, stratified, hedged in by prescriptions, by the primacy of the communal good over individual rights and interests. Therefore to what extent can rights (such as those contained in LAMA) premised upon the primacy of the individual over the group be relevant or useful? How are the group obligations separated from individual rights when family connections and obligations are not just based on rationality and practical considerations, but also on emotion, which is often stronger than reason and logic?

Would it be better to retain the group rights mould and try to strengthen women's position within it? If so, how is this achieved? In other words, what other socially supportive structures need to be constructed to underpin some of these purely legislative gains.

The Immovable Property (Prevention of Discrimination) Act, 19 of 1982

The Immovable Property (Prevention of Discrimination) (IPPD) Act prohibits sexual discrimination in relation to immovable property. By implication, therefore, discrimination against women in relation to movable property has not been removed from this Act. The Act also allows discrimination on grounds of gender if the discrimination is justified in the interests of decency or morality or in the light of any legal disability to which women are already subject; or the immovable property concerned has been reserved for the use of one sex and the person against whom the allegedly discriminatory act was committed belonged to the other sex. Questions of decency and morality are highly volatile, and there is very little societal consensus on the issues. But societal perceptions are likely to be loaded against women since over the years a moral code, stricter for women and more lenient for men, has evolved.

This indeterminate ground may be used to camouflage discriminatory acts against women. More unacceptable, however, is the provision that women can be discriminated against on account of any legal disabilities to which they are already subject. Here one kind of inequality is used as a justification for legitimising another. The accused is bound to prove that his actions were not discriminatory. However, if he is acting under any other law which requires or mandates the discriminatory treatment then that discrimination is not actionable in terms of the IPPD Act. Nor does the IPPD Act limit the effects to those passed prior to the enactment of the IPPD Act. In this way the legislature has managed to create and maintain a facade of frowning upon discrimination while actually allowing it, a fact about which women's rights groups should be vigilant.

The Communal Land Act, 20 of 1982

This Act regulates the use of the communal land. It does not mention women as such, but its provisions have direct relevance for women. Section 8 of this Act provides that:

> (1) [A] person may occupy and use communal land for agricultural or residential purposes with the consent of the district council established for the area concerned...
>
> (2)(b) When granting consent in terms of subsection (1) a district council shall grant consent only to persons who according to the customary law of the community that has traditionally and continuously occupied and used land in the area concerned, are regarded as forming part of such community or who, according to such customary law, may be permitted to occupy and use such land: 'Provided that, if no community has traditionally and continuously occupied and used land in the area concerned, the district council should grant consent only to such class of persons as the Minister by notice in writing to the district council, may specify.'

Under customary law usufructuary rights in land – as opposed to ownership rights which were unknown to customary law – are allocated to adult, married, males. Women are therefore denied an individual right to land. Their entitlement is a secondary one, predicated upon one of the many relationships that identify them, but mainly as wives.

Communal land areas should be easily accessible to all people. Unlike other types of land where criteria such as wealth or collateral determine access, it should be enough in establishing entitlement to land in communal areas for someone to prove that they are members of the community which has traditionally and continuously occupied that land. However, this only holds for men. Women must both prove the existence of a relationship entitling them to use such land, and the relevant related male must allow her to use his allocation of land.

The law thus makes women's access to land a privilege dependent on the magnanimity of their male counterparts. This gives major cause for concern because women constitute the majority living in communal areas and actually working the land. In the words of Gary Magadzire, president of the Zimbabwe National Farmers Union:

> I could tell you quite categorically that there would be no agriculture in this country without women. The role of women in this country is paramount – in fact, it is the central pin to agricultural advancement. If, for any reason women went on strike, agriculture in this country would fall to pieces.[25]

Women feel both their subjugation and the insecurity of their situation. A relative of mine who was helping her husband erect a durawall around their Chitungwiza house through eliciting monetary contributions recently said to me:

> What I am doing is just preparing the house for those who will come after me when I am gone. When you are a married woman, you are really on a temporary job [kungogadzirira vachauya kana uri mukadzi uri patembarari].[26]

It is thus women's experience of life which makes them feminists. For feminism springs from a conviction that women too are human beings entitled to inherent human dignity and human rights. But in terms of Zimbabwean customary law relating to land use, women are reduced to propertyless dependents relying on the magnanimity of their menfolk. Clearly provision should be made ensuring individual land-use rights for women. It is no answer to point to 'culture, custom and tradition' for customs such as this are a real throwback to an age when women were no more than vehicles through which men obtained rights and obligations. As Teurai Ropa (alia Joyce Mujuru) observes:

> Cultures and traditions are not static but change as circumstances and situations change. Customs are made by people and it is people who can change them. They are fashioned to suit the prevailing socio-economic order and it is on this basis that women feel certain aspects of customary law are simply obsolete and out of step with the situation in Zimbabwe today.[27]

As Simbi Mubako, the then minister of Justice, Legal and Parliamentary Affairs, once said: '[A]ny system of law which does not develop with the times in the manner of its administration and in substantive content will be discredited and will decay.'[28]

The Labour Relations Act, 16 of 1985

The Labour Relations Act (LRA), 16/85 was the next in line to be promulgated. Prior to its enactment employers enjoyed, subject to the terms of the contract of employment, an unfettered right to hire and fire their employees. And although female employees were entitled to maternity leave, it was unpaid.

Now the LRA lays down minimum standards which employers must adhere to. The LRA: (a) Criminalises discrimination on the basis of, inter alia, sex, in employment matters; (b) provides for partially-paid maternity leave; (c) entitles nursing mothers to breastfeeding time during working hours; (d) severely limits the employer's right to dismiss employees; and (e) gives the relevant minister power to pass minimum wage regulations.

The criminalisation of sexual discrimination

Zimbabwean women are not as qualified as – or at least qualified in the same respects as – men. Their lower or different educational qualifications and experiences are used to justify not only differences between men's and women's pay but also their consignment to non-decision making and lower status jobs. This means the protection offered by the sexual discrimination provision is unlikely to benefit significant numbers of women. The decision to hire a prospective employee ultimately rests with the employer and may well be influenced by such inarticulate premises as a person's carriage, the firmness of their handshake, the cut of their clothes, the directness of their look, and so on. It is not possible to legislate against these biases.

While we should concede the importance of such a law at the ideological level, we must also accept its limitations. As Liz Gwaunza says: 'A law may be perfect but unless it is matched with appropriate structures to administer it, such law may fail to benefit those whom it may have been intended to benefit.'[29]

This demonstrates the need to understand how law interacts with women's lives in order to 'subvert' this process to women's advantage. It also highlights the dangers of trying to fit women into the straitjacket of the law, when the law should be there to serve people, not be their master.

Maternity provisions

The LRA provides that unless a woman is already working under better conditions, she is entitled to partially-paid maternity leave of 90 days – 45 days before delivery and 45 days after. If the woman agrees to forfeit any annual leave due to her, she is entitled to 75 per cent of her normal salary during the maternity leave period. If she refuses to forfeit her leave days or does not have any, she is entitled to 60 per cent of her usual salary.

This provision is a bitter-sweet achievement for women because in practice it has shown itself to be a double-edged sword. It represents a break-away from the tradition of 'penalising' women for following the 'traditionally female' path of having children. However, women on maternity leave get only a portion of their normal salary, which means some of the old thinking remains: paying a woman on maternity leave is really doing her a favour. Such thinking seems to presume a male breadwinner which itself presupposes that all women will marry and be either wholly or partially supported by a man. This seems a logical explanation for the law sanctioning a decrease in the women's earnings at a time when there is an increase in her actual expenditure.

The only other logical explanation for such a position is the economics of the situation. In deciding the percentage of a woman's salary payable during maternity leave, the legislature must have balanced the average ability of employers to pay with the average needs of the female employees.

Although maternity payments are not enough to cover their increased expenses, one can also appreciate the possible dangers of fully-paid maternity leave for women: to entrench, justify and reinforce male preference in job opportunities and promotion. It cannot seriously be argued that it is in the employer's interest to pay a woman's salary at a time when she is not productive in the enterprise and when her absence may have forced the employment of a replacement who might not be as good, experienced or 'cheap' as the woman herself.

Laws conceived of as assets for women may reveal themselves, in reality, to be assegais. This is especially so given the context of high unemployment. While fully-paid maternity leave would benefit women already in employment, it might also have the effect of excluding those presently unemployed. It may also limit women's access to promotions. So the law tried to produce a compromise. By definition, a compromise always involves choice and it cannot satisfy every person's legitimate expectations.

If women want their claims to be taken seriously, they must locate them realistically within current contexts, and couch them in terms which show an awareness and appreciation of the national as well as global issues involved. For instance, it would be foolhardy to claim absolute financial independence for women when our countries are mortgaged to the hilt to the World Bank and the International Monetary Fund, so that even as nations we do not have economic independence! There are no painless choices in women's issues.

Breastfeeding provisions

The LRA entitles a breastfeeding employee to either one hour or two half-hour periods during normal working hours. Though legislatively a major gain, this provision presupposes the existence of nurseries and créches at workplaces, or alternatively, an efficient, reliable and affordable public transport system. I have yet to hear of a Zimbabwean workplace which boasts such facilities. And Zimbabwe's transport system, both public and private, is notorious for its high cost, inefficiency and unreliability.

The situation is exacerbated by the fact that most employees live a long way away from their places of employment. In most cases the two half-hour periods, or the combined one hour is spent waiting for the bus or emergency taxi. Only those who can afford their own transport can exercise this right.

The Zimbabwean experience has been that this provision has remained out of reach of the majority of those whom it was meant to benefit. This is a classic example what happens with the wholesale transplantation of western ideas without first determining how they fit in to an African context.

We must strive to break away from the 'western/imported/good, local/indigenous/bad' philosophy. To use that tired cliché, we should cut our jacket to our own cloth, not that of the colonial master or the developed world. In many ways our societies are like the human body: they reject foreign bodies which do not agree with them. The 'homebrew' very often works better precisely because it is specifically designed to meet our specific conditions. This research should begin with a social rather than legal definition of the issue. An issue which is defined and addressed legally may remain a social issue.

A good illustration in the Zimbabwean context is the law relating to maintenance. Prior to the current laws, the problem appeared to be the absence of a law giving illegitimate children a right to maintenance from their fathers. However, when the legal problem was removed by the enactment of the current laws, it became obvious that people's attitudes were the real barrier to women mobilising these laws to their advantage. Maintenance remains a problem in practice.

Protection against unjustified dismissal

Section 17 of the LRA gives the minister responsible for labour issues extensive regulatory powers over the whole field of employment. Exercising these powers, the minister passed regulations severely restricting the employer's right to fire employees. Thus the Labour Relations (General Conditions of Employment) (Termination of Employment) Regulations, 1985, provide in section 2 that:

> (1) No employer shall, summarily or otherwise, terminate a contract of employment with an employee unless:
> (a) he has obtained the prior written approval of the minister to do so; or
> (b) he and the employee mutually agree, in writing, to the termination of the contract; or

(c) the employee was engaged for a fixed duration or for the performance of a specific task, and the contract of employment is terminated on the expiry of such period or on the performance of such task; or

(d) the contract of employment is terminated in terms of Section 3.[30]

This protection is a major legislative gain for women who are most vulnerable to dismissal, whether justified or not. However, this is only of limited value because protection against dismissal is not the same thing as a guarantee of employment. Women comprise only about 6,8 per cent of the total workforce even though they form 51 per cent of the total Zimbabwean population. Employers in fact, do not have to employ women at all. The probabilities of this happening, especially given the backdrop of the *prima facie* 'anti-employers' and 'pro-women' provisions discussed above, are quite high. The challenge lies in minimising such a risk, if not eliminating it altogether.

Minimum wage regulations

In terms of section 17 of the LRA, the minister has made regulations setting out the salaries payable to different categories of employees. Recognising that not every employer can afford the statutory minimum wage, the regulations provide for a graduated scale whereby employers can apply for exemption from prescribed wages.

Women are major employers of other women, especially as domestics. Given the employers situation it is not realistic to expect them to afford to pay the statutory wage. Consequently, it is mainly women employers who need minimum wage exemptions and it is also mostly women who are paid less than the stipulated wage as a result.

Apart from calling for an improvement in the gross national product, the only other claim women can make is that however small the national cake available, it must be shared fairly among the deserving people. Whatever the case, we must understand the full implications and possible repercussions on women, whatever programmes are embarked upon.

Two other observations need to be made about the LRA. It does not expressly cover the recently unveiled issue of sexual harassment. There are currently attempts to rectify this by bringing sexual harassment within the general prohibition of sexual discrimination in section 5 of the LRA on the basis that it entails different qualifications and/or conditions of employment for the different sexes. Importantly, the arguments are not women-specific but gender-neutral. It is not just that women who refuse sexual favour demands are prejudiced, sexual harassment also prejudices men: because they cannot provide sexual favours, they either have to be better qualified or put in more effort than their female counterparts who do give bosses sexual favours. This is an attempt to build alliances through showing that in some cases there are similar interests at stake.

The lessons here are that reality requires ever-changing and expanding strategies borne out of concrete situations, that it is important to shun arguments which portray women as being at war with men, and that it is better not to isolate and thereby weaken women.

In Zimbabwe, as elsewhere, attempts to make labour legislation more 'women friendly' have apparently been premised upon an underlying assumption that women's 'working' day is similar to men's. This is shown by the fact that women whose lifestyles bear the strongest resemblance to men's find it easiest to mobilise labour law to their advantage. A woman who is not a mother is spared. A married woman with children has to juggle multiple demands to accommodate her many commitments. Women often start working long before the official hour of 8 am and stop working long after 5 pm. Thus, in reality, women are either full-time housewives, part-time housewives/part-time wage earners, or full-time wage earners/over-time housewives.

This argument has tended to reinforce the logic of feminist demands. But it does not, in the long run, augur well for the theoretical and ideological basis of feminist jurisprudence in terms of formulating women's claims in a coherent theoretical framework. No matter how educated, busy or demanding her career may be, an African woman almost always has to execute her domestic chores, or at least manage or supervise the person employed to do this who, incidentally, is usually paid by the woman herself, because she is employed to relieve the woman of some of these chores. Her male colleague does not have the same demands on his time.

The quantity of time and effort put into an endeavour usually translates directly into the quality of the product. For those seeking a theoretical basis for women's rights, the challenge lies in how to justify the same salary for a man and woman doing the same work when realistically a woman splits her time and energies between her job and her family responsibilities. Such an argument would be particularly strong in cases involving people at senior management levels who work according to the demands of the job and not necessarily according to the 'eight to five' model.

A deregulation warning

This is the labour law position in Zimbabwe today. However, as of 1 October 1990, Zimbabwe abandoned its strict trade controls over trade liberalisation. In anticipation of the new economic order, the senior minister of Finance, Economic Planning and Development, Politburo

Member and member of parliament for Harare Central, Dr Bernard T Chidzero said:

> While economic regulations have their advantages, these should be weighed against the costs incurred in enforcing them and other possible economic gains which the country has to forego as a result of such controls. With trade liberalisation and general structural programmes in place, Government has seen this to be the opportune time to do away with most of the economic regulations by allowing market forces to operate in directing the pace and course of economic activities in Zimbabwe.
>
> The other area where decontrol is necessary is the area of wage and salary determination and the employment regulations. Following the aspiration of growth with equity and the protection of the worker from exploitation and unfair retrenchment, Government introduced regulations on minimum wages and withdrew the employer's right to fire.
>
> In 1989, Government started moving away from statutory wage increments to collective bargaining which takes into account the firm's ability to pay. However, this was done within set parameters. In 1990 the parameters were reduced further such that collective bargaining is now a permanent feature in wage and salary increment negotiations. On the issue of hiring and firing, Government is going to streamline procedures so as to reduce the time lag between the time an employer applies to retrench and when the responsible Minister grants permission to fire. Both the employers' and workers' representatives are being consulted on this issue.
>
> In addition to reviewing price and income controls, Government will be studying other controls in the economy, with a view to introducing flexibility in areas where control acts as constraints on investment.[31]

Such statements flash a warning light. Deregulation does not bode well for women as (prospective) employees. Women from free trade zones have been at pains to make us learn from their experiences. When she attended the Women, Law and Development Inter-regional Meeting in Washington DC in June 1990, Manouri Muttetuwegama, a lawyer from Sri Lanka, also the president of the Women Lawyers Federation of Colombo and general secretary of the Women's Front of Sri Lanka, stressed the plight of Sri Lankan women in free trade zones and the dangers of free trade zones for women's issues.[32]

At home other people share these sentiments. In an interview, Miriro Pswarayi, head of the women's wing of the Zimbabwe Congress of Trade Unions (ZCTU), said the trade liberalisation programme, together with the proposed changes in the labour laws, were set to create a dangerous working environment in which many vulnerable women might not survive.[33] All the gains made so far would vanish and women would be more concerned about keeping their jobs rather than asserting their rights. In her own words, trade liberalisation

> is a regrettable development as far as women at the workplace are concerned. We are still in the process of organising and educating our women. Now with this programme the light which was beginning to show at the end of the tunnel is gone.[34]

Analyses of how deregulation programmes affected women should have been done before the problems arose. It is now rather late to demand the necessary guarantees and protections. As it is we have lost the initiative and are now limited to reacting to what authorities initiate. It is important to maintain, or at least resuscitate, the initiative.

The Matrimonial Causes Act, 33 of 1983

Prior to the enactment of the Matrimonial Causes Act, 1985 (MCA 85), the situation on divorce depended on whether customary law or general law governed a particular property dispute. If the parties involved were Africans married in Zimbabwe customary law applied.[35] If the couple were non-Africans, or the marriage was an inter-racial one, or the parties involved were Africans married outside Zimbabwe and whose mode of life was westernised, general law applied.

Where general law applied, the outcome on divorce depended on whether the marriage was in or out of community of property. Where the marriage was out of community of property there was never a merger of property. Each spouse retained his/her own separate property and on divorce each spouse got what he or she had acquired. Where the marriage was in community of property, the matrimonial property was jointly owned by the spouses in equal undivided shares. On divorce the matrimonial property had to be shared equally between them.

Where customary law applied, all property acquired during the subsistence of a marriage belonged to the husband whether acquired by him or by his wife.[36] On divorce the wife left the marriage empty-handed. There were a few exceptions to this general rule. The motherhood beast given to a woman on the marriage of her daughter; 'mavoko' (hands) property acquired through the exercise of the wife's skills or the proceeds of agricultural produce in excess of her family's needs; and household goods such as her sleeping mat, cooking stones and water pot. In most cases such property did not amount to much and bore little relation to her contribution to the acquisition of her 'husband's' property. The courts had no power to redistribute the property on grounds of equity. It was the injustice of this rule that the MCA 85 sought to redress.

The MCA 85 was interpreted as applying only to marriages contracted in terms of the Marriage Act[37] which brings about monogamous marriages. This view concluded that the MCA 85 did not apply to (potentially) polygamous marriages contracted in terms of the African Marriages Act.[38] The MCA 85 was amended by the Matrimonial Causes Amendments Act[39] to state that the MCA 85 applied to both monogamous and (potentially) polygamous marriages.

With the MCA 85, if a marriage ends in divorce, the court is empowered to order equitable division of matrimonial property. The court takes into account, inter alia, the respective parties' contributions in kind such as housework and caring work as a mother, wife, daughter-in-law, etc, which is not always expressed in monetary terms. This change is noteworthy because it provides women with a legal right which can be enforced in a court of law. The change is also important ideologically in that it reflects a dawning recognition of the economic dimensions of the domestic and caring work women perform.

Admittedly, the MCA 85 is a major legislative victory for women. However, property redistribution on divorce remains a major social problem for women. The more progressive judges have interpreted the provisions liberally, holding that a woman's contribution in kind through the execution of domestic and caring work entitles her to a substantial portion of the matrimonial property. The more conservative judges, on the other hand, have tended to place a very low monetary value upon such contributions and some are on record as saying this type of contribution should only be given weight where it goes beyond what a wife would normally put into a normal marital relationship.

Prima facie, the problem is that the monetary valuation of such contributions is left entirely within the individual judge's discretion, without any guidelines whatsoever, whether statutory or judge-made. Perhaps this approach was intended to provide flexibility and adaptability to each individual case. In practice it is not the flexibility which is the problem, but the negative attitudes of those administering the law which leads to an abuse of the flexibility of the provisions and a consequent negation of the spirit underlying those provisions.

Two important lessons emerge from this. The law is not always the all-important phenomenon it is sometimes made out to be. And sometimes the law only works when it is pulling in the same direction as other non-legal factors (for example, social, economic, political, ideological, emotional, cultural, etc). To make law work in the manner it was intended it is sometimes necessary to construct socially supportive measures to underpin legislative moves. Exactly what these supportive structures are is best identified by adopting a social definition of the problem. In our quest for a better life for women, we need to identify those factors which facilitate effective law/policy formulation and implementation. In most cases we lose sight of this fact and find when we have broken down one wall, we are still encased, or, worse still, we have actually created another wall. Hence, as Kishwar and Vanita aptly note:

> Today we (should) no longer say: 'Give us more jobs, more rights, consider us your equals or allow us to compete with you better.' But rather: 'Let us re-examine the whole question, all the questions. Let us take nothing for granted. Let us not only redefine ourselves, our role, our image but also the kind of society we want to live in...'[40]

A problem with the MCA 85 is that it only relates to 'matrimonial' property which presupposes the existence of a union recognised as a valid marriage by the MCA 85. Because the MCA 85 is part of general law, this means the union must be recognised under general law. Of all unions contracted in Zimbabwe, only parties married in terms of the African Marriages Act[41] and the Marriage Act[42] are covered by the MCA 85. Conspicuously outside its ambit is the unregistered customary law union (UCLU).

A UCLU is a union between a man and a woman recognised as a marriage in terms of customary law but regarded as invalid by general law. In practice parties to a UCLU conduct themselves and their lives in much the same manner as parties to registered marriages. The only difference is that they do not have a piece of paper attesting to the fact that they are spouses. In substance the only difference between a UCLU and the English common law marriage is that a UCLU is recognised by African customary law while a common law marriage is recognised by non-African customary law.

Most unions in Zimbabwe are unregistered. The exclusion of UCLUs from the coverage of the MCA 85 indicates an unnecessary and unwarranted preoccupation with form rather than substance. A piece of legal paper should not determine whether spouses are entitled to an equitable share of matrimonial property. In fact, the formulation of the relevant MCA 85 provisions shows that it is the respective parties' actual contributions, and not the marital knot as such which gives them a stake in the matrimonial property.

Once this argument is accepted in principle there should be no ideological justification for not extending the MCA 85 provisions to cover UCLUs. Admittedly, registration of marriages helps administratively. However, a slavish adherence to form rather than substance might cause unnecessary and avoidable injustice and hardship. The challenge lies in promoting registration of marriages without necessarily making non-registration fatal to a woman's entitlement to an equitable share in property which she has helped acquire and accumulate.

Evidentiary problems should not be used to justify retention and/or perpetuation of the status quo. The courts have a duty to make findings as to whether or not a particular relationship amounts to a marital relationship, and courts are currently being called upon to resolve far more difficult questions than this. At the moment for a woman in a UCLU to get any of the property jointly acquired with her 'husband', she has to prove the existence of a universal partnership. This means she must prove that the two of them pooled their earning and resources and created a kind of business partnership that is something more than a marital relationship. Because most UCLUs are in reality no more than ordinary marriages, it is impossible for most of the women to prove the existence of a universal partnership. It seems both inconsistent and illogical not to let the parties' conduct determine whether or not the relationship amounts to a marriage and therefore covered by the MCA 85.

The Zimbabwean Supreme Court has already provided a precedent for just this kind of argument. The court recently stated that, in so far as a woman in a UCLU is already entitled to maintenance from her customary law 'husband', and to the extent that the mischief sought to be corrected by the common law remedy of damages for loss of support was, in substance, the same as where a breadwinner in a marriage has been wrongfully killed, the question of form – that is whether or not a marriage exists – should not override considerations of justice.[43] It is further held that although the remedy involved may have been conceived of in relation to registered marriages and a UCLU is an unregistered union, since there is nothing inherently immoral or contrary to public policy about UCLUs, and since UCLUs are legally recognised in a number of cases, that this remedy should now be construed as extending to UCLUs.

People can use this kind of 'alternative' jurisprudence to force the legal fraternity to deal creatively with problems. Such judgements can also be used as the basis for other, further, differing claims which require original and even novel reasoning in order to build up an alternative jurisprudence more consistent with the value of equality.

Another problem with the MCA 85 is that it only applies in the event of divorce, not in the event of the death of a spouse. In this event customary law with its heavy bias against women applies if the parties involved are Africans who married in Zimbabwe. In so far as inheritance is concerned, a woman who divorces her husband is better off than the one whose marriage is dissolved by death. 'Practical' people have observed that it is therefore better for a woman to divorce her husband each time he becomes seriously ill and remarry him on his recovery if he does not die.

Once it has been accepted in principle that contribution of whatever kind to the accumulation of matrimonial property entitles a wife to a proportionate share in that property, it does not make sense to limit the principle to situations of divorce. The obvious conclusion is to extend it to cover succession and inheritance cases as well. Indeed, it might have made more sense to start by changing the situation on death, then move on to divorce. But in fairness to the legislature the problem has largely been the conflict of interest between the different women's interest groups and their failure to present a common position on this issue.

Deceased Persons Family Maintenance Act, 39 of 1978

In cases of inheritance, if the deceased left a valid will the estate devolves according to the terms of the will. If there is no will then either customary law or general law applies. If general law applies the widow stands to inherit a portion of her late husband's property: a child's share, or Z$30 000, whichever is the greater. If customary law applies then the widow herself is part of her husband's inheritable property.

The effect of these rules has been ameliorated considerably by the Deceased Persons Family Maintenance (DPFM) Act. The DPFM Act changed the legal position, not on inheritance but on maintenance. In effect it provides that even if the widow does not inherit from her late husband, her maintenance should put her largely in the same position she would be in if the marriage ended in divorce. This entitles her to a share in the matrimonial property commensurate with her actual contribution (in cash and kind) to its acquisition and her needs, both current and prospective. The factors taken into account in quantifying her maintenance entitlements on death of a spouse are the same as those the court factors in when overseeing a divorce action.

This is a very circuitous route to the same destination. The point to note, however, is that this route makes not only the journey but the destination appealing and acceptable to those to whom it applies and, therefore, worthwhile. As already stated, a law has optimum effect when those who apply it and those to whom it relates agree with not only its letter and spirit but the rationale underlying it. This circuitous route was chosen specifically because women failed to come up with a consensus position on inheritance.

The now-stalled Succession Bill had sought to give an African woman a right to inherit from her husband. In line with the recognition of polygamy contained in customary law, the proposed Succession Bill tried to make provision for this by allowing each wife a share in the matrimonial property. The size of each wife's share depended not only on the size of the estate and the number of the deceased's dependents, but also on whether the widow was first, second or subsequent wife.

Women's reception to this Bill showed that women are not a homogeneous group and that rules of law do not necessarily affect them in the same manner. Therefore, provided that what is sought is genuine justice, it does not matter if some women lose certain privileges where these privileges emerge from the same patriarchal structures which spawn, nurture, reinforce and perpetuate male privilege.

The struggle for justice is not directed at people as such but the bulwarks of injustice whether these be people, structures or institutions. People who resist struggles for justice are those who have identified themselves and their interests with the preservation of these oppressive structures.

The Finance Act (No 1), 11 of 1988

Prior to the enactment of the Finance Act, a wife was not a taxpayer for income tax purposes. Any income she earned was deemed to have accrued to her husband. This meant the Income Tax Department could take all or some of her salary to pay off any shortfall her husband might have. The disadvantages were varied and manifold. All the allowances for married people such as child allowances and the lower rates of taxation went to the husband. With the husband and wife's salaries taxed as a single income unit, the tax taken off the wife's salary was substantial. Given women's generally poor salary packages when compared with their husband's this reduced a married woman's net income to a mere fraction of that of other people in the same income bracket.

When Zimbabwean married women started calling for a change in this law, they gathered support from men by making them see how they, too, were prejudiced by these provisions. Taxation of married women was not portrayed as a women's issue but as a family issue. Men put their full weight behind women's clamours for change. Now every employee is taxed as an individual taxpayer. However, all tax credits for children still automatically go to the father unless the parents have agreed otherwise. This shows the presumption that it is the man who shoulders the responsibility for supporting children. Growing evidence, however, points to the contrary.

The Zimbabwean experience illustrates that the approach to an issue might have a significant impact on the success or failure of the claims being made. It also argues against unnecessary alienation of sectors of society whose sympathy and support might influence an outcome.

Women's participation in the liberation struggle

Equality is a basic human right. Women are therefore entitled to equal treatment because they are human beings and not because they participated in the national liberation struggle.

This is not to deny that women's participation in the liberation struggle helped women's emancipation in Zimbabwe. Women could point to some tangible proof of their equality with men, and the architects of the liberation struggle used this as a rallying point to garner support for the struggle. They cannot afford to be seen to renege on the issue for fear of being labelled political 'back-trackers'. But the claims usually made about women's participation in Zimbabwe's liberation cloud the real issues.

It is necessary to avoid being drawn into issues which do not really improve women's position. We have seen this happen in Zimbabwe as women have been drawn more and more into politics. This is not to say women should not engage in politics, nor that women's issues are divorced from politics. Indeed, women's claims are very much political issues and it is important that women participate in politics if they are to solve their problems. However, the women have not yet begun to make politics work for them as women.

For decades women have seen their sheer numbers as a weakness. There are more women than men, and the culture which makes marriage a woman's proper vocation means men can pick and choose their marriage partners whereas women often have to share a husband. Now the tables are being turned: these same numbers are transforming women into a political force to be reckoned with.

Women's numerical strength gives them decisive political power. Those who aspire to parliament have to sell themselves to women. This strength can be used not only as a power base for those women politicians who are prepared to champion women's causes: it can also be used to force those people, both men and women, who want to ride into parliament on female support not only to put women's issues on their political agenda but to prioritise such issues in the programme they sell to the electorate.

Women must reach political maturity before they can make the political process really work for them. In Zimbabwe it is only now that women are beginning to realise that politics should be their slave, not their master. It is only now that they are awakening to the fact that they can use politics to actualise their needs as women. But women are not yet politically mature. For example, in the aftermath of the 1990 general elections, it was women who demonstrated nation-wide against various people for no other 'crime' than that they had dared to support or sympathise with the newly formed political party, Zimbabwean Unity Movement (ZUM). In some cases they went as far as demanding the resignation or dismissal from employment of ZUM supporters, directly violating these individuals' rights to free political thought, expression and association. As one of our women activists observed:

> If we, the women of Zimbabwe, want our rights to be recognised as basic human rights, then we have to stop being at the centre of some of the violations of basic human rights. No one should ever have to refrain from expressing their political thoughts for fear that after election a group of women will demand that person's resignation from their job. We cannot ask with one hand and take away with the other. Victimising an individual for their political affiliation has never guaranteed anyone appropriate health care, access to credit, or an end to violence, to mention only a few. Yet these are the things that should concern us and should be paramount at our political gatherings.[44]

We cannot condone human rights violations just because they were perpetuated by women. We must be careful about the increasing danger of being waylaid or channelled into avenues which do not benefit women and may even support and provide a power base for structures which might be prejudicial to women as a group. Therefore, women need to be well organised in the exercise of their new-found strength and to do this they need to network with other groups and individuals such as researchers, academics and activists working on women's issues.

Notes

1. Zimbabwe African National Union (Patriotic Front) (ZANU PF) 1980 Election Manifesto.
2. The aims and objects of the party (ZANU PF) which is currently in power and, therefore, holding the reigns of state power, shall be
    (b) to create and preserve a just social order in Zimbabwe;
    (c) to establish and sustain a Socialist State in Zimbabwe based on Marxist-Leninist principles but firmly based on our historical, cultural and social experience in which the Political Order is based on Adult Universal Suffrage under the Vanguard Leadership of the workers, peasants and intellectuals;
    (d) to oppose resolutely, tribalism, regionalism, racism, sexism, religious bigotry, corruption, and all forms of exploitation, and all forms of exploitation of man by man.

3. SI 1600/1979.
4. Section 23 of the Customary Law and Primary Courts Act.
5. Charles Samupindi quoting John Updike and Chinua Achebe in 'Wrestling With An Alien Culture,' The *Herald*, 24.9.1990, p2.
6. Sections 2 and 3 of the African Law and Tribal Courts Act 24/69.
7. *M'pambiwa v M'pambiwa* 1974 (2) RLR 20.
8. Section 3 of Act 24/69.
9. Act No 24 of 1969.
10. Section 3 of 24/69.
11. M Maboreke, 'The Legal Status of Women in Zimbabwe: The Laws Relating to Violence Against Women and Child Custody As Illustrations', MPhil thesis, University of Zimbabwe, Faculty of Law, July 1987, chapter 2.
12. Chapter 34 of the Laws of Zimbabwe.
13. Chapter 238 of the Laws of Zimbabwe.
14. Chapter 301 of the Laws of Zimbabwe.
15. Chapter 37 of the Laws of Zimbabwe.
16. Act 2 of 1990.
17. Act 15 of 1982.
18. SC 87/84.
19. *Hansard*, Parliamentary Debates, 12 September 1984.
20. *Hansard*, 12 September 1984.
21. The *Herald*, 7.11.1984.
22. Opening Speech at the Colloquium on the Rights of Women in Zimbabwe, 14 November 1984, in the Report of the Colloquium.
23. An avenging spirit of a person wronged during their lifetime, now coming back to exact satisfaction.
24. Speeches and Documents of the National Women's League Conference, Harare, City Sports Centre, 4–5 November, 1989, p14.
25. *Mahogany* Magazine, June 1986, p42.
26. MBKM Chivu Nyanga.
27. In her opening speech to the Colloquium on the Rights of Women in Zimbabwe.
28. *Hansard*, 1980–81, p1485.
29. Elizabeth Gwaunza, 'Moves to Improve Maintenance Law', The *Sunday Mail*, 14.10.1990, p9.
30. SI 371/85, 'Labour Relations (General Conditions of Employment) (Termination of Employment) Regulations, 1985. Note all reference to 'employers' as 'he'.
31. The Hon Dr BTG Chidzero, MP Republic of Zimbabwe, 'Economic Policy: Macro-economic Adjustment and Trade Statement: Liberalisation including the Budget Statement 1990', presented to the Parliament of Zimbabwe on 26 July 1990, published by the Government Printers, Harare.
32. See Margaret A Schuler (ed), 'Report of the Proceedings of the (WLD) Inter-regional Meeting: Women, Law and Development: Action for Change', *Series on Women, Law and Development: Issues and Strategies for Change*, 2, Washington DC: Overseas Educational Fund International, 1989.

33. 'Trade liberalisation to bring misery – Pswarayi', The *Sunday Mail*, 14.10.1990, p1.
34. 'Trade liberalisation to bring misery'.
35. This is the combined effect of Section 13 of the African Marriages Act and Section 69 of the Administration of Estates Act.
36. *Ettie Nyemba v Joshua Jena*, SC 49/86.
37. Chapter 37 of the Laws of Zimbabwe.
38. Chapter 238 of the Laws of Zimbabwe.
39. Act 21 of 1987.
40. Quoted in *The Tribune: A Women and Development Quarterly*, 45, New York: International Women's Tribune Centre, July 1990, p45.
41. Chapter 238 of the Laws of Zimbabwe.
42. Chapter 37 of the Laws of Zimbabwe.
43. *Zimnat Insurance Company Ltd v Joyce Chawanda*, SC 107/90.
44. Amy S Tsanga, 'As I see it, Zimbabwe should ratify CEDAW and follow its principles', The *Sunday Mail*, 3.6.1990, p8.

Namibian Independence

Bience Gawanas

*N*amibia's declaration of independence on 21 March was not only the most important milestone in the history of the country; it was also significant in the development of the women's movement in Namibia and in the southern African region. The issue of women's rights has been with us for years, but changes in favour of women are still far away. As a Namibian women recently said: 'It is quite undeniable that we cannot escape change any more – women's liberation is right in our midst and it is unquestionably here to stay.'

The reconstruction of the economic, organisational and social structures is inescapable in view of the changing role and status of women. The basic premise of this paper is that the formal equality as provided for in the new Namibian constitution will remain ineffective unless there are accompanied structural changes.

Namibian women are entering a new phase in their struggle. The agenda during the national liberation struggle highlighted the need to fight for the liberation of *all* the people – despite the fact that women have suffered under multiple forms of the oppression of apartheid. This was aggravated by the sexual or gender prejudices embedded in the Roman-Dutch legal system[1] which reduces all women to the status of legal minors.

The inevitable result of giving precedence to the national liberation struggle has meant women's struggle for liberation has taken second place. As women involved in a struggle, great achievements have been made. Whatever the shortcomings, the fact that after independence women were regarded as citizens with equal rights that can never be taken away from them is significant. Women also never lived under an illusion that independence by itself would bring about their liberation as women. Neither did they believe that it would bring about the elimination of sexual oppression and gender discrimination.

The election process

The independence process provided the opportunity to redraft priorities – explicitly putting gender issues on the agenda. For example, women voted in great numbers in the November 1989 elections for the constituent assembly. As one observer noted, women were courted as never before to participate in the elections, which they demonstrably did.

The woman as a voter has shown that she can and will be a dominant factor in influencing the pace of change. She also realises that to elect others to bring about change is one thing but the need to be elected to bring about change by herself is another. Unless women do something themselves to dictate the agenda for change, the status quo will remain untouched.

Many parties dealt with women's rights in their political manifestos, but it was obvious that this was done with a view only to win the votes of women. Women make up 51 per cent of the population. There were no public debates on exactly what these rights of women were or how the issue of women's subordination, or strategies for achieving emancipation, would be dealt with. The momentum of the women's movement was lost because many parties were restructured in line with the election campaign. Therefore, women's energies were geared more towards making their respective parties the victors than towards making the women's issue part of the campaign. Women failed to combine their resources in an effort to speak out on issues which affected their lives as women and to reorganise themselves in the process. This is not to deny the fact that women saw the election process as an opportunity to make people aware that women were on the march or that they were impressing upon their parties to make the women's issue part of their election platform.

The presence of women from various countries as part of the UNTAG contingent[2] enabled women, especially those who had never left the country, to share experiences and obtain visions of what is happening with women all over the world. This made women aware of many issues in ways that they had not been able to before, and raised the level of public debate on gender issues to new heights. In fact, shortly before the adoption of the constitution, meetings were held to look at the shortcomings and advantages of the provisions in that document for women. Women were aware that at the final stages they would probably not be able to change the constitution. But they resolved to adopt strategies which could ensure their full participation in issues which affected them as women from the onset of independence.

Participation in constitutional drafting

It is generally agreed that the constitution, which is the basic law of the land and which affects the lives of every Namibian, should be shaped by the people themselves. Although it was assumed that it was the responsibility of their elected representatives to the constituent assembly[3] to draw up the constitution, people nevertheless questioned what their own roles should be both in constitution-making and in the national reconstruction of their country. This is important in that Namibians have now secured for themselves constitutional guarantees. Yet many women, who ought to be the beneficiaries of these rights, are still unaware of them. In addition, these rights, and for that matter, laws, in and by themselves cannot address or redress the question of injustice unless women participate in their enforcement.

It was clear that the few women in the constituent assembly were not merely there to represent women's interest but rather their party interest. This is not to dismiss the contributions they made in shaping the constitution. There was one woman (who is also now a cabinet minister)[4] in the select committee on the constitution who gave tremendous input, and one wonders what a significant difference it could have made had there been more women.

The constitution

The constitution of the Republic of Namibia is based upon the principles of multi-party democracy, the rule of law and strong guarantees for protecting fundamental human rights and freedoms. It also reflects the doctrine of separation of powers with the government headed by an executive president and composed of cabinet ministers; the bicameral parliament which is the legislative branch of government; and an independent judiciary.

There are a number of fundamental rights and freedoms, including the right to equality, freedom from discrimination and the rights of the family, which have a direct bearing on women. Although the constitution is couched in non-sexist language with strong constitutional guarantees, women are yet to benefit from them.

Affirmative action

There is an important provision which empowers the government to implement affirmative action policies and mechanisms to advance people who had been disadvantaged by past discriminatory laws and practices.[5]

A casual glance at the position of women in Namibia reveals the following: There are seven women in the national assembly out of a total of 72 voting members; there are 16 ministers in the cabinet of whom only one is a woman, Dr Albertine Amathila; only two of the seven members of the Public Service Commission are women, one of whom is the author; two of the ten members of the Board of the Namibian Broadcasting Corporation are women; and so on. These women in leadership positions are still disadvantaged in advancing the women's cause in real terms because of their numbers, and the very real fact that they will be operating within a culture that discriminates against them. These structures are designed so that women cannot occupy or be promoted to influential positions which would challenge such male-dominated structures.

For example, structures in the inherited civil service are in the main dominated by white males. The influential role that civil servants play in shaping the policies and programmes of the government cannot be overlooked. It is possible that these positions will remain unaltered for some time because of the guarantees provided in the constitution. It is therefore important to bear in mind that any progressive policies emanating from the government to advance the position of the disadvantaged, and especially women, will be severely hampered unless the civil service is injected with black people and with women.

Another structural problem is traditions and customs. There are postcolonial legacies to deal with. The majority of people are uneducated and illiterate; a majority of those are women. The great majority of women still find themselves on the last rungs of the ladder. It is in this regard that the provision on affirmative action becomes essential in redressing these past colonial legacies. Article 23(3) says that parliament should

> have regard to the fact that women in Namibia have traditionally suffered
> special discrimination and that they need to be encouraged and enabled
> to play a full, equal and effective role in the political, social, economic
> and cultural life of the nation.[6]

If independence is to be meaningful to the majority of Namibian women, it has to be accompanied by reform and transformation of the social and economic structures which mitigate against women. Economic reconstruction must include land reform, provision of education and training, housing and employment. All discriminatory laws and practices must be abolished. Women must call for the revision of laws pertaining to the family, as family relationships are still premised on patriarchal attitudes. They must demand the democratisation of society, cultural practices and political parties so that they can have a say. But affirmative action is being attacked in some quarters as discriminatory against white people. Similarly, the policy of national reconciliation is purposely being misinterpreted to mean 'retaining the status quo provided there is internal peace'.

In discussing the issues of equality, there is a need to question assumptions that because men and women are biologically different, they need different treatment and therefore cannot be equal. By analogy can we say that because black and white people are different, they cannot be equal? This is a fallacy and it destroys the whole basis of our struggle.

Teaching and practising sexual and gender equality is a fundamental issue as it is a major value embodied in the constitution. Suffice is to state that in the search for equality, we should not struggle for openings for the privileged ones who have choices and opportunities. After all, only a few will make it. We should fight on behalf of the most disadvantaged women. We should help to empower them to use their own voices and make their own demands. Too many times 'we' have spoken on behalf of 'them'. Too many times 'we' spoke about 'them' as if the most disadvantaged women were merely objects. But how many times do 'we' allow 'them' to speak for themselves? How many times do women in positions of power fall into the same trap of not soliciting the views of those for whom changes would matter most?

Human rights

Law in and of itself cannot address the question of injustice. Indeed, it often strengthens the status quo because it is obliged to be neutral. Once it is accepted that society is neither just nor egalitarian, then one must reject the neutrality in favour of supporting the weak in their confrontation with the strong.

Namibian courts must embark on a process of evolving a new constitutional jurisprudence: one that breathes life into the fundamental rights' provisions of the constitution. In developing human rights law, a participatory approach must be adopted which enables those most in need of the rights to have the greatest say in delineating the content of the rights.

This will entail looking at human rights with new eyes, the eyes of the victims, the 'eyes of the down-trodden'. Human rights must be seen as a source of empowerment and as a means for securing public and social accountability.

Human rights can also play a significant role in securing the account-ability of those who wield power and control the resources essential to the satisfaction of basic human needs. Such rights are also important as a means for securing participation. Human rights approaches should repre-sent a vital expression of values.

Human rights often stress rights of value to dominant groups, such as the right of property interests. What this means for the majority of people who were dispossessed and left landless is that these rights have been used to frustrate land reforms or resist attempts to enforce laws dealing with money lending. Government policies and programmes undertaken to bring about development must be assessed in terms of their impact on helping realise the human rights of the poorest and the most disadvantaged in the area of the project.

Women will have to form a strong lobby or pressure group in order to exert influence on policies. A Women's Desk has recently been set up in the Office of the President but its function, powers and duties have not as yet been finalised. As women, we see this desk as a means to get involved in activities which are of direct and immediate benefit to women. In addition, there are numerous women's organisations ranging form political party women's wings to women organising themselves in co-operatives or projects. There is talk of the formation of a federation of Namibian women with the aim of carrying out an awareness campaign, drawing up a charter of women's rights and a committee to advise gov-ernment on the necessary revision of many discriminatory laws which are still on the statute book. In the final analysis, the enforcement of the constitution and any other legislative measures adopted by the govern-ment will depend on how vigilant women are in safeguarding their newly acquired rights and making use of opportunities open to them.

Unity of purpose is a precondition for the advancement of women. In a divided society such as ours, our resolve to fight for our rights is so often weakened by disunity and hence we are prevented from finding solutions to problems that are common to all women. The past has been witnessed by inferiority complexes, lack of self-esteem and destructive tendencies amongst women themselves. Looking at the overall policy of national reconciliation, I would strongly argue that women should accept that policy as also relating to them – to us!

Conclusion

The women of Namibia have entered the most important phase of their struggle. The remnants of colonialism will be felt for years to come but the conditions under which women continue their struggle are more favourable. Any attempts to create a better deal for women on the part of the government through affirmative action will no doubt be valuable and prove the government's sincerity to change the status quo.

An unquestioning or complacent acceptance of the status quo conveys a message that inequality is acceptable. It also helps to discourage any attempts to search for and discuss serious alternatives. While there are ongoing discussions, these should be accompanied by concrete actions. Already there are women who have been elected or appointed to government, boards, commissions and committees. It is hoped that their presence, although numerically small, will make a difference. What we all hope to strive for in the long run is to create equal opportunities for all men and women, to create peaceful conditions under which our children can grow up and to create an economic structure which will value the active participation of women and the productive role which they already play in the economic life of Namibia.

Notes

1. Roman-Dutch laws were inherited from the legacy of the apartheid laws of South Africa.
2. UNTAG was the United Nations Assistance Transition Group which was appointed in terms of Resolution 435 to oversee the election process and the transition to independence in Namibia.
3. More than 97 per cent of the Namibian population eligible to vote elected the 72 member constituent assembly, from seven political parties, from 7–11 November 1989. The constituent assembly began to meet on 21 November 1989. A fully democratic constitution was approved by consensus of the assembly on 9 February 1990, and 21 March 1990 was the official date of independence.
4. Dr Libertine Amathila, minister for Local Government and Housing, and the only woman cabinet minister. She was one of the two key note speakers at the Lawyers for Human Rights conference.
5. Article 23 of the Namibian constitution reads as follows:
    Apartheid and Affirmative Action
    (1) The practice of racial discrimination and the practice and ideology of apartheid from which the majority of the people of Namibia have suffered for so long shall be prohibited and by Act of Parliament such practices, and the propagation of such practices, may be rendered criminally punishable by

the ordinary Courts by means of such punishment as Parliament deems necessary for the purposes of expressing the revulsion of the Namibian people at such practices.

(2) Nothing contained in Article 10 hereof shall prevent Parliament from enacting legislation providing directly or indirectly for the advancement of persons within Namibia who have been socially, economically or educationally disadvantaged by past discriminatory laws or practices, or for the implementation of policies and programmes aimed at redressing social, economic, or educational imbalances in the Namibian society arising out of past discriminatory laws or practices, or for achieving a balanced structuring of the public service, the police force, the defence force, and the prison service.

(3) In the enactment of legislation and the application of any policies and practices contemplated by Sub-Article (2) hereof, it shall be permissible to have regard to the fact that women in Namibia have traditionally suffered special discrimination and that they need to be encouraged and enable to play a full, equal and effective role in the political, social, economic and cultural life of the nation.

Article 10 reads:

Equality and Freedom from Discrimination

(1) All persons shall be equal before the law.

(2) No persons maybe discriminated against on the grounds of sex, race, colour, ethnic origin, religion, creed or social or economic status.

6. Article 23 of the Namibian constitution.

Gender Equality Under the Botswana Constitution

Unity Dow

Mosadi o a nyalwa, monna o a nyala – a man marries, while a woman is married by the man.

Is a Motswana man more Motswana than a Motswana woman? A Motswana male and a Motswana female should have equal rights and privileges.[1]

The wife and children belong to the husband hence the adoption of his surname. They must therefore reside in the man's country, not a foreign country.[2]

The citizenship law is fine as it is, it should not be changed in order to accommodate a handful of women in Gaborone... They should not be taken seriously as this might mislead some Batswana women who still respect their tradition.[3]

How did woman first become subject to man as she now is all over the world? By her nature, her sex, just as the Negro is, and always will be, to the end of time, inferior to the white race, and therefore doomed to subjection, but happier than she would be in any other condition, just because it is the law of nature. The women themselves would not have this law reversed.[4]

Botswana constitution

The constitution of Botswana came into force in 1966 when the country gained independence from Britain. It starts off with a bill of rights[5] which specifically states that every person in Botswana is entitled to the fundamental rights and freedoms of the individual. It goes on to detail prohibited grounds for discrimination, including race, place of origin, political opinions, colour, creed or sex. Article 3 further provides that

> the provisions of this chapter shall have the effect for the purpose of affording protection to those rights and freedoms subject to such limitations of that protection as are contained in those provisions, being limitations designed to ensure that the enjoyment of the said rights and freedoms by any individual does not prejudice the rights and freedoms of others or the public interest.[6]

The rights, freedoms and protections guaranteed under the constitution are: i) the right to life, liberty, security of the person and protection of the law; ii) the protections of the privacy of the home and other property and from the deprivation of property without compensation.

Equality and non-discrimination in the enjoyment of these rights seem to be guaranteed by the use of such expressions as 'every person', 'no person' and 'any person' found in articles 3–14.

On the other hand, article 15, which provides that no law shall make any provision that is discriminatory either of itself or in its effect, defines discrimination as 'affording different treatment to different persons, attributable wholly or mainly to their respective descriptions by race, tribe, place of origin, political opinions, colour or creed…' Sex is not included in the list of categories.

Because of this narrow definition of 'discrimination', it has often been argued that sex-based discrimination is not outlawed by the constitution and thus it was never the intention of the drafters to guarantee equal rights for men and women.

It has been said that in view of the customary and common law rules in existence at the time of the adoption of the constitution, gender equality was never intended. This argument seems to suggest no greater rights and protections were granted by the constitution than existed prior to its adoption. To attempt to interpret the constitution within the narrow confines of customary and common law is, in my opinion, to go against the very purpose of a constitution enshrining fundamental rights.

In the words of Kentridge JA in the case *Attorney General v Moagi*:

> [A] constitution such as a Constitution of Botswana, embodying fundamental rights, should as far as its language permits be given a broad

construction. Constitutional rights conferred without express limitation should not be cut down by reading implicit restrictions into them, so as to bring them into line with common law...[7]

Immediately after independence Botswana became a part of the United Nations Charter. Article I of the UN Charter lists among its main purposes the achievement of international co-operation 'in promoting and encouraging respect for human rights and fundamental freedoms for all without distinction as to race, sex, language or religion'.

The UN's Universal Declaration of Human Rights affirms the principle of the inadmissibility of discrimination and proclaims that all human beings are born free and equal in dignity and rights and that everyone is entitled to all the rights and freedoms set forth therein, without distinction of any kind, including distinction based on sex.

Furthermore, Botswana is a signatory to the African Charter on Human and People's Rights. The African Charter reaffirms the human rights commitments of the UN Charter and the Universal Declaration of Human Rights. It specifically provides that all persons are equal before the law and guarantees equal protection of the law without distinction of any kind, including distinction based on sex.

In view of Botswana's apparent commitment to the observance of human rights, there seems to be no justification to continue undermining the bill of rights in the constitution by interpreting it in the context of our gender-discriminatory customary and common law notions. But then perhaps there is no commitment to the observance of human rights if human rights are to include 'women's rights'. That would explain Botswana's failure to sign the UN Convention on the Elimination of All Forms of Discrimination Against Women.

The Unity Dow challenge to the citizenship law

The case of *Unity Dow v The Attorney General of the Republic of Botswana*,[8] which was heard by the High Court of Botswana on 1 and 2 November 1990, raised these issues. The case is *sub-judice* as judgment is still to be pronounced. An attempt will be made to report on the facts and issues addressed without comment.

The writer hereof made application to the High Court of Botswana alleging that certain provisions of the Citizenship Act of 1982 offended against the constitution. According to the challenged provisions, a Motswana woman married to a foreigner cannot pass on Botswana citizenship to the children of the marriage regardless of where the children are born.[9] Further, the challenged provisions give foreign women, but not foreign men, who marry Botswana citizens special status for purposes of naturalisation.

The argument by the applicant was essentially that the distinction between sexes in this case was unjustified and offended against the constitution which guarantees all persons the rights amongst others, to liberty and the protection of the law. It was argued further by the applicant that the Citizenship Act curtailed her right to enter and reside in Botswana since female citizens do not have an unrestricted right to live in Botswana if they marry a foreigner, whereas male citizens have an unrestricted right to do so. A further argument by the applicant was that discrimination against women, violating as it does the principle of equality of rights and respect for human dignity, offended against the constitution as it subjects women to degrading treatment.

The argument advanced by the state was that sex-based discrimination was not outlawed nor was it intended to be outlawed. It was further argued that none of the rights alleged by the applicant to be contravened had been so contravened. A list of discriminatory laws (customary, common law and statute) was supplied as justification for the existence of the Citizenship Act.

This is an incredible argument in the 1990s. All over the world discrimination against women has been rationalised by paternalistic, outdated, notions like the following:

> [M]an is/or should be women's protector and defender. The natural and proper timidity and delicacy which belongs to the female sex evidently unfit it to the many of the occupations of civil life... The paramount destiny and mission of women are to fulfil the noble and benign offices of wife and mother. This is the law of the creator.[10]

The state's representative in the citizenship case to some extent endorsed this age-old argument and stated,[11] in reference to the various discriminatory laws in our statute books, that these 'are there for sound and practical reasons, such as protection of privacy, morality and recognition of child-bearing capacity'. He lamented: 'it is not unfair to say that if gender discrimination were outlawed in customary law, very little of customary law would be left at all.'[12]

The arguments advanced by the state in this case indicate the great reluctance by men in Botswana to see women as anything other than wives and mothers (or potential wives and mothers). This continued relegation of women to a status lower than that of men is obviously an obstacle to full participation of women in the political, economic, social and cultural aspects of their societies. Very often those who support discriminatory laws consider it sufficient to defend them by simply stating 'it is our culture'.

It is always difficult to fight cultural and traditional practices and a constitution which fails clearly and specifically to outlaw sex-based discrimination, especially as it relates to rights of nationality, education, employment and within marriage, is inadequate. The adequacy or otherwise of the Botswana constitution in this respect will soon be determined by the High Court when it pronounces judgement on the citizenship case.

Postscript

Judgement in the case was finally delivered on 11 June 1991. The court decided in favour of the applicant reasoning inter alia that:

> '[T]he effect of Section 4 (3) of the Citizenship Act is to hamper unnecessarily free choice, the liberty of the subject to exercise her rights in terms of the constitution...'[13]

> '[T]he time when women were treated as chattels or were there to obey the whims and wishes of males is long past and would be offensive to modern thinking...'[14]

> 'What is considered degrading treatment today has changed from former conceptions. Discrimination against women, denying or limiting as it does their equality of rights with men is fundamentally unjust and constitutes an offence against human dignity!...'[15]

The court declared Sections 4 and 5 of the Citizenship Act *ultra vires* to the constitution in that the said sections violated the applicants rights to liberty, protection of the law, immunity from expulsion from Botswana, protection from degrading treatment and protection against discrimination on the basis of her sex.[16]

Notes

1. Unity Dow quoted in *Report of the Law Reform Committee*, Gaborone: Botswana Government Printers, 1989.
2. Gudu Muhinda quoted in *Report of the Law Reform Committee*, p19.
3. T Malale quoted in *Report of the Law Reform Committee*, p37.
4. *New York Herald* in 1852 quoted by A Kraditor, in *Up From the Pedestal: Selected Writing in the History of American Feminism*, 1968, p190.
5. Bill of Rights at Chapter II and Article 3.

6. Bill of Rights, Article 3.
7. Kentridge JA in *Attorney General v Moagi* 1981 BIR 1, p28.
8. *Unity Dow v The Attorney General of the Republic of Botswana* Msc 134/90.
9. Prior to Unity Dow's challenge to the Botswana citizenship laws under the Botswana constitution, this discriminatory practice was documented fully by Ataliah Molokomme, 'Discrimination Under the Guise of Tradition: Women's Citizenship Rights in Botswana', in Alice Armstrong (ed), *Women and Law in Southern Africa*, Harare: Zimbabwe Publishing House, 1987, pp210–20.
10. *Bradwell v Illinois*, 83 US 130, 141 (1872 (upholding prohibition of law practice by women)).
11. Respondents' Heads of Argument in the case of *Unity Dow v The Attorney General*, p15.
12. Respondents' Heads of Argument in the case of *Unity Dow v The Attorney General, p15.*
13. The judgement in the case of *Unity Dow v The Attorney General*, p15.
14. The judgement in the case of *Unity Dow v The Attorney General*, p17.
15. The judgement in the case of *Unity Dow v The Attorney General*, p23.
16. For more information on this case see 'A Big Win for Unity Dow – And for Women Everywhere' in *The Women's Watch*, 5(1), International Women's Rights Action Watch, July 1991.

Women and Equality Rights in Canada

Sobering reflections, impossible choices

Elizabeth A Sheehy

[R]ights are not inherently progressive, but rather depend upon the politics
informing them . . . The Canadian Charter comes to dominate political discourse
and thus defines the universe within which political struggle occurs.
– Judy Fudge[1]

*C*anadian women have a history of turning to the courts to challenge
discriminatory legislation resulting from the 'democratic' process. Our
democratic process has been and remains markedly unrepresentative of
women, black people, Aboriginal peoples, and the poor, both in numbers
in the legislative and administrative branches of the state, and in the
concrete policies pursued. In spite of women's corresponding
under-representation in the judiciary and in spite of the continuity of
interest among these various manifestations of the state, women valiantly
put our grievances to the courts under the Canadian Bill of Rights[2]
during its short life span. We lost virtually[3] every case litigated.[4]

When the Canadian government announced its intention to enact a
new constitutional document, which would clearly authorise judges to
invalidate parliament's legislation if it contravened constitutional rights,
women's organisations had no choice but to intervene to try to have their
interests represented in this new document. We were, however, forced to

fit our demands into the framework of the pre-existing agenda of those (exclusively white) men charged with negotiation and drafting of the new Canadian Charter of Rights and Freedoms.[5]

A lengthy and often bitter struggle ensued as women fought to have sexual equality added to the list of protected rights in the charter in un-equivocal language.[6] Aboriginal women waged a parallel battle to have their rights to sexual equality restored to them through these same con-stitutional negotiations.[7]

Aboriginal and non-Aboriginal women achieved sex equality rights in some form through the enactment of bill C-31[8] and section 15 in the charter:

> Section 15 (1): Every individual is equal before and under the law and has the right to the equal protection and equal benefit of the law without discrimination and, in particular, without discrimination based on race, national or ethnic origin, colour, religion, sex, age or mental or physical disability.
> (2) Subsection (1) does not preclude any law, program or activity that has as its object the amelioration of conditions of disadvantaged individuals or groups including those that are disadvantaged because of race, national or ethnic origin, colour, religion, sex, age or mental or physical disability.
> Section 28: Notwithstanding anything in this Charter, the rights and freedoms referred to in it are guaranteed equally to male and female persons.

Although section 15 marks a victory for Canadian women, many de-mands were ultimately abandoned in the negotiation process. Further, women were not allowed to provide any input at the ground level of creating the parameters and concepts of the charter. Worse, perhaps, is that women's fate has once more been placed in the hands of the Cana-dian judiciary through their power to interpret the meaning of constitutional guarantees.

The results of women's litigation under the new charter are not quite as dismal as the cases decided under the old bill of rights. But the Cana-dian courts nonetheless have a questionable record in advancing women's rights. This paper considers whether the creation of equality rights in a constitutional document was the best route by which to em-power or preserve the gains of Canadian women in light of this record.

Women have in fact brought very few equality cases and this re-strained participation is structurally conditioned: women have won an even smaller number of cases; these few cases represent narrow vic-tories, couched within the framework of the liberal state and beneficial to those women who most closely resemble the male model (that is, white and elite); men are winning more charter cases, including equality cases, which means that the few gains which women have managed to achieve in the legislative process are being struck down as contrary to men's equality and fair trial rights. In the light of these facts we cannot even begin to expect that our courts will move beyond a monolithic understanding of 'women's' rights to recognise as issues of equality the more complex questions represented by the structures of ethnocentrism, white supremacy, homophobia, colonialism, able-bodied privilege, and the grinding poverty of the lives of women and their children.

The experience of Canadian women offers important information for South African women who have also had to insert themselves into a process of constitutional negotiations undertaken without adequate representation of women, on terms which are not of women's making. In the context of the imminent defeat of the apartheid government in South Africa, a bill of rights is imperative; South African women do not have the luxury of saying 'no' to sex equality rights at this stage. However, Canadian experience highlights trouble spots, additional measures which must be undertaken to make constitutional rights mean something, and suggests some minimum criteria which South African women might want to insist upon in their bill of rights. Most importantly, charter litigation in Canada makes clear the importance of women's continued political struggle, and the limits of sex equality 'rights' in a society which remains premised upon and preoccupied with differentiation on the basis of race, class, and gender.

In what follows, I first survey the results of equality litigation in Canada. Second, I present a tally of the costs of these cases for women. Third, I describe some of the potentialities which a bill of rights may hold for South African women, and I make suggestions for promising strategies.

Equality litigation under the charter

A major study commissioned by the Canadian Advisory Council on the Status of Women, *Women and the Canadian Charter of Rights and Freedoms: One Step Forward or Two Steps Back?*[9] found that in the first three years after the charter was enacted, only a minuscule fraction of the equality claims were brought by or on behalf of 'disadvantaged' persons. Of the 591 cases argued, only 17 involved claims by the 'disadvantaged':[10] seven by women; four by members of ethnic minorities; four by mentally disabled persons; one by a member of a racial minority; and one by an Aboriginal person. The remaining cases were brought by corporations and men!

Sex equality cases comprised only ten per cent of the equality litigation in the first three years.[11] Of the 52 claims, nine were made by or on behalf of women and 35 by or on behalf of men,[12]. This latter number is even higher if men's interventions on behalf of unborn foetuses are included. While women's success rate of 50 per cent was somewhat higher than men's with respect to these cases,[13] the rate of men's claims still means men are winning at least twice as many sex equality cases as women.

The structural barriers which inhibit women from bringing equality claims are economic, practical, and ideological. Charter cases are extremely costly. For example, one important case[14] took two-and-a-half years and $200 000 to litigate in 1985; the costs will be even higher in 1991.[15] When women's claims challenge entrenched and powerful structures such as the police, they will probably be fought on every minute point to the highest courts of the land. For example, in a tort suit by a rape victim who claims sex discrimination on the part of the police in failing to adequately investigate rape, the plaintiff was forced to take her case to the highest court in Ontario. It took four years to win the right to bring the case to trial![16] Her lawyers have not yet even *begun* to argue the substance of her claim.

Organisations such as the federally funded Court Challenges Program[17] and the Women's Legal Education and Action Fund (LEAF)[18] finance litigation for some women who could not otherwise pursue claims. Such assistance is constrained by several factors. First, these groups have extremely limited resources and must constantly set priorities and make difficult decisions. Second, these organisations tend to respond to requests for assistance rather than to pursue a particular agenda. This means they are oriented towards the interests and claims of women who view the issues in their lives as legal, involving a denial of 'rights', and who have the ability and willingness to pursue a legal remedy. Third, these groups have tended to fund the winnable cases which are also usually the less costly cases.

Few barriers remaining for women are found in overt legislative form. Therefore novel claims require gathering and even creating statistical information. Funders have to assist in case development, expending even more of their limited resources.

Several practical barriers to sex equality claims which challenge societal structures – money, years to litigate, and endurance – are implicit in the information just described. We must add to this list the impediments (sometimes harassment) offered by the Canadian media,[19] competing demands on women's time and energy, ongoing fund-raising struggles for such lawsuits,[20] the narrow remedies which courts can or will offer, the fact that not all women are either able or willing to assume the role of 'victim' by initiating complaints of sex oppression,[21] and, finally but significantly, the fact of retaliatory male violence.[22]

The ideological barriers to sex equality claims by women are founded in the nature and structure of the judiciary. Authors such as John Griffith[23] and Terence Ison[24] have examined the composition, training, and values of the judiciary both in Canada and in the United Kingdom, and have argued that the products of judicial decision making will inevitably reflect class interests. Albie Sachs and Joan Hoff Wilson[25] have suggested that not only class but also patriarchal interests are served by the cases decided by male judges. Mary Jane Mossman[26], in analysing the tools of legal reasoning, concluded that these tools rely upon and thus reinforce the status quo. Catharine MacKinnon[27] has argued that legal principles are conceptualised from an essentially male perspective, and that the values which law reifies reflect what we take to be masculine qualities. Brettel Dawson[28] has suggested that men's power is also encoded in our underlying legal structures and concepts, and Carol Smart[29] has argued that law itself contributes to women's disempowerment through its replication of gender ideologies and relations in legal principles and outcomes.

These analyses have further implications for progressive efforts to use charter litigation. Mary Jane Mossman noted that an important feature of legal method is malleability: the tools of legal reasoning offer great latitude for judicial choice while producing legal results which appear inevitable and are therefore very powerful conveyors of ideologies.[30] Charter critics such as Judy Fudge,[31] Terence Ison,[32] Andrew Petter,[33] Reuben Hasson,[34] Harry Glasbeek and Michael Mandel,[35] and Sheila McIntyre[36] have expressed the fear that the charter vests even more concealed power in the hands of the judiciary: judges are empowered to strike down legislation based on the promises of an essentially liberal constitutional document, drafted and passed by legislators who reflect the dominant interests in Canadian society. Judicial decisions in charter cases thus carry power without political accountability and renewed legitimacy in spite of the fact that the race, class, and gender composition of the judiciary remains unchanged, as do the underlying legal structures, doctrines, methodologies, and values.

To what extent do these ideological constraints prevent women benefitting from the charter's guarantee of sex equality?

First, the experience of United States litigators suggests sex equality claims are most likely to succeed when the claimant is a man, when the claim highlights the impact of a law upon men, or when a woman demonstrates that she meets the (*male*) standard and therefore deserves 'equal' treatment.[37] In Canada, there is the example of the adoptive parents benefits case, heralded as a feminist victory.[38] The court held that denying parental leave benefits to an adoptive father amounted to a denial of his sex equality rights.[39] What is noteworthy is that this case is of primary benefit to men and that any advantages conferred on women through, for instance, a broadening of social notions of responsibility for child care, are secondary and certainly speculative. Another example is the case of female hockey player Justine Blainey, who won the right not to be barred from a boys' hockey team because she could meet their level of competitive play and thus demonstrated her exceptional ability in terms of a male standard.[40] These cases raise questions about how many women will in fact benefit from equality litigation, since many women cannot meet the standards designed by and for men.

Second, in Canada, in order to make their arguments understood by and acceptable to judges, feminist litigators are driven to soften the language and power of their analyses.[41] Thus, propositions and results which are most compatible with the current legal, political, and economic structures will be offered up as alternative arguments, and, unfortunately, these are likely to provide the most appealing bases for any positive judicial decisions.[42]

Examples can be found in many cases: the women teachers' case where a last ditch effort by feminist litigators protected the women-only teachers' union against a sex discrimination claim;[43] the same-sex partners case, where a lesbian argued that her partner should be able to claim health care benefits as a dependent because their relationship met all of the features of a traditional heterosexual marriage;[44] the abortion decision of the Supreme Court of Canada where the challenge to the constitutionality of the criminal prohibition against abortion was won on the basis that the offence violated principles of procedural fairness to accused persons rather than any substantive rights possessed by women;[45] and the balcony rapist case where LEAF argued that the police failure to warn a woman about the threat posed by a serial rapist was based upon stereotypes about hysterical women. This is more likely to succeed than the claim that the police systematically fail to investigate and prosecute assaults upon women.[46]

Third, the work of critical legal scholars suggests that judges are inclined towards charter rulings which enhance the authority and power of the common law and thus the bench.[47] For example, Canadian judges have been reluctant to invalidate their *own* common law rules on the basis of the charter. The Supreme Court of Canada upheld the use of judicial powers of contempt against legal picketers outside a court house[48] in spite of the charter right to freedom of association.

In the specific context of sex equality claims, it is true that LEAF successfully defended criminal law provisions which protect the woman who has been raped from questions regarding her past sexual history against a charter challenge by accused men.[49] However, LEAF's 'winning' argument conceded important ground by accepting that in some cases there should be a 'constitutional exemption'[50] to the absolute bar in criminal legislation on such evidence.

The costs of charter litigation

The barriers identified above do not necessarily take away from women's status although they do suggest limits to the promise of the charter. However, a 'rights' document such as the charter also has its costs, as it inspires many groups to utilise concepts of 'fundamental freedoms' to their own ends.

Men use 'their' equality rights and other charter rights to invalidate legislation which was intended to benefit women. For example, several criminal code provisions drafted in sex-specific language to capture abusive sexual behaviour by males upon females have been struck down as offending men's equality rights;[51] statutes which conferred social welfare benefits exclusively upon female recipients have been invalidated on the same basis.[52] Accused men have also asserted other charter rights to undercut criminal law provisions which protect women who have been raped against harassing and misleading questions regarding their past sexual histories.[53] The success of these arguments in some provincial lower and appellate courts,[54] leaves women uncertain about their privacy in rape trials.

One aspect of this effort by men to appropriate charter and equality rights to their own ends has involved the coalescing of 'men's rights' groups and anti-feminist 'women's rights' groups. Their main objectives are attacking gains made by women and asserting the 'rights' of the foetus.[55] These groups have been successful in securing media attention, tapping into male fear and backlash against feminism generally, and cloaking their campaigns in legal rhetoric, forcing feminists to respond to these essentially anti-intellectual positions in rational terms.

Much of the misogynistic violence which occurs across Canada would be unfolding in some form whether or not the charter existed. But the language of equality lends legitimacy, moral authority, and legal literacy to an otherwise pathetic effort to halt women's empowerment.

Women risk further losses through charter litigation. For instance, in the adoptive parents benefits case, plaintiff Shalom Schachter argued for the expansion of the state's obligations to provide income support for adoptive parents to take time off from work to spend with their new arrivals.[56] However, there was a serious risk that the government might have responded to these increased financial obligations by cutting back on maternity benefits already available to women. Schachter's own argument acknowledged this as a possible government response.[57]

The charter holds further hidden costs for women: the erosion of much of the legislation intended to provide consumer[58] and worker protection[59] and to prevent the concentration of corporate power, through charter litigation by corporations.[60] Women will be increasingly vulnerable to the excesses and abuses of advertising and marketing practices for the beauty and health industries, through weakened health, safety, and collective bargaining rights for women workers, and through the 'privatisation of the costs of reproduction'[61] effected by successful charter challenges to social welfare schemes.

Equality litigation pursued by or on behalf of women has its own costs. If these cases are lost, the government can easily then avoid political responsibility for law making in the name of women's fundamental rights and freedoms.[62] Further, individual women and women's groups engaged in charter battles invest their meagre resources and divert precious political energy away from other organising strategies. Women's groups can be left depleted, disorganised, and dispirited when such heavy reliance is counterproductive to social change.

Even worse, women's struggles have sometimes divided along race and class lines because the chances of success of charter claims may be enhanced by one-dimensional arguments.[63] Thus, women's groups have tended to concentrate on straightforward sex discrimination claims, as opposed to complex, multi-dimensional claims which constitute serious challenges to legal structures. However, LEAF is currently litigating a claim based on race, class, immigrant status, and sex discrimination regarding the exclusion of domestic and farm workers from minimum employment standards legislation.[64] This is an important effort to fund claims which serve the interests of all women. Such claims require much more by way of creative energy, risk-taking, and new forms of evidence and argumentation.

An example of the divisiveness of sex equality claims involves the case where the claimant, a well-known feminist lawyer, challenged the non-deductibility of the expenses of employing a nanny against her professional income.[65] It has been argued that this claim reinforces class divisions within the scheme of income taxation because non-professional women cannot deduct their child care expenses: it thus confers a differential benefit upon Canadian women according to professional status, wealth, and race.[66] This case has also fed further anti-feminist sentiments, from the left, and has widened the gap between liberal and other feminists.

Another sex equality claim, this one launched against the federal Prison for Women,[67] illustrates that charter cases may undercut other important feminist concerns. The complaint in this suit is that the programs and services provided to female inmates are sex-stereotyped and far inferior to those provided to male inmates,[68] and that because there is only one federal women's prison, women, and particularly Aboriginal women, are further punished by loss of contact with their families and communities as they serve their sentences. While this complaint is absolutely justified and raises very serious concerns, the problem with an equality argument is that we may well get 'equal' prisons for women! In response to pressure from many sources, the federal government has just announced the closure of the Prison for Women[69] and the plans for *more*, albeit smaller prisons, for women across Canada. Is 'equality' what we want in the context of a prison system which effectively destroys human beings?

When women's sex equality claims succeed, they are often won on narrow, technical grounds. Some of that technical language may come back to haunt us. After the Supreme Court of Canada struck down the criminal prohibition against abortion in 1987, the federal government responded by re-introducing criminal legislation[70] which carefully avoided the pitfalls identified in the ruling. Luckily for Canadian women, the unexpected occurred: while our elected representatives passed the Bill, it was stopped in the senate by a tie vote.[71]

A further example can be found in the women teachers' union case. The judicial reasoning behind the women teachers' victory was that unions are *private* organisations immune from the charter.[72] This reinvocation of the inviolability of the 'private sphere' from government intervention will surely have a negative impact on women's claims to be protected in that sphere.

In another case involving a man's discrimination claim against sex-specific sexual assault legislation, Madam Justice Wilson, women's strongest advocate on the Supreme Court of Canada, upheld the legislation partly on the basis that equality is not violated when the offence matches *biological differences*.[73] Such an analysis fails to acknowledge that sexual assault is not biologically determined but rather socially constructed. This reliance upon biological difference as underlying female victimisation poses serious threats to women's advancement in other domains, including legal discourse and equality litigation. We may, in fact, have to count these two technical victories as losses.

Future struggles

In Canada the charter is there to stay. In countries such as South Africa a bill of rights seems inevitable. What then are the potentialities of a bill of rights and how can the most be made of them?

The passage of a bill of rights can create the imperative for legislative reform. In Canada governments undertook statute audits[74] to assess the shortfall between the charter equality guarantee and all legislation on the books. Although many government committees took a narrow view of the meaning of equality and reformed statutes only when sexism in language use was glaring,[75] the process of statute review does have a great deal of potential for creative input and political organising by women, outside of the confines of test case litigation.

A bill of rights can set minimum constitutional requirements for women's participation in political parties, in government, and in the judiciary. Gender representation guaranteed by a bill of rights might be the best way to provide for women's empowerment in the long term.[76] In countries such as the United States and Canada where rights are essentially dependent upon judicial interpretations, rights have been narrowed and even retracted by new judicial appointments to the bench. In Canada, some leading women judges bring a different set of values to their judging and are thus, to some extent, transforming the face of Canadian law.[77] But the recent retirement of Madam Justice Wilson, the strongest feminist on the Supreme Court of Canada, leaves only two women on a bench of nine appointed by a conservative government. This must have implications for the interpretation of upcoming charter issues. If our constitution required that women be represented proportionately in all branches of the government, including institutions such as the judiciary and the police, we would be much closer to creating a society which reflects the needs and concerns of both sexes.

A bill of rights may be most effective at undermining the relations of dominance which maintain women's subordinate position if it gives more power to democratic structures which themselves serve women's interests and if it protects basic political and social rights. Constitutional provisions which protect the right to bargain collectively, which ensure that the right to vote can be exercised easily by the entire population, and which protect democratic processes from corporate power provide important underpinnings for the creation of a society in which women are equal participants.

Women must be promised some basic conditions, apart from any provision guaranteeing sexual equality, if a constitutional document is to be meaningful for women's lives. Issues such as wages for housework and child care, day care, and full access to reproductive choice and services must be part of the foundational political document for a society which claims a commitment to women's equality. Failing to address these issues in a bill of rights involves a deliberate choice to perpetuate economic, legal, and political structures which ensure that women bear these costs and that they carry the full load of any protracted effort to alter the status quo through the 'democratic' processes offered by the courts and the legislature.

South African women have been presented with an important opportunity for political struggle through having their interests represented in a bill of rights. Lessons from countries such as Canada may be helpful for the negotiations over women's equality rights, but women must conserve their energy and resources. Long-term struggle lies ahead in fighting off 'rights' challenges to women's few and fragile gains, and in the implementation of sex equality through structural change outside of the arena of litigation.

Notes

1. Judy Fudge, 'The Effect of Entrenching a Bill of Rights Upon Political Discourse: Feminist Demands and Sexual Violence in Canada', *International Journal of the Sociology of Law*, 17, 1989, pp445, 460.
2. Canadian Bill of Rights, SC 1960, c 44, RSC 1970, Appendix III.
3. For a rare example of a case where a woman was able to invoke the bill of rights successfully, see *R v Lavoie*, [1971] 1 WWR 690 (BCCoCt).
4. See, for example, *Attorney-General of Canada v Lavell*, (1973), [1974] SCR 1349; *Bliss v Attorney-General of Canada*, (1978), 23 NR 527 (SCC); and *R v MacKay*; *R v Willington*, (1977), 36 CCC (2d) 349 (Alta SC).
5. Canadian Charter of Rights and Freedoms, Part I of Constitution Act, 1982, as enacted by Canada Act (UK) 1982, c 11, Schedule B.
6. Chaviva Hosek, 'Women and Constitutional Process' in Keith Banting and Richard Simeon (eds), *And No One Cheered: Federalism, Democracy and the Constitution Act*, Toronto: Methuen, 1983, pp280–300.
7. For descriptions of the struggles of Aboriginal women to overturn the federal legislation which provided that women, but not men, lost their 'Indian' status at law when they married non-Aboriginal partners, see Janet Silman, *Enough is Enough: Aboriginal Women Speak Out*, Toronto: Women's Press, 1987; and Teressa A Nahanee, 'Indian Women, Sexual Equality and the Charter', paper delivered at the conference on Canadian Women and the State, University of Ottawa, October 1990. On file with the author.
8. Indian Act, RSC, c I–6 as amended c 10 (2nd Supp); 1974–76, c 48; 1978–79, c 11; 1980–82, cc 47, 110; 1985, c 27. This legislation goes some distance towards restoring 'Indian' status to Aboriginal women and their children.
9. Gwen Brodsky and Shelagh Day, *Canadian Charter Equality Rights for Women: One Step Forward or Two Steps Back?*, Ottawa: Canadian Advisory Council on the Status of Women, 1989.
10. Brodsky and Day, *Canadian Charter Equality Rights*, pp118–19.
11. Brodsky and Day, *Canadian Charter Equality Rights*, p119.
12. Brodsky and Day, *Canadian Charter Equality Rights*, p128.
13. Brodsky and Day, *Canadian Charter Equality Rights*, p56.
14. *Hunter v Southam Inc*, [1984] 2 SCR 145.

15. Brodsky and Day, *Canadian Charter Equality Rights*, p44, footnote 39. Note that the 1989 cost of litigation was estimated at between $250 000 and $300 000.
16. *Jane Doe v Metropolitan Toronto (Municipality) Commissioners of Police*, (1989), 58 DLR (4th) 396 (HCJ), affirmed, (1990), 74 OR (2d) 225 (HCJ), leave to appeal denied, (1991), 1 OR (3d) 416 (CA).
17. Canada, Parliament, House of Commons, Standing Committee on Human Rights, *Court Challenges Program: First Report of the Standing Committee on Human Rights and the Status of Disabled Persons*, Ottawa: Speaker of the House of Commons, 1989.
18. For example, see Women's Legal Education and Action Fund, *LEAF Litigation: Year One,* Toronto: LEAF, 1986.
19. *Canadian Newspapers Co v A-G Canada*, [1988] 2 SCR 122. In this case a group of newspapers challenged (unsuccessfully) the Criminal Code press ban on the publication of identifying information about rape victims on the basis of the charter right to freedom of expression.
20. *Robichaud et al v The Queen*, (1987), 40 DLR (4th) 577 (SCC). Bonnie Robichaud fought a *ten year* legal battle, which she finally won in the Supreme Court of Canada, against sexual harassment perpetrated by her supervisor in the federal government. Since her victory in 1987, she has spent *another* four years trying to recoup her financial losses and to enforce new guidelines regarding sexual harassment for federal employees.
21. Kristin Bumiller, 'Victims in the Shadow of the Law: A Critique of the Model of Legal Protection', *Signs: Journal of Women in Culture and Society*, 12, 1987, pp421, 433.
22. For descriptions of anti-feminist violence in Canada see Janet Bagnall, 'Women in Fear', *The Montreal Gazette*, 6.10.1990, pA1; Dan Hogan, 'Kingston Vigil: Sexism at Queen's Linked to Killings', *The Whig Standard*, 8.12.1989, p1; Cathy Campbell, 'Queen's men mock slayings firing "mimic machine- guns"', *The Whig Standard*, 8.12.1989, p11; and Victor Malarek, 'Killer's letter blames feminists: Suicide note contains apparent hit list of 15 women', *The Globe and Mail*, 8.12.1989, ppA1, A2.
23. John Aneurin Grey Griffith, *The Politics of the Judiciary*, London: Fontana, 1985, p198.
24. Terence George Ison, 'The Sovereignty of the Judiciary', *Adelaide Law Review*, 10, 1985–86, p1.
25. Albie Sachs and Joan Hoff Wilson, *Sexism and the Law: A Study of Male Beliefs and Legal Bias in Britain and the United States*, New York: The Free Press, 1979.
26. Mary Jane Mossman, 'Feminism and Legal Method: The Difference It Makes', *Australian Journal of Law and Society*, 3, 1986, p30.
27. Catharine A MacKinnon, 'Feminism, Marxism, Method, and the State', *Signs: Journal of Women in Culture and Society*, 8, 1983, p657.
28. T Brettel Dawson, 'Legal Structures: A Feminist Critique of Sexual Assault Reform', *Resources for Feminist Research*, 14, 1985, p40.
29. Carol Smart, *Feminism and the Power of Law*, London: Routledge, 1989.
30. Mossman, 'Feminism and Legal Method', pp37, 42, 45.

31. Judy Fudge, 'The Privatization of the Costs of Social Reproduction: Some Recent Charter Cases', *Canadian Journal of Women and the Law*, 3(1), 1989, p246.
32. Ison, 'The Sovereignty of the Judiciary', p17.
33. Andrew Petter, 'Immaculate Deception: The Charter's Hidden Agenda', *The Advocate*, 45(6), 1987, p857; 'The Politics of the Charter', *Supreme Court Law Review*, 8, 1986, p473; 'Canada's Charter Flight: Soaring Backwards into the Future', *Journal of Law and Society*, 16(2), 1989, pp151, 157–8.
34. Reuben Hasson, 'What's Your Favourite Right?: The Charter and Income Maintenance Legislation', *Journal of Law and Social Policy*, 5, Fall 1989, p1.
35. Harry J Glasbeek and Michael Mandel, 'The Legalisation of Politics in Advanced Capitalism: The Canadian Charter of Rights and Freedoms', *Socialist Studies*, 2, 1984, p84.
36. Sheila McIntyre, 'The Charter: Driving Women to Abstraction', *Broadside*, 6(5), 1985, p8; 'Journey Through Unchartered Territory', *Broadside*, 4(5), 1983, p8.
37. David Cole, 'Strategies of Difference: Litigating for Women's Rights in a Man's World', *Law and Inequality*, 1(2), 1984, p33.
38. Women's Legal Education and Action Fund, 'Schachter: Landmark decision upholds the power of the courts to extend benefits', *Leaf Lines*, 3(3), 1990, p1.
39. *Schachter v Canada Employment and Immigration Commission*, (1988), 18 FTR 199 (FCTD), affirmed [1990] 2 FC 129 (CA).
40. *Re Blainey and Ontario Hockey Association*, (1986), 54 OR (2d) 513 (CA). This insight is the contribution of Andrew Petter, 'Legitimizing Sexual Inequality: Three Early Charter Cases', *McGill Law Journal*, 34, 1989, pp358, 364.
41. McIntyre, 'The Charter'.
42. Fudge, 'The Privatization of the Costs of Social Reproduction'.
43. *Re Tomen and Federation of Women Teachers' Association of Ontario*, (1987), 61 OR (2d) 489, 506-07 (HC), affirmed, (1989), 70 OR (2d) 48 (CA). Again, this observation is from Petter, 'Legitimizing Sexual Inequality', p366.
44. *Andrews et al v Ontario (Minister of Health)*, (1989), 49 DLR (4th) 584 (Ont HC). See also Mary Eaton and Cynthia Peterson, 'Comment: *Andrews v Ontario (Minister of Health)*', *Canadian Journal of Women and the Law*, 2(2), 1987–88, p416.
45. *R v Morgentaler*, [1988] 1 SCR 30.
46. *Jane Doe*, (1989), 58 DLR (4th), 398.
47. Ison, 'The Sovereignty of the Judiciary', p17.
48. *BC Government Employees Union v AGBC and A-G Canada*, (1988), 53 DLR (4th) 1 (SCC); *Newfoundland Association of Public Employees v A-G Newfoundland*, (1988), 53 DLR (4th) 39 (SCC).
49. *R v Seaboyer; R v Gayme*, (1987), 37 CCC (3d) 53 (Ont CA). This case is currently under appeal to the Supreme Court of Canada.
50. *Seaboyer; Gayme*, 68, where availability of the 'constitutional exemption' doctrine was approved of by the court. This doctrine would mean that in

future cases, the rape shield provision of the Criminal Code could be declared inoperative with respect to individual cases where trial judges detect a constitutional violation on the facts.

51. Male accused were successful in having a section of the Criminal Code of Canada invalidated as offending sexual equality provisions of the charter in: *R v Howell*, (1986), 57 Nfld & PEIR 198, 203 (Nfld Dist Ct) and *R v Paquette*, (1988), 14 CRD 350, 70-01 (BCSC).

52. *Re Phillips and Lynch*, (1986), 27 DLR (4th) 156 (NSSC), affirmed, (1986), 76 NSR (2d) 240 (CA) (legislation providing benefits to single mothers and not to single fathers was struck down as inoperative because it offended section 15(1) of the charter and could not be saved by section 1).

53. *R v Wald*, [1989] 3 WWR 324 (Alta CA). See also *Seaboyer* and *Gayme*.

54. The rape shield provision in the Criminal Code of Canada was held to be invalid in the following cases: *R v Coombs*, (1985), 23 CCC (3d) 356 (Nfld SC); *R v Oquataq*, (1985), 18 CCC (3d) 440 (NWTSC); *R v Brun*, (1986), 28 CCC (3d) 397 (NBQB); *R v LeGallant*, (1985), 47 CR (3d) 170 (BCCA); *Seaboyer; Gayme* and *Wald*.

55. See, for example, *Borowski v A.G. Canada*, [1989] 1 SCR 342 and *Tremblay v Daigle*, [1989] 2 SCR 530, where men attempted unsuccessfully to intervene to prevent women's abortions.

56. See Cristin Schmitz, 'Charter Can Extend UI Benefits to Natural Parents, Fed. Court Holds', *The Lawyers Weekly*, 24.6.1988, p24, which quotes Shalom Schachter's social objective of wanting to assist women.

57. Brodsky and Day, *Canadian Charter Equality Rights*, p60. Note, '[o]nly the Women's Legal Education and Action Fund (L.E.A.F.), an intervenor in the case, argued consistently against reducing or eliminating pregnancy benefits.'

58. See *R v Quest Vitamin Supplies Ltd*, [1988] 6 WWR 374 (BCCoCt) and *R v Wholesale Travel Group Inc*, (1989), 70 OR (2d) 545 (CA) (burden of proof regarding regulatory offences violates the presumption of innocence in the charter).

59. See *Reference Re Public Service Employee Relations Act (Alta)*, [1987] 1 SCR 313; *Public Service Alliance of Canada v The Queen*, [1987] 1 SCR 424; and *Saskatchewan v Retail Wholesale and Department Store Union, Locals 544, 496, 635, and 955*, [1987] 1 SCR 460 (right to freedom of association for unions given a more restrictive interpretation than for individuals); *R v Cancoil Thermal Corporation and Parkinson*, (1986), 52 CR (3d) 188; and *R v Ellis-Don Ltd*, (1990), 1 OR (3d) 193 (CA) (offences in the legislation regulating health and safety in the workplace offend the presumption of innocence and fair trial rights in the charter).

60. *Hunter v Southam Inc*, [1984] 2 SCR 145 (corporation entitled to rights regarding search and seizure); *R v Big M Drug Mart Ltd*, [1985] 1 SCR 295 (corporation is entitled to freedom of religion).

61. Fudge, 'The Privatization of the Costs of Social Reproduction'.

62. Fudge, 'The Effect of Entrenching a Bill of Rights'.

63. See Sherene Razack, 'Speaking for Ourselves: Feminism and Minority Women', *Canadian Journal of Women and the Law*, 4(2), 1991 (forthcoming), for her analysis of the work of LEAF from the perspective of

'minority' women. See also the work of Professor Nitya Duclos of the
University of British Columbia who is completing a study on double or
multiple discrimination in human rights litigation. (Paper delivered to
conference on the Canadian State and Women, University of Ottawa,
October 1990. Available from the author.)

64. Women's Legal Education and Action Fund, 'Immigrant Women's
Organization Joins Challenge of Language Training Program', *Leaf Lines*,
3(3), 1990, p4.

65. *Symes v The Queen*, [1989] CTC 476 (FCTD).

66. Faye Woodman, 'A Child Care Expenses Deduction, Tax Reform and the
Charter: Some Modest Proposals', *Canadian Journal of Family Law*, 8,
1990, pp371, 377, 383. See also Maureen Maloney, '*Symes*: A Case By
Yuppies, For Yuppies, and About Yuppies', unpublished manuscript
available from the author at the University of Victoria Faculty of Law,
Victoria, British Columbia.

67. Linda Hossie, 'Women charge discrimination at prison', *The Globe and
Mail*, 23.6.1990, pA5.

68. Ellen Adelburg and Claudia Currie (eds), *Too Few To Count*, Vancouver:
Press Gang, 1987, pp67–102.

69. Sherri Barron, 'Life and Death in the Cage', *The Ottawa Citizen*, 9.3.1991,
pB3.

70. Abortion Act (Bill C-43, 1989).

71. William Walker, 'Senate kills abortion bill by a tie vote', *Toronto Star*,
1.2.1991, pA1.

72. *Tomen*, (1987), 61 OR (2d), 506-507.

73. *R v Hess*; *R v Nguyen*, [1990] 2 SCR 906, 929: '[T]here are certain
biological realities that one cannot ignore and that may legitimately shape
the definition of particular offences.'

74. See for example, Diana M Majury, *Report on the Statute Audit Project: A
Preliminary Analysis of Selected Federal and Ontario Laws Based on the
Sex Equality Provisions of the Canadian Charter of Rights and Freedoms*,
Toronto: Charter of Rights Educational Fund, 1985.

75. Salina Shrofel, 'Equality Rights and Law Reform in Saskatchewan: An
Analysis of the Charter Compliance Process', *Canadian Journal of Women
and the Law*, 1(1), 1985, p108.

76. Christine Boyle, 'Home Rule For Women: Power-Sharing Between Men
and Women', *Dalhousie Law Journal*, 7, 1983, p790.

77. See the judgments of Madam Justice Wilson in the following cases:
Morgentaler, Smoling and Scott v R, (1988), 37 CCC (3d) 449, 546 (SCC);
and *Lavallee v R*, (1990), 55 CCC (3d) 97, 100 (SCC). See also Bertha
Wilson, 'Will Women Judges Really Make A Difference?', *Osgoode Hall
Law Journal*, 28, 1990, p507 and Christine Boyle, 'Sexual Assault and the
Feminist Judge', *Canadian Journal of Women and the Law*, 1(1), 1985,
p93.

Appendix 1

Statement of the National Executive Committee of the African National Congress on the emancipation of women in South Africa

2 May 1990

*T*he African National Congress's commitment to eliminate racism, oppression and exploitation from our society cannot fail to address also the question of the emancipation of women.

The experience of other societies has shown that the emancipation of women is not a by-product of a struggle for democracy, national liberation or socialism. It has to be addressed in its own right within our organisation, the mass democratic movement and in the society as a whole.

The majority of South African women, who are black, are the most oppressed section of our people, suffering under a triple yoke of oppression. The liberation of women is central to our people's struggle for freedom.

In 1985 Presidents Sam Nujoma and Oliver Tambo made a joint pledge to the women of Namibia and South Africa that we would not 'consider our objectives achieved, our task completed, or our struggle at an end until the women of Namibia and South Africa are fully liberated'. We consider it long overdue that our organisation and the entire democratic movement establishes principles and initiates practices which will guide us in fulfilling this pledge.

Accordingly, the ANC NEC submits for discussion our views on how to advance and ensure the emancipation and development of women in every sphere of our existence now and in the future.

To achieve genuine equality, our policies must be based on a real understanding of gender oppression and the way it manifests itself in our society. From such a base we will be able to work towards creating the necessary conditions for truly liberating women in the practical reality of our daily lives.

Gender oppression is everywhere rooted in a material base and is expressed in socio-cultural traditions and attitudes all of which are supported and perpetuated by an ideology which subordinates women. In South Africa it is institutionalised in the laws as well as the customs and practices of all our people. Within our racially and ethnically divided society, all women have a lower status than men of the same group in both law and practice. And as with racism, the disadvantage imposed on them ranges across the political, economic, social, domestic, cultural and civil spheres.

The manipulation of gender relations has been an important feature of state control over, especially, the African people and the effects have impinged most harshly upon women. Their mobility has been rigidly controlled, and the unpaid labour of African women in the rural areas has underpinned the migrant labour system and subsidised the profits of the mining industry.

Within apartheid ideology African women have been perceived simply as the breeders of future generations of labour. With the creation of the bantustans large numbers have been confined to deteriorating rural environments, dependent on the commitment of absent breadwinners for small cash remittances. Many have been made the sole minders of the elderly, the disabled and the children. Women have carried the main load of responsibility for survival and generational reproduction even though they are often still subject to the legal authority of absent men who are removed from day to day decision making.

Centuries of women's subjugation have deprived and marginalised them in different ways. Nationally, women have the lowest levels of health, education and skills. The majority still bear the sole burden of domestic labour. Their contribution to the creation of our country's wealth is unrecognised and mostly unpaid. Women make up the majority of the unemployed, while those in waged work are channelled into the worst-paid lowest status jobs. Even white, but especially black, women do not participate fully in the decision and policy-making organs of our country.

Notwithstanding these oppressive conditions, women have made significant contributions to our liberation struggle. But, as is evident among the youth, the people's army and elsewhere in our ranks, we have to acknowledge that their full potential has not been realised. We have not, as yet, fully integrated women's concerns and the emancipation of women into the practice of our liberation struggle.

The prevalence of patriarchal attitudes in South African society permeates our own organisations. The absence of sufficient numbers of women in our organisations, especially at decision-making levels, and the lack of a strong mass women's organisation has been to the detriment of our struggle. As a consequence the particular concerns of more than half of our people are hardly heard when we define our strategies and determine our tactics. President Tambo summed the problem up when he opened the ANC Women's Conference in 1981:

> The struggle to conquer oppression in our country is the weaker for the traditionalist, conservative and primitive restraints imposed on women by man-dominated structures within our Movement, as also because of equally traditionalist attitudes of surrender and submission on the part of women.

The realisation of our objective of a non-racial and democratic South Africa is dependent upon the extent to which we are able to address and mobilise all the people of South Africa: men and women.

ANC policy

In this new phase of open organisational 'legality', the ANC commits itself to the development and implementation of a wide range of policies for restructuring the organisation to meet the tasks of the day. In this we believe it imperative to address the inequalities women face in every aspect of our work. By adopting such an approach we will bring women in their millions into active participation in all forms of struggle and at all levels. In this process we will, at the same time, facilitate their own upliftment and advance to freedom.

The NEC together with the NEWC is re-examining the functions of the ANC Women's Section as part of the overall restructuring of the ANC. We are determined to ensure that our pronouncements are consistent with our practices and that gender issues are integrated in all spheres of our movement.

We consider the formation of the ANC Women's League essential to fulfilling the tasks of mobilising and organising women into the liberation struggle.

As recommended by the 1987 ANC Women's Conference we are actively considering the appointment of a National Commission on the

Emancipation of Women to sensitise, monitor, stimulate and report on the women's position.

Highest priority must be given to finding the means to facilitate women's participation in the struggle and within all the political, administrative and military sectors of the ANC from the grassroots throught to the NEC.

Patterns of discrimination and inequality are not self-correcting. Rather, they tend to replicate themselves, as those already in leading positions acquire necessary experience and confidence and appear better equipped to bear responsibility. To break this cycle we need to take affirmative action within the ANC to supplement and reinforce education and advancement programmes based on the principle of full equality.

The Department of Political Education has been instructed to embark on a systematic programme of formal and informal education to promote an understanding of the origin and effects of gender oppression on our people. The ANC Educational Council has been asked to re-examine our education policy to ensure that its style and content is non-sexist and avoids gender-stereotyping.

The demands of the struggle now and in a post-apartheid South Africa

Our policies have to address simultaneously the material base, the legal system, the political and other institutions and the ideological and cultural underpinnings of gender-oppression now and in the future. In this regard the NEC is giving urgent consideration to the recommendations of a recent internal seminar which examined the formulation of national policy regarding the emancipation of women and the promotion of women's development in our country.

Among these recommendations are amendments to the ANC Constitutional Guidelines, including the categorisation of South Africa as an independent, united, democratic, non-racial and non-sexist state. Laws, customs, traditions and practices which discriminate against women shall be held to be unconstitutional. Patriarchal rights, especially but not only with regard to family, land and the economy need serious re-examination so that they are not entrenched or reinforced.

In the new South Africa women will not immediately have the education, skills and resources to claim the rights provided in the constitution and laws. It shall therefore be the duty of the state to take appropriate measures to ensure the principle of gender-equality. Equally, our legal system must be easily accessible, with a judiciary which is familiar with the experience and has the confidence of the least privileged sections of our people. Women's right to democratic participation in all decision making must be there in principle and in practice. These and other recommendations, which will be circulated in the seminar's report should provide a basis for thorough discussion amongst the people so that we can adopt policies which will help create a society free of gender-oppression.

The Charter of Women's Rights

Men and women alike bear the responsibility for eliminating gender-oppression. However, women must take the lead in creating a non-sexist South Africa. They must move the ANC and the MDM to adopt policies and forms of organisation that facilitate the participation of women in the struggle that still lies before us.

Women must lead the national debate for a Charter of Women's Rights which will elaborate and reinforce our new constitution, so that in their own voice women define the issues of greatest concern to them and establish procedures for ensuring that the rights claimed are made effective.

We call upon the ANC Women's League to initiate a campaign for the Charter involving all other structures of our organisation, the membership and supporters throughout South Africa. The campaign should involve millions of women directly in the process of determining how their rights would be protected in a new legal and constitutional order. Such an initiative will provide the opportunity to set an example of democracy in practice, and be a major agency for stimulating women to break the silence imposed on them.

Based upon the demands and needs of African women, the great majority and the most oppressed, it should draw in and represent the wishes of women from all sections of South African society, and as such be an important step in preparing over half the population for full citizenship and equality.

Although the principal themes of the Charter must be guided by women, men must be engaged in the process, so that we ensure that the Charter has the backing of the widest strata of society.

Although the dominant always find it difficult in the short term to give up age-old privileges and habits, in the long run they only stand to gain from living in a world in which the health, happiness and welfare of all is guaranteed.

Appendix 2
ANC Constitutional Guidelines

*T*he Freedom Charter, adopted in 1955 by the Congress of the People at Kliptown near Johannesburg, was the first systematic statement in the history of our country of the political and constitutional vision of a free, democratic and non-racial South Africa.

The Freedom Charter remains today unique as the only South African document of its kind that adheres firmly to democratic principles as accepted throughout the world. Amongst South Africans it has become by far the most widely accepted programme for a post-apartheid country.

The stage is now approaching where the Freedom Charter must be converted from a vision of the future into a constitutional reality.

We in the African National Congress submit to the people of South Africa, and all those throughout the world who wish to see an end of apartheid, our basic guidelines for the foundations of government in a post-apartheid South Africa.

Extensive and democratic debate on these guidelines will mobilise the widest sections of our population to achieve agreement on how to put an end to the tyranny and oppression under which our people live, thus enabling them to lead normal decent lives as free citizens in a free country.

The immediate aim is to create a just and democratic society that will sweep away the country's old legacy of colonial conquest and white domination, and abolish all laws imposing racial oppression and discrimination.

The removal of discriminatory laws and eradication of the vestiges of the illegitimate regime are, however, not enough. The structures and institutions of apartheid must be dismantled and be replaced by democratic ones. Steps must be taken to ensure that apartheid ideas and practices are not permitted to appear in old or new forms.

In addition, the effects of centuries of racial domination and inequality must be overcome by constitutional visions for collective action which guarantees a rapid and irreversible redistribution of wealth and opening of facilities to all. The constitution must also be such to promote the habits of non-racial and non-sexist thinking, the practice of anti-racist behaviour and the acquisition of genuinely shared patriotic consciousness.

The constitution must give firm protection to the fundamental human rights of all citizens. There shall be equal rights for all individuals irrespective of race, colour, sex or creed. In addition, the constitution must entrench equal cultural linguistic and religious rights for all.

Under the conditions of contemporary South Africa 87% of the land and 95% of the instruments of production are in the hands of the ruling class, which is drawn solely from the white community.

It follows, therefore that constitutional protection for group rights would perpetuate the status quo and would mean that the mass of the people continue to be constitutionally trapped in poverty and remain as outsiders in the land of their birth.

Finally, the efficacy of the constitution will, to a large extent, be determined by the degree to which it promotes conditions for the active involvement of all sectors of the population at all levels in government and in the economic and cultural life.

Bearing these fundamental objectives in mind, we declare that the elimination of apartheid and the creation of a truly just and democratic South Africa requires a constitution based on the following principles:

The State

(a) South Africa shall be an independent, unitary, democratic and non-racial state.

(b) Sovereignty shall belong to the people as a whole and shall be exercised through one central legislature, executive, judiciary and adminstration. Provision shall be made for delegation of the powers of the central authority to subordinate administrative units for purposes of more efficient administration and democratic participation.

(c) The institution of hereditary rulers and chiefs shall be transformed to serve the interests of the people as a whole in conformity with the democratic principles embodied in the constitution.

(d) All organs of government, including justice, security and armed forces, shall be representative of the people as a whole, democratic in their structure and functioning, and dedicated to defending the principles of the constitution.

Franchise

(e) In the exercise of their sovereignty, the people shall have the right to vote under a system of universal suffrage based on the principle of one person/one vote.

(f) Every voter shall have the right to stand for election and to be elected to all legislative bodies.

National identity

(g) It shall be state policy to promote the growth of a single national identity and loyalty binding on all South Africans. At the same time, the state shall recognise the linguistic and cultural diversity of the people and provide facilities for free linguistic and cultural development.

Bill of rights and affirmative action

(h) The constitution shall include a Bill of Rights based on the Freedom Charter. Such a Bill of Rights shall guarantee the fundamental human rights of all citizens, irrespective of race, colour, sex or creed, and shall provide appropriate mechanisms for their protection and enforcement.

(i) The state and all social institutions shall be under a constitutional duty to eradicate race discrimination in all its forms.

(j) The state and all social institutions shall be under a constitutional duty to take active steps to eradicate speedily, the economic and social inequalities produced by racial discrimination.

(k)The advocacy or practice of racism, fascism, nazism or the incitement of ethnic or regional exclusiveness or hatred shall be outlawed.

(l) Subject to clause (i) and (k) above, the democratic state shall guarantee the basic rights and freedoms, such as freedom of association, thought, worship and the press. Furthermore, the state shall have the duty to protect the right to work and guarantee the right to education and social security.

(m) All parties which conform to the provisions of (i) and (k) above shall have the legal right to exist and to take part in the political life of the country.

Economy

(n) The state shall ensure the entire economy serves the interests and well-being of the entire population.

(o) The state shall have the right to determine the general context in which economic life takes place and define and limit the rights and obligations attaching to the ownership and use of productive capacity.

(p) The private sector of the economy shall be obliged to co-operate with the state in realising the objectives of the Freedom Charter in promoting social well-being.

(q) The economy shall be a mixed one, with a public sector, a private sector, a co-operative sector and a small scale family sector.

(r) Co-operative forms of economic enterprise, village industries and small scale family activities shall be supported by the state.

(s) The state shall promote the acquisition of managerial, technical and scientific skills among all sections of the population, especially the blacks.

(t) Property for personal use and consumption shall be constitutionally protected.

Land

(u) The state shall devise and implement a land reform programme that will include and address the following issues: abolition of all racial restrictions on ownership and use of land, implementation of land reform in conformity with the principle of affirmative action, taking into account the victims of forced removals.

Workers

(v) A Charter protecting workers' trade union rights, especially the right to strike and collective bargaining, shall be incorporated into the constitution.

Women

(w) Women shall have equal rights in all spheres of public and private life and the state shall take affirmative action to eliminate inequalities and discrimination between the sexes.

The family

(x) The family, parenthood and childrens' rights shall be protected.

International

(y) South Africa shall be a non-aligned state committed to the principles of the Charter of the Organisation of African Unity and the Charter of the United Nations and to achievement of national liberation, world peace and disarmament.

Appendix 3

The ANC Constitutional Guidelines for a democratic South Africa – proposed amendments after seminar on gender*

*T*he Freedom Charter, adopted in 1955 by the Congress of the People at Kliptown near Johannesburg, was the first systematic statement in the history of our country of the political and constitutional vision of a free, democratic and non-racial South Africa.

The Freedom Charter remains today unique as the only South African document of its kind that adheres firmly to democratic principles as accepted throughout the world. Amongst South Africans it has become by far the most widely accepted programme for a post-apartheid country.

We are now approaching the stage where the Freedom Charter must be converted from a vision of the future into a constitutional reality.

We in the African National Congress submit to the people of South Africa, and all those throughout the world who wish to see an end to apartheid, our basic guidelines for the foundations of government in a post-apartheid South Africa. Extensive and democratic debate on these guidelines will mobilise the widest sections of our population to achieve agreement on how to put an end to the tyranny and oppression under which our people live, thus enabling them to lead normal decent lives as free citizens in a free country.

---

* *The full text was previously published in Albie Sachs, Protecting Human Rights in a New South Africa, Cape Town: Oxford University Press, 1990.*

The immediate aim is to create a just and democratic society that will sweep away the centuries-old legacy of colonial conquest and white domination, and abolish all laws imposing racial oppression and discrimination. The removal of discriminatory laws and eradication of all vestiges of the illegitimate regime are, however, not enough; the structures and institutions of apartheid must be dismantled and be replaced by democratic ones. Steps must be taken to ensure that apartheid ideas and practices are not permitted to appear in old forms or new.

In addition, the effects of centuries of racial domination and inequality must be overcome by constitutional provisions for corrective action which guarantees a rapid and irreversible redistribution of wealth and opening of facilities to all. The constitution must also promote the habits of non-racial and non-sexist thinking, the practice of anti-racist behaviour and the acquisition of genuinely shared patriotic consciousness.

The constitution must give firm protection to the fundamental human rights of all citizens. There shall be equal rights for all individuals, irrespective of race, colour, sex or creed. In addition, it requires the entrenching of equal cultural, linguistic, and religious rights for all. *Special attention has to be paid to combatting sexism, which is even more ancient and as pervasive as racism.**

Under the conditions of contemporary South Africa eighty-seven per cent of the land and ninety-five per cent of the instruments of production are in the hands of the ruling class, which is solely drawn from the white community. It follows, therefore, that constitutional protection for group rights would perpetuate the status quo and would mean that the mass of the people would continue to be constitutionally trapped in poverty and remain as outsiders in the land of their birth.

Finally, success of the constitution will be, to a large extent, determined by the degree to which it promotes conditions for the active involvement of all sectors of the population at all levels in government and in the economic and cultural life. Bearing these fundamental objectives in mind, we declare that the elimination of apartheid and the creation of a truly just and democratic South Africa requires a constitution based on the following principles:

---

* *The italics represent amendments proposed at a seminar jointly organised by the women's section and the constitutional committee of the ANC. The changes were adopted after four days of discussion informed by comments and papers received from inside and outside South Africa. About 70 persons, roughly two-thirds women, one-third men, attended. The italicised amendments correspond to the author's record of the proceedings and should not be regarded as the official text.*

The State

(a) South Africa shall be an independent, unitary, democratic, non-racial and non-sexist state, *based on the principle of equal rights for all.*

(b) Sovereignty shall belong to the people as a whole and shall be exercised through one central legislature, executive, and adminstration. Provision shall be made for the delegation of the powers of the central authority to subordinate administrative units for purposes of more efficient administration and democratic participation.

(c) The institution of hereditary rulers, chiefs, *and chieftainesses*, shall be transformed to serve the interests of the people as a whole in conformity with the democratic principles embodied in the constitution.

(d) All organs of government, including justice, security, and armed forces shall be representative of the people as a whole, *men and women*, democratic in their structure and functioning, and dedicated to defending the principles of the constitution.

Franchise

(e) In the exercise of their sovereignty, *all men and women* shall have the right to vote under a system of universal suffrage based on the principle of one person, one vote.

(f) Every voter shall have the right to stand for election and to be elected to all legislative bodies.

National identity

(g) It shall be state policy to promote the growth of a single national identity and loyalty binding on all South Africans. At the same time, the state shall recognise the linguistic and cultural diversity of the people and provide facilities for free linguistic and cultural development. *Such cultural diversity shall not be the basis for discrimination.*

A Bill of Rights and affirmative action

(h) The constitution shall include a Bill of Rights based on the Freedom Charter. Such a Bill of Rights shall guarantee the fundamental human rights of all citizens irrespective of race, colour, sex or creed, and shall provide appropriate mechanisms for their enforcement.

(i) The state and all social institutions shall be under a constitutional duty to eradicate race discrimination in all its forms.

(i) *(bis) The state and all social institutions shall be under a constitutional duty to work towards the rapid elimination of inequality based on gender and to combat sexism in all its forms.*

(j) The state and all social institutions shall be under a constitutional duty to take active steps to eradicate, speedily, the economic and social inequalities produced by racial discrimination.

(k) The advocacy or practice of racism, fascism, nazism, or the incitement of ethnic or regional exclusiveness or hatred shall be outlawed.

(l) Subject to clauses (i) and (k) above, the democratic state shall guarantee the basic rights and freedoms, such as freedom of association, expression, thought, worship, and the press. Furthermore, the state shall have the duty to protect the right to work, and guarantee education and social security.

(m) All parties which conform to the provisions of paragraphs (i) to (k) shall have the legal right to exist and to take part in the political life of the country.

(n) (*bis*) *The basic rights and freedoms set out above shall be enforceable through the courts and the principle of ensuring equal access to the legal system shall be followed.*

Economy

(n) The state shall ensure the entire economy serves the interests and well-being of all sections of the population.

(o) The state shall have the right to determine the general context in which economic life takes place and define and limit the rights and obligations attaching to the ownership and use of productive capacity.

(p) The private sector of the economy shall be obliged to co-operate with the state in realising the objectives of the Freedom Charter in promoting social well-being.

(q) The economy shall be a mixed one, with a public sector, a private sector, a co-operative sector and a small-scale family sector.

(r) Co-operative forms of economic enterprise, village industries, and small-scale family activities shall be supported by the state.

(s) The state shall promote the acquisition of managerial, technical, and scientific skills among all sections of the population, especially the blacks, *and shall take special steps to remove the barriers to women participating fully in economic life.*

(t) Property for personal use and consumption shall be constitutionally protected.

Land

(u) The state shall devise and implement a Land Reform Programme that will include and address the following issues: abolition of all racial and gender-based restrictions on ownership and use of land, implementation of land reform in conformity with the principle of affirmative action, taking into account the status of victims of forced removals.

Workers

(v) A Charter protecting workers' trade union rights, especially the right to strike and collective bargaining, shall be incorporated into the constitution.

Women and men

(w) *A charter of gender rights shall be incorporated into the constitution guaranteeing* equal rights *between men and women* in all spheres of public and private life and requiring the state *and social institutions* to take affirmative action to eliminate inequalities, discrimination, and *abusive behaviour based on gender.*

The family

(x) The family, parenthood and *equal rights within the family* shall be protected.

Children's rights

(y) *The principles of the International Convention on the Rights of the Child shall recieve constitutional respect.*

International

(z) South Africa shall be a non-aligned state committed to the principles of the Charter of the Organisation of African Unity and the Charter of the United Nations and to the achievements of national liberation, world peace and disarmament.